Religion in America

ADVISORY EDITOR

Edwin S. Gaustad

SKETCHES

OF THE

EARLY CATHOLIC MISSIONS

OF

KENTUCKY;

FROM THEIR

COMMENCEMENT IN 1787,

TO THE

JUBILEE OF 1826-7

M[artin] J. Spalding

ARNO PRESS
A NEW YORK TIMES COMPANY
New York • 1972

Reprint Edition 1972 by Arno Press Inc.

Reprinted from a copy in
The State Historical Society of Wisconsin Library

RELIGION IN AMERICA - Series II
ISBN for complete set: 0-405-04050-4
See last pages of this volume for titles.

Manufactured in the United States of America

Library of Congress Cataloging in Publication Data

Spalding, Martin John, Abp., 1810-1872.
   Sketches of the early Catholic missions of Kentucky.

  (Religion in America, series II)
  Reprint of the 1844 ed.
  1. Catholic Church in Kentucky. 2. Catholic
Church in Kentucky--Biography. 3. Kentucky--Church
history. I. Title.
BX1415.K4S6 1972   282.769   70-38548
ISBN 0-405-04087-3

SKETCHES

OF THE

EARLY CATHOLIC MISSIONS

OF

KENTUCKY;

FROM THEIR

COMMENCEMENT IN 1787,

TO THE

JUBILEE OF 1826-7:

EMBRACING A SUMMARY OF THE EARLY HISTORY OF THE STATE.; THE AD-VENTURES OF THE FIRST CATHOLIC EMIGRANTS ; BIOGRAPHICAL NOTICES OF THE EARLY MISSIONARIES ; THE EARLY HISTORY OF THE PRINCIPAL PROTESTANT SECTS IN KENTUCKY; WITH SOME ACCOUNT OF THE ES-TABLISHMENT OF THE EPISCOPAL SEE AT BARDSTOWN, OF THE VA-RIOUS RELIGIOUS SOCIETIES, AND OF THE GENERAL STATE OF THE CATHOLIC RELIGION IN KENTUCKY.

COMPILED FROM AUTHENTIC SOURCES, WITH THE ASSISTANCE OF

THE VERY REV. STEPHEN THEODORE BADIN,

THE FIRST PRIEST ORDAINED IN THE UNITED STATES.

By M. J. SPALDING, D. D.

Colligite fragmenta quo manent, ne pereant.
Gather up the fragments that remain, lest they be lost.—St. John vi. 12.

LOUISVILLE:
B. J. WEBB & BROTHER.
JOHN MURPHY,—BALTIMORE.

COPY RIGHT SECURED ACCORDING TO LAW.

B. J. WEBB AND BROTHER, PRINTERS.

TO THE

Rt. Rev. *Benedict Joseph Flaget*, D. D.
BISHOP OF LOUISVILLE,
And the Venerable Patriarch of the West,
THESE SKETCHES OF A HISTORY,
IN WHICH HE WAS A PRINCIPAL ACTOR,
AND OF WHICH HE WAS THE BRIGHTEST ORNAMENT,
Are Respectfully Inscribed,
AS SOME SLIGHT TRIBUTE TO HIS MANY EMINENT VIRTUES,
AND TO HIS PROTRACTED APOSTOLICAL LABORS IN KENTUCKY,
AND AS A SMALL PLEDGE OF GRATITUDE
FOR HIS PARENTAL SOLICITUDE,
AND FOR HIS MANY ACTS OF AFFECTIONATE KINDNESS,
BY HIS FAITHFUL SERVANT,
AND GRATEFUL CHILD IN CHRIST.

THE AUTHOR.

PREFACE

THE writer of the following pages has not intended to give a full and connected history of the early Catholic Missions of Kentucky. His only object has been, to collect together, and to record, in a series of sketches, such facts as might prove interesting to the general reader, and serve as materials for the future church historian of the United States, and especially of the West, to which Kentucky has been, in a religious, if not in a political, point of view, the great pioneer and *alma mater*.

Of all the Western States Kentucky is the oldest; and it was in this State, that the first Episcopal See of the West was erected. At the time of its establishment, the See of Bardstown held spiritual jurisdiction over all the States and Territories of the United States, lying between the thirty-fifth degree of North Latitude and the Lakes of the North, and between the States bordering on the Atlantic Ocean and the Rocky Mountains. This vast original diocese of the West is now divided into ten different flourishing dioceses, under ten different prelates, all of whom look up to the venerable Bishop Flaget as their Patriarch.

Most of the early Catholic settlers of Kentucky, and almost all the older missionaries, have already disappeared from the stage of life; and the scanty remnant of these venerable pioneers is now fast hastening to the tomb. They belonged to a class; which did much, and wrote little. The dangers and hardships, through which they had to pass, left them little time; and gave them little inclination, to write their memoirs. Almost the only means of learning the early religious history of Kentucky, of which their lives constitute the principal part, is to take down their own statements of facts, and their own reminiscences of early times, while they still linger above the horizon of life.

This is what the writer of these hasty and imperfect sketches has attempted to do. How well he has succeeded, the public will best judge. The only merit he can claim is that of some industry and patient research. He has sought information from almost every living source within his reach; he has noted down, and compared with one another the different statements of numerous aged persons; he has labored to supply the deficiencies, or to correct the mistakes, of some of these statements, by the more copious or accurate details furnished by others: in a word, he has endeavoured to derive from all of them an accurate, and, as far as was practicable, a connected account of the early Catholic Missions of Kentucky.

But he did not stop here. He endeavoured to examine all the written and printed documents, bearing on the subject, to which he could have access. The statements furnished by these papers, were diligently compared with those contained in the notes of the oral accounts just alluded to: and the comparison served to shed additional light upon both.

The published accounts of our early missions, besides

being, in general, unconnected and fragmentary, are meagre enough. Scattered over the pages of the many volumes comprising the "Annals of the French Association for the propagation of the Faith," or published in various religious journals of Europe and America, they are sometimes inaccurate in point of facts and dates. Some of them are overburdened with unimportant details, too trivial for history; while others by far the most valuable—are much too brief and summary. To the former class belong many of the letters written by our early missionaries; to the latter, a few succinct and well-written accounts of our early missions.

To this class belongs the admirable account of the early missions of Kentucky drawn up by the very Rev. M. Badin, while residing in Paris, in 1822. This sketch has the good qualities of nearly all the other writings of the venerable "first-ordained" of the United States. It is clear, connected, accurate in point of facts and dates, well written, and in good taste. The only matter of regret is, that it is so brief, and that it enters into so few details. Yet, withal, it has been found of great utility in the composition of the following sketches, which have in fact, been based on it, at least, in that portion of the early religious history of Kentucky of which it professes to treat.

The author deeply regrets, that this is almost the only writing of M. Badin to which he could have access. In the numerous peregrinations and wanderings of this venerable missionary pioneer, most of his notes and papers, connected with his early labors in the West, have been entirely lost.* Yet the writer of these sketches has derived invaluable assistance from him otherwise. In fact, it was he who, in a great measure, originated the work, which would not probably have been undertaken, but for his promised aid and co-operation. His clear memory of facts and dates furnished much valuable information on the earlier portion of our missionary history; and supplied many of the links that were wanting in the chain of printed documents.

The later portion of our religious history, comprised in these sketches, might have been much more copious and detailed, had another venerable personage not been prevented by his modesty and humility from allowing the writer access to his copious notes and papers. However much this may be regretted, it may, perhaps, be thought that the time had not yet come for writing this portion of our missionary history. When that time shall come, the necessary materials will probably not be wanting; nor will they be deficient, either in copiousness, or in interest.

One of the greatest difficulties, perhaps, which the writer of these pages had to encounter, arose from his having undertaken to write the history of recent events, many of the actors in which are still living. If it is a difficult and delicate task to write the history even of the dead; it is manifestly much more so, to write that of the living. A man's actions and motives cannot be properly appreciated, until after he has completed his career, and finished all the acts in the drama of life. Influenced by these considerations, the author has determined to say as little as possi-

---

* This loss occurred chiefly while he was laboring among the Potowatomy Indians of the North West, about twelve years ago.

ble of the living, and to confine himself almost entirely to the dead. He has however felt compelled to make two axceptions to this rule; and to speak at some length of two venerable living octogenarians, without an account of whose lives and labors, any history of the early missions of Kentucky would be meagre and incomplete indeed.

The chief thing aimed at by the author has been accuracy in facts and dates. He is, however, sensible that, from the difficulties he had to encounter in regard to the materials of the history, as well as from numerous interruptions by heavy missionary duties while engaged in writing it out, he may have been betrayed into some errors. These he will willingly correct, whenever they will be pointed out by any kind friend. To enable his readers the more easily, to know the sources whence he borrowed his information, he has also thought it better to indicate his authorities as he proceeded.

To such as might be inclined to think, that many incidents and anecdotes related in these pages are too trivial in their character, and had better have been omitted, he would beg leave to say, that these things may have a local, if not a general interest; and that many details, which would be wholly out of place in a regular history, may be pardoned in mere desultory sketches.

BARDSTOWN, KENTUCKY,
Feast of Corpus Christi, 1844.

CONTENTS.

CHAPTER I.

PAGE.

INTRODUCTION.—BRIEF SUMMARY OF THE EARLY HISTORY OF KENTUCKY.—Necessity of this Introduction—The two Historians of Kentucky—The original Indian claimants of Kentucky—Treaties with them—The Pioneers—Dr. Walker—John Finley—Daniel Boone—The "Long Hunters"—The Surveyors—The first man burned in Kentucky—James Harrod—Stations of Boonesborough and Harrod's Town—Other Stations—Difficulties and dangers of the Emigrants—James Rogers Clark—Takes Kaskaskias and Post St. Vincent's—Battle of the Blue Licks—Expedition of Clark—Kentucky a State—Gen'l. Harmar's Expedition—Gen'l. St. Clair's Defeat—Gen'l. Wayne's Victory—Treaty of Greenville—General Peace.......................... 1

CHAPTER II.

THE EARLY CATHOLIC EMIGRANTS TO KENTUCKY.—Glowing reports of the Pioneers—Virginia and Maryland in motion towards the West—The first Catholic Emigrants to Kentucky—Dr. Hart—Wm. Coomes—The first Physician and the first School—The Successive Catholic Colonies—Dangers on the way—Running the gauntlet—Indian attacks—Death of McManus, of Cox, and of Buckman—The Savages and the Cross—Thrilling incident of the late war—Mode of procuring salt—Domestic manners of the Early Emigrants to Kentucky—Furniture, food, and apparel—Hospitality—Singular Adventures and hair-breadth escapes of Wm. Coomes—Incidents in the early history of Harrod's Town......... 22

CHAPTER III.

THE FIRST CATHOLIC MISSIONARY IN KENTUCKY—HIS LIFE AND TIMES.—FROM 1787, TO 1793.—Father Whelan—His early history—His appointment to the Mission of Kentucky—His arrival and missionary labours—Promiscuous meetings and dancing—Prejudices of Sectarians—Anecdotes—Father Whelan's trials and difficulties—His return to Maryland and subsequent life—Rev. Wm. De Rohan—Remarkable adventures of John Lancaster.. 41

CHAPTER IV.

REVEREND M. BADIN IN KENTUCKY.—FROM 1793 TO 1797. —The French Revolution—Virtues of the exiled French Clergy—M. Badin—His early studies—Anecdote—His firm attachment to the faith—He sails for America—Singular coincidence—Anecdote of Bishop Carroll—M. Badin appointed to the missions of Kentucky—Characteristic conversation between him and Bishop Carroll—Departure for Kentucky—Delay at Gallopolis—Arrival of M. Barrieres—M. Badin alone in Kentucky—His troubles—Christian friendship—M. Rivet—M. Badin's labours in Kentucky—His missionary stations—Teaching Catechism—Morning and evening prayer—His Maxims—Curious anecdote—Hearing confessions—Dancing—Anecdotes—Strange notions respecting Catholic priests—M. Badin's privations—His disinterested zeal—His dangers and adventures—How to cure the Pleurisy—St. Paul.. 55

CHAPTER V.

ARRIVAL OF OTHER MISSIONARIES.—FROM 1797 TO 1803.—Rev. M. Fournier—Traits and facts of his early life—His arrival in Kentucky—His stations and labours—His character—His sudden death—Rev. Mr. Salmon—His zeal and labours—Humorous incident—His tragical death—His Epitaph—Rev. M. Thayer—Anecdote of Franklin—Mr. Thayer's conversion—His labours in Boston—in Kentucky—And in Limerick—His death...... 73

CHAPTER VI.

EARLY HISTORY OF THE CHIEF PROTESTANT SECTS IN KENTUCKY.—FROM 1784 TO 1820.—Our authorities—Father Rice—His opinion of the first Protestant preachers in

Kentucky—A "speck" of Religion—Wrangling and Sectarism—A frightful picture—Causes of religious decline—Avarice in preachers—The great hurricane of religion—Origin and doctrines of the Cumberland Presbyterians—Fierce and indomitable spirit of Presbyterianism—Origin of the "New-Lights"—Singular *manifesto*—Sentence of deposition—A curious document—Origin of the Campbellites—Presbyterian dissensions—A preacher twice convicted of slander—Another condemned—Disunion among Baptists—The "great revival" in Kentucky—Col. Stone's description of it—Farther particulars—*Jerking, jumping, falling*, and *barking* exercises—The Shakers in Kentucky—Curious religious statistics—Reflections.......................... 82

CHAPTER VII.

M. BADIN AGAIN ALONE.—FROM 1803 TO 1805.—Death of missionaries—M. Rivet and General Harrison—But three Catholic missionaries in the whole West—Labors of M. Badin increase—No rest in this life—Anecdote of Bishop David—M. Badin *not* dead—Fruits of his labours—Piety of early Catholics—Zeal to attend church "Uncle Harry," a pious negro—Hospitable Catholics of the olden time—Distinguished men of Kentucky, friends of M. Badin—Joe Daviess—Converts—Judge Twyman—Mrs. Onan—Singular charge against Catholics—Is the Pope antichrist?—Zealous Catholic laymen—Anecdotes—Celibacy—Having two wives—The "Water-witch"—Asking a sign—Divorces—Praying by proclamation—How many Commandments—"Principles of Catholics"—Discussion with preacher McHenry—Famous Sermon on Baptism................... 111

CHAPTER VIII.

THE REV. CHARLES NERINCKX—HIS EARLY LIFE AND LABOURS—FROM 1805 TO 1811.—M. Nerinckx—His childhood and early history—Curate at Malines—And at Everbery Meerbeke—His care of children—Revival of piety—His austerity—Is persecuted and compelled to fly—His retreat at Terremonde—Escapes to the United States—A "floating hell"—Reaches Baltimore—Sent to Kentucky—His arrival and early labours—His spirit of prayer and mortification—His courage and zeal—His cheerfulness and kindness to the poor—His narrow escapes in crossing rivers—His wolf adventure—His adventure with Hardin—His bodily strength and toils—The churches he built—His labours in the confessional—A touching devotion—The fruits of his zeal—The secret of his success—A touching incident................ 130

CHAPTER IX.

THE DOMINICANS IN KENTUCKY.—FROM 1805 TO 1824.—
Early missionary labours of the Dominican Order—The
English Dominicans—College at Bornheim—Departure
for America—Arrival in Kentucky—Founding of St.
Rose—The new noviciate—Bishop Concannon—Father
Wilson's learning, virtues, labours and death—Father
Edward Fenwick—His zeal and labours—'Stray sheep'
—Humorous adventure with an old lady—His missionary labours in Ohio—Founding of St. Joseph's, Somerset—Nominated first Bishop of Cincinnati—His success
and death—The missionary labours of the Dominicans
in Kentucky—Father Willet—College of St. Thomas
Aquinas—Monastery of St. Magdalen's................ 149

CHAPTER X.

THE TRAPPISTS IN KENTUCKY.—FROM 1805 TO 1809.—
Goodness of Providence toward the Missions of Kentucky—The Cistercian and Carthusian Monks—The
Abbe De Rance—His early life, disorders, and conversion—His exemplary penance—Attempts a reform of
the Order—The Trappists—Their rules and austerities
—Dispersed by the French Revolution—Some of them
escape to America—Father Urban Guillet—The Trappists at the Pigeon Hills, in Pennsylvania—Their arrival in Kentucky—Their edifying life and austerities—
The number who died in Kentucky—Cross in the moon
—Departure for Missouri—Delay at the mouth of the
Ohio—Sublime spectacle—Ascent of the Mississippi—
Curious accident—The Trappists at Flourissant—And
at Monk's Mound—The Indians—Curious fact in
acoustics—Deaths at Monk's Mound—Return to Europe—Incidents of travel—Remarks on a passage in
the "American Notes" of Charles Dickens............. 162

CHAPTER XI.

THE ARRIVAL OF THE BISHOP IN KENTUCKY.—Efforts of M.
Badin to have a Bishop nominated for Kentucky—His
Journey to Baltimore—Edifying incident at Brownsville
Pennsylvania—The Rev. M. Flaget—His early life—
Arrival in America—Labours at Vincennes—In Havana—And at Baltimore—His qualities—Appointed first
Bishop of Bardstown—Firmly declines accepting—
Compelled to yield—Consecrated—The Rev. M. David
—Difficulties and delay at Baltimore—Extracts from the
Bishop's correspondence—Incidents of the journey to

CONTENTS. xv

Kentucky—The arrival—The ceremonies of taking possession of his See—Apostolical poverty—Religious statistics of Kentucky on his arrival—And of the Northwest—The Bishop removes to St. Thomas', and to Bardstown—The first priest ordained in Kentucky—His zeal and labours—Eulogy of Bishop Flaget............ 178

CHAPTER XII.

REV. M. NERINCKX AGAIN.—HIS ESTABLISHMENTS AND DEATH—FROM 1811 TO 1824.—Rev. M. Nerinckx—Faithful unto death—A good soldier of the cross—His merits testified by Bishop Flaget—His success in making converts—Appointed administrator of New Orleans—Declines the honor—Affection of his old parishioners—His spirit and character—Founds the Society of Loretto—The objects of the Sisterhood—The Mother House—And branch establishments—Bishop Flaget's testimony—Utility of the Society—Christian perfection—Reliance on Providence—Love of Poverty—Continual prayer—Mortification—Rules modified—Journey of M. Nerinckx to Missouri—His edifying death—Translation of his remains—His monument and epitaph................ 196

CHAPTER XIII.

FATHER DAVID—HIS EARLY LIFE—THE THEOLOGICAL SEMINARY.—Father David—His parentage and early youth—He studies for the Church—And is ordained—Joins the Sulpicians—Is forced to fly from France—Sails for America—Becomes a missionary in Maryland—Gives Retreats with great fruit—Resides in Georgetown College—And in Baltimore—Accompanies Bishop Flaget to Kentucky—Founds our Theological Seminary—Its early history sketched—Virtues and labours of the Seminarians—Instructions and Maxims of Father David—His character—His missionary labours............... 215

CHAPTER XIV.

THE SISTERS OF CHARITY IN KENTUCKY.—Father David, their Founder—The objects of the Sisterhood—Its humble beginning—And early history—Its rapid growth—And extended usefulness—Branch establishments—Removal to the present situation—Present condition of the Society—A precious legacy...................... 229

CHAPTER XV.

THE NEW CATHEDRAL OF ST. JOSEPH'S—CONSECRATION OF FATHER DAVID—HIS WRITINGS, DEATH, AND CHARAC-

xvi   CONTENTS.

TER.—Removal of the Seminary to Bardstown—Erection of the Cathedral—Liberal subscriptions—Obstacles—Dedication of the Cathedral—The edifice described—Its paintings and ornaments—Father David named Bishop—Accepts with reluctance—His poverty—His Consecration—His zeal redoubles—His zeal for the rubrics—And taste for Music—His qualities as pastor of the Cathedral—As a preacher—And as a confessor—The splendid services of the Cathedral—A refreshing reminiscence—Testimony of eye-witnesses—The remainder of Father David's life—His zeal for the faith—His oral discussion with Hall—His controversial sermons and writings—His other writings—His happy death—And character................................ 242

CHAPTER XVI.

REV. MESSRS. O'FLYNN AND DERIGAUD.—Rev. F. O'Flynn—His early life—Emigration to America—And arrival in Kentucky—His appearance and piety—Incident showing his eloquence—His infirm health—And return to France—Rev. M. Derigaud—His early life—Ordination—Virtues—Zeal and labours—A religious brotherhood—His edifying death...................... 259

CHAPTER XVII.

REV. WM. BYRNE AND REV. GEORGE A. M. ELDER.—Two Christian friends—Two founders of Colleges—Rev. Wm. Byrne—His early life—His ordination—His zeal and missionary labours—Founds St. Mary's College—His unshaken constancy in adversity—His qualities as a preacher—His virtues and instructions—Falls a martyr of charity—Rev. G. A. M. Elder—His early life—And missionary labours—His amiability of character—Founds St. Joseph's College—A touching incident—His indefatigable zeal—His pious and edifying death... 265

CHAPTER XVIII.

THE JUBILEE OF 1826-7.—STATISTICS OF THE DIOCESS AT ITS CLOSE—CONCLUSION.—The nature of a Jubilee—And of an Indulgence in general—The utility of Indulgences shown—The Jubilee of 1826-7 in Kentucky—Its commencement—Progress—And astonishing results—Edifying examples—Conversions of Protestants—Statistics of the Diocess—The Rev. Mr. Kenrick—Reflections—The Patriarch of the West............... 288

APPENDIX... 303

SKETCHES
OF THE
EARLY CATHOLIC MISSIONS OF KENTUCKY.

CHAPTER I.
INTRODUCTION.

Brief Summary of the Early History of Kentucky.

Necessity of this Introduction—The two Historians of Kentucky—The original Indian claimants of Kentucky—Treaties with them—The Pioneers—Dr. Walker—John Finley—Daniel Boone—The "Long Hunters"—The Surveyors—The first man burned in Kentucky—James Harrod—Stations of Boonesborough and Harrod's Town—Other Stations—Difficulties and dangers of the Emigrants—James Rogers Clark—Takes Kaskaskias and Post St. Vincent's—Battle of the Blue Licks—Expedition of Clark—Kentucky a State—Gen'l. Harmar's Expedition—Gen'l. St. Clair's Defeat—Gen'l. Wayne's Victory—Treaty of Greenville—General Peace.

BEFORE we attempt to sketch the early religious history of Kentucky, it will be necessary, for the better understanding of the subject, rapidly to trace the chief events connected with the first settlement of this Commonwealth. Our plan will call for and permit only a very brief summary. Those who may wish a more detailed account are referred to the two Histories of Kentucky written by Humphrey Marshall and Mann Butler.* The

---

* The former in 2 vols. 8vo.; and the latter in 1 vol. 12mo. The edition of Marshall, to which reference may be made in the sequel, is that of Frankfort, 1824: and of Butler, that of Louisville, 1834.

latter, though more concise than his predecessor, will be found in general more accurate, more impartial, more learned, and more satisfactory. His style also, though far from being faultless, or even always grammatical, is more simple and in better taste than that of Marshall, who often indulges in fustian and school-boy declamation.

Kentucky is the oldest of all the States west of the Alleghany Mountains. She became a State and was admitted into the Union in 1792, four years sooner than Tennessee, and ten years before Ohio. The first hardy adventurers who travelled westward came to Kentucky; and the first Catholic missions in the west, if we except those at the French stations on the Wabash and the Mississippi, were those established in Kentucky. So that, both in a political and in a religious point of view, Kentucky pioneered the way for the other western States of our confederacy.

Nor does the interest which attaches to her early history stop here. This history is rich in examples of lofty daring, hardy adventure, and stirring incident. It tells of dangers encountered, and of difficulties overcome, which would have appalled the stoutest hearts. It speaks of the deeds of an iron race of pioneers, now fast disappearing from the theatre of life, who fed on difficulties and dangers, as their daily bread, and were thus nerved for the difficult mission they had to accomplish. They never faltered in their purpose for a moment, but ceaselessly marched on, planting farther and farther in the unreclaimed forests the outposts of civilization. When Kentucky had been settled by a white population, we find many of them moving still farther westward, with Daniel Boone, never satisfied unless their houses were built in the very midst of the waving forests!

HISTORICAL SUMMARY.

The land of Kentucky—or, as the Indians called it, *Kantuckee*—seems not, within the memory of the white man, ever to have been permanently settled by any Indian tribe. The hunters from North Carolina and Virginia, who visited it after the year 1767, could discover no trace of any Indian habitation.* It was a kind of neutral territory, and a common hunting-ground for the various Indian tribes. It became also, from this very circumstance, a great Indian battle-ground. The Miamis, Shawnees, and Illinois, from the banks of the Miami, the Scioto, and the Illinois rivers, of the north; and the Cherokes and Tuscaroras from the south, repeatedly met and struggled for the mastery on the "Dark and Bloody Ground." Thus it happened, that the various Indian tribes successively swept over Kentucky, leaving no trace of their passage behind them. This also explains to us the many conflicting claims to the proprietorship of its territory put in by the different Indian nations.

From an early period of their history, the Indian tribes of the northwest had been seeking to conquer or exterminate one another. The most powerful of these was the great confederation of the Five Nations of New York; of which the Mohawks, or *Iroquois*—as the French historians style them—were the principal. Like the ancient Romans, they were in the habit of incorporating into their own body the various tribes whom they successively subdued. They gradually extended their conquests towards the west and the south. As early as 1672, after having subdued

---

* In the beginning of his first volume (p. 13, seqq.,) Mr. Marshall indulges in a long and somewhat rhapsodical account of the Indian "annals of Kentucky;" Noah's Flood being the *fifth* period of his annals!! This is *one* way to write history!

the Indian tribes on both sides of Lake Huron, they had conquered the Chawanons, or Shawnese, on the Illinois river; and in 1685, the Twightees, subsequently called the Miamis. In 1711, they conquered and incorporated into their own body the Tuscaroras of the south, who from that period constituted the *sixth* nation of this powerful confederacy.*

This confederation claimed by right of conquest the proprietorship of Kentucky, and of all the lands lying on both sides of the Ohio river. Governor Pownal testifies, that the Six Nations were in actual possession of all these lands at the peace of Ryswick, in 1697.† In their treaty with the British Colonies, in 1744, they put in this claim.‡ They had already put themselves and their vast territories under the protection of the British government, in the year 1701, and again in 1726:|| and in the treaty of Fort Stanwix, in 1768, they had ceded their rights to the British government, for the sum of £10,460 7s. 6d., paid them by Dr. Franklin.

Subsequently, after the conclusion of the French and British war of 1755-1763, the Six Nations seem to have practically relinquished all claim to Kentucky and to the whole territory of the northwest. The two great confederacies of the Miamis and of the Illinois appear, from this period, to have covered the entire northwest, from the banks of the Scioto to those of the Mississippi. The former occupied part of Ohio and the whole of Indiana; the latter, the present State of Illinois. This state-

---

* Thatcher's "Lives of the Indians," (p. 39) quoted by Butler, p. 2. Edit. Louisville, 1834.
† Report of Administration of British Colonies—apud. Butler page 3.
‡ Franklin's Works, vol, iv. p. 271., || Butler, p. 4.

HISTORICAL SUMMARY.

ment is confirmed by General Harrison,* who farther remarks, that the Miamis were the original occupants of the soil, and that the other tribes were viewed as intruders. The Six Nations were called the northern, and those of whom we have just spoken, the western, confederacy. By these two powerful confederations the minor Indian tribes were either successively exterminated, or driven farther into the wilderness.

The right of proprietorship to the soil of Kentucky was obtained by different treaties with the Indian tribes, who successively laid claim to it. The principal of these treaties were: that of Fort Stanwix with the Six Nations, in 1768, already alluded to; that of Lord Dunmore with the Shawnese, in 1744; and that of Col. Henderson with the Cherokees, who ceded their rights to the soil, for the consideration of £10,000, in the year 1775. This last treaty interfered greatly with those previously made; and the conflicting claims which it originated were a fruitful source of litigation among the early emigrants to Kentucky. It was finally set aside and declared illegal by the legislature of Virginia, which however, by way of compensation, assigned ample territory to the Henderson Land Company, in the northwestern part of Kentucky.†

The first settlement of Kentucky by the white people was commenced under circumstances of great difficulty and danger. The first who visited it were either hunters or mere roving adventurers. As early as the year 1747, Dr. Walker of Virginia led a party of hardy adventurers as far as the banks of the Cumberland river, a name which he gave to that stream, after the "bloody Duke" of Eng-

* In his reports to Sec'ry. Armstrong, 1814. Amer. state papers.
† The present county of Henderson is a portion of this territory.

land, in place of its old denomination of *Shawanee*. It is also known, that in the year 1767, the country was visited by John Finley, with a party of hunters from North Carolina; though no written account of this visit has been preserved. Its only result seems to have been to stimulate others to enter on the same perilous career of adventure.

Among those to whom Finley related the thrilling story of his visit to this hitherto unexplored region, was a man, whose life is identified with the early history of Kentucky, and whose name shines conspicuous among the pioneers of the west. For bold enterprise and lofty daring; for unfaltering courage and utter contempt of danger; for firmness of purpose and coolness of execution; for all the qualities necessary for a successful pioneer, few men deserve to rank higher than Daniel Boone. He was the very man for the emergency. His soul was fired with the prospect opened to him by the relation of Finley; and he entered upon the new career which lay before him, with all the ardour of his soul—an ardour which was however qualified by the cool determination to do or to die.

On the first day of May, 1769, Daniel Boone, accompanied by John Finley, John Stewart and three others, left his residence on the Yadkin river, in North Carolina, with the determination to explore Kentucky. On the 7th of June, he reached Red river, a branch of the Kentucky river. From an eminence, he descried the beautiful level of Kentucky, about Lexington; and his soul was charmed with the prospect. He represents the whole country as swarming with buffalo, deer, elk, and all kinds of game, and filled with wild beasts. He continued hunting with his companions until the 22nd of December, soon after which John Stewart was killed by the Indians;

HISTORICAL SUMMARY. 7

the first white man who is known to have fallen by their hands in Kentucky. His comrades, probably alarmed by this circumstance, returned to their homes in North Carolina; but Daniel Boone, with his brother who had lately come out, remained in Kentucky during the winter. He pitched his camp on a creek in the present Estill county, called, from this circumstance, Station Camp Creek. Here he continued until the following May, undisturbed by the Indians, who seldom visited Kentucky in the winter.* He then returned to his friends on Yadkin river.

In this same year, 1769, Col. James Knox led out a party of about forty hunters through the unexplored regions of Tennessee and Kentucky. In Kentucky, nine of this party penetrated as far as the Green and Cumberland rivers, and were designated "the Long Hunters," from the length of time they were absent from their homes.†

The bounty lands awarded by the British government to those who had served in the war against the French, furnished another keen incentive to emigration. For, though the royal proclamation granting the bounty, forbade that the lands should be laid off on the Ohio river, yet its prohibition was disregarded. Surveyors, employed by the claimants of these bounty lands, penetrated to all parts of Kentucky. The most conspicuous of these land surveyors were Thomas Bullit and Hancock Taylor, who came out to Kentucky from Virginia, in 1773. On their route they were overtaken by the M'Afees, whose names are so closely connected with the history of the early settlement

* See Boone's Narrative, written from his dictation, by John Filson, in 1784: and Butler, p. 18. seqq.
† Butler, pp. 18-19.

INTRODUCTION.

of our State.* Bullit was elected Captain of the party, which proceeded to mark off the site of the present city of Louisville, in August, 1773.

During the same year, James Douglass, another surveyor, visited Kentucky. He was the first man who discovered the celebrated collection of mammoth bones, in the place known since by the name of the Big Bone Lick. "Douglass formed his tent poles of the ribs of some of the enormous animals, which formerly frequented this remarkable spot, and on these ribs blankets were stretched for a shelter from the sun and the rain. Many teeth were from eight to nine, and some ten feet in length; one in particular was fastened in a perpendicular direction in the clay and mud, with the end six feet above the surface of the ground; an effort was made by six men in vain to extract it from its mortise. The lick extended to about ten acres of land, bare of timber, and of grass or herbage; much trodden, eaten, and depressed below the original surface, with here and there a knob remaining to show its former elevation."†

About the year 1774, another surveyor, Simon Kenton, with two companions, landed a few miles above Maysville, or *Limestone*, as it was then called. This party penetrated to May's Lick, and visited the Upper and Lower Blue Licks. They saw immense herds of Buffalo, in the vicinity of the licks. On returning to his camp, near May's Lick, from one of his exploring expeditions, Kenton found it sacked and burned by the Indians; and, at a little distance from it, he discovered the mangled remains of Hendricks, one of his com-

---

* For an interesting account of the adventures of the M'Afees, in Kentucky, see Butler, p. 22. segg. His account is drawn from the M'Afee papers, to which he had access.

† Butler, p. 22.

panions, who had been tied to a stake and burned. He was the first and the last white man who suffered this cruel manner of death at the hands of the Indians on the soil of Kentucky.*

The parties who had hitherto visited Kentucky were either hunters, land surveyors, or mere adventurers. No attempt had as yet been made to settle down on the soil and to establish regular colonies. On the 25th of September, 1773, Daniel Boone attempted to remove five families to Kentucky, with a view to their permanent location in the territory which he had already explored. But he had not advanced far when, according to his own account, "the rear of his company was attacked by the Indians, who killed six men and wounded one."† The party returned to their homes, in North Carolina, and the attempt was given over for the present.

Another hardy adventurer from Virginia, was more fortunate. James Harrod came out to Kentucky with several families, in the year 1774. He built the first log cabin in Kentucky, on the site of the present town of Harrodsburgh, then called Harrod's Town. This colony was soon dispersed by the Indians; but, after a brief interval, it was re-established under more favourable auspices.‡

Early in 1775, Daniel Boone again visited Kentucky, in the capacity of guide to a party sent out by the Henderson Land Company, which had purchased the Cherokee title to all the lands south of the Kentucky river. The party was often attacked by the Indians, but finally succeeded in reaching the Kentucky river. To protect themselves from Indian invasion, they immediately set about erecting a fort, which was called Boonesbo-

* Butler, p. 23–4.   † Id. p. 29.   ‡ Id. p. 26.

rough. It was commenced on the 1st of April of that year, and completed on the 14th of June following. This was the first fort erected in Kentucky. It consisted of a stockade, with block houses at the four angles of the quadrangular inclosure.*

The next fort erected was that at Harrod's Town. The colony in the vicinity of this place had been greatly sterngthened by a party led out from North Carolina, by Hugh M'Gary, in the fall of 1775. At Powell's valley he had united his party to another conducted by Daniel Boone; and the whole body numbered twenty-seven *guns*, or fighting men, besides women and children. The parties again divided on reaching Dick's river; that under Boone repairing to Boonesborough, and that under M'Gary, to Harrod's Town. The fort in this latter place was commenced in the winter of 1775-6.†

Wherever a colony was planted, there a fort was also erected, as a protection against the Indians. They were called Stations. These multiplied in proportion as the new territory became settled. The principal and most ancient of them, besides those already named, were: Logan's Station, established by Col. Benjamin Logan, about the same year as that at Harrod's Town, at the distance of one mile from the present town of Stanford, in Lincoln county; Bryant's Station, about twelve miles from Lexington; Floyd's Station, on Beargrass Creek, about six miles from Louisville, and another at Lexington.

Many were the difficulties and terrible the dangers encountered by the first emigrants to Kentucky. They carried their lives in their hands:

* Butler, p. 27.   Id. p. 29. seq.

HISTORICAL SUMMARY. 11

the Indians gave them no rest day or night. From the date of the first settlement in 1774, to that of Wayne's decisive victory and the subsequent treaty of Greenville, in 1795—a period of twenty-one years—Kentucky was a continual battle-ground between the whites and the Indians, the latter ceaselessly endeavouring to break up the colonies, and the former struggling to maintain their position. The savages viewed with an evil eye the encroachment on their favourite hunting grounds, and employed every effort to dislodge the new comers. To effect their purpose, they resorted to every means of stratagem and of open warfare. Their principal efforts were, however, directed against the forts, which they rightly viewed as the rallying points of the emigrants. For nearly four years they besieged, at brief intervals, the forts of Harrod's Town and Boonesborough, especially the former, which they made almost superhuman exertion to break up.

The colonists were often reduced to the greatest straits. Their provisions were exhausted, and all means of obtaining a new supply seemed hopelessly cut off. Their chief resource lay in the game with which the forests abounded. But hunting was hazardous in the extreme, while their wily enemies lay in ambush in the vicinity of the forts. The hunters were often shot down, or dragged into a dreadful captivity, with the prospect of being burned at the stake, staring them in the face. Did they attempt to cultivate the soil, the husbandmen were often attacked by the Indians. The labourers in the field were under the necessity of being constantly armed: they were generally divided into two parties, one of which kept guard, while the other cultivated the soil. But during the four years' siege, above referred to, even this method of tilling the land became too hazardous, and was, at least to a great extent, abandoned.

Besides, their ammunition was often exhausted, and the obtaining of a new supply was extremely difficult and dangerous. The road to the old settlements lay through a wilderness beset with lurking savages. All these difficulties taken together, became truly appalling. Still the hardy pioneers were not cast down. They were struggling for their new homes, for their families, for their very existence. Prodigies of valour were achieved by individuals, and by small parties, to detail which would greatly exceed the limits of this brief summary.* It was the heroic age of Kentucky.

But the rude military tactics of the savage could not cope with the superior organization and higher civilization of the white man. Succours continued to pour into the stations, from Virginia, North Carolina and Maryland, in spite of all Indian opposition. In 1775, there arrived in Harrod's Town a man who was destined to exercise a powerful influence on the rising destinies of Kentucky and of the whole west. James Rogers Clark was a native of Virginia, whence he emigrated to join the bands of hardy adventurers who were seeking their fortunes in the west. He was young, bold, and adventurous; was active in body and mind; and was gifted with great coolness, forecast, and military talent.

In the fall of the year, 1775, Clark returned to Virginia, but he revisited Harrod's Town in the following spring. A meeting of the citizens was held, and he and Gabriel John Jones were appointed delegates to the legislature of Virginia.

---

* We refer those who may wish to see more on this interesting subject, to the two histories of Kentucky aboved named.

HISTORICAL SUMMARY.

They succeeded in obtaining from the Governor and Council of that Commonwealth a loan of 500 pounds of gunpowder, which Clark was charged to transport to Harrod's Town. Clark executed this difficult commission with wonderful intrepidity and success. After having been pursued through almost the entire journey by the Indians, who compelled him to conceal the gunpowder for some time near Maysville, or Limestone, he finally succeeded in delivering it safely at Harrod's Town. The drooping spirits of the garrison rallied on receiving this most fortunate supply, which, had it fallen into the hands of their enemies, would have been employed for their destruction.

The active mind of Clark soon led him to the conviction, that unless some decisive blow were struck, the infant colonies could not hope long to struggle successfully against their savage invaders. He determined to carry the war into the heart of their own territory, and to wrest, if possible, from the hands of the British the military stations of Kaskaskias and St. Vincents, or Post Vincennes. These his quick eye soon discovered were the great rallying points of the Indian invaders. Accordingly, he obtained a Colonel's commission from the Commonwealth of Virginia, with men and military supplies for the expedition. The commission was dated January 2nd, 1778. It was drawn up by Patrick Henry, then Governor of Virginia, who gave Colonol Clark two sets of instructions: one public, ordering him to repair to Kentucky for its defence; and the other private, directing an attack on the British Post of Kaskaskias. The war of the Revolution was then raging; and the success or failure of Clark's expedition was destined to have an important bearing on the question, whether Great Britain or the United

States should be able to claim the proprietorship of the northwest.

Col. Clark showed by his conduct that the confidence reposed in him was not ill-placed. He conducted the expedition with singular prudence and secrecy. He landed his small army near fort Massac, on the Ohio river; marched through Illinois; and, on the fourth of July, 1778, he took Kaskaskias by surprise, without shedding a drop of blood! On the sixth of July, he detached Col. Bowman with a company of men, who surprised and captured the neighbouring military post of Cahokias.*

Col. Clark determined to follow up the advantages thus secured. After a long and painful march through Illinois, in the most inclement season of the year, he appeared, on the 23rd of February, 1779, with 170 men, before Post St. Vincent's, on the Wabash, then also in possession of the British. He compelled the British commandant, Hamilton, to surrender at discretion, after a slight previous skirmishing.† Thus were the British driven from the northwest, by a mere handful of men, under a gallant and skillful commander. And thus also were the great centres of Indian invasion broken up.

Still, notwithstanding this terrible blow struck in their strongest rallying points of the northwest, the Indians, especially the Miamis and the Shawnese, continued to carry on the war with unabated fury, against the white settlers of Kentucky,

---

* We have condensed the detailed statement of Butler, derived from the papers of Gen'l. Clark. p. 48. seqq.

† For a full account of this remarkable expedition, see Butler, p. 81. seqq.; and for a more detailed and interesting one still, see Judge Law's able discourse, delivered before the "Vincennes Historical Society," on the 22nd of Feb. 1839, p. 31. seqq.

HISTORICAL SUMMARY.

They united their forces at Chilicothe, and determined to strike one more blow for the recovery of their favourite hunting grounds, which they beheld fast escaping from their grasp.

On the 14th of August, 1782, an army of about 500 warriors suddenly appeared before Bryant's Station, twelve miles from Lexington. So cautious had been their movements, that they made their appearance in the very heart of Kentucky without exciting any alarm. They closely encompassed the place, killing or driving away the cattle and horses, and shooting down or taking prisoners chance stragglers from the station. The siege continued for only two days; for happily on the first appearance of the savages, a few intrepid men had escaped, who carried the alarm to the neighbouring stations of Lexington, Boonesborough, and Harrod's Town; and also to Logan's Station. So prompt were the movements of the men in these stations, for the succour of their brethren, that on the 18th of August, a force of 182 chosen men from Lexington, Boonesborough, and Harrod's Town, assembled at Bryant's Station. The Indians, anticipating, or cognizant of this movement, had already fled. They were hotly pursued to the Lower Blue Licks, a distance of about 40 miles, where they were speedily overtaken. Daniel Boone and some other officers, fearing an ambuscade, endeavoured to check the ardour of the pursuit, in order to await the arrival of reinforcements under Col. Benjamin Logan from Logan's Station. But this wise course was prevented by the imprudent impetuosity of Major Hugh M'Gary, who, plunging his horse into Licking river, cried out, with a loud voice, that "all who were not cowards should follow him, and he would show them where the Indians were."

INTRODUCTION.

The whole body of the pursuers shared in his impetuosity, and followed after him in disorder. But they had not advanced more than a mile, when they received, throughout their whole front line, a murderous volley from the Indians, who lay concealed in a deep ravine, extending on both sides of the road at right angles to it. The ranks of the white men were thrown into confusion, and, though they fought with desperation, could not withstand the assault for more than a few minutes. They fled precipitately, the Indians following them with loud shouts and uplifted tomahawks. Many were killed in the attempt to recross Licking river. The route was complete, and the Indians pursued them for many miles, killing or taking prisoners the straggling parties whom they were able to overtake.

Never, in the whole annals of Indian warfare in Kentucky, had the white people experienced so overwhelming a defeat. Besides the wounded, about sixty of them were killed, and seven taken prisoners; most of them from Harrod's Station. Among the slain were Col. Todd from Lexington, and Majors Trigg, M'Bride, and Harland, from Harrod's Town. Major M'Gary escaped.

Shortly after the action, Col. Benjamin Logan reached the battle ground with 450 chosen men; but only in time to bury the mangled bodies of the dead. The Indians had already fled into the interior of Ohio. Had the pursuing army patiently awaited his arrival, the disastrous defeat of the Blue Licks might never have occurred. But petty jealousies among the officers, and their desire to win the laurels of victory without the presence and assistance of their senior officer, Col. Logan, prevented their taking the prudent advice of

Daniel Boone: and bitterly did they rue their rashness, when it was too late.*

In the midst of the despondency occasioned by this ruinous defeat, all eyes were turned on Col. James Rogers Clark, who had recently been promoted to the rank of General. He immediately called a meeting of the superior officers, at the Falls of the Ohio river; and it was unanimously resolved to organize a large body of mounted riflemen, for the purpose of attacking the Indian towns in the interior of Ohio.

On the last day of September, 1782, 1000 mounted riflemen appeared at the appointed place of rendezvous, the mouth of Licking river, under the command of Cols. Floyd and Logan, who were the officers next in rank to General Clark. The expedition proceeded with great secrecy to the neighbourhood of Chilicothe. But some Indian stragglers had already communicated the alarm; and on the approach of the army, the Indian towns were found already evacuated. The expedition was enabled only to burn the towns and to destroy the Indian crops; after which the soldiers returned to their respective stations in Kentucky.†

Notwithstanding the constant attacks of the savages, and all the horrors of Indian warfare, the white population continued to pour into Kentucky. But seven years had elapsed since the first attempt to colonize the country, and already, with little more than a month's warning, the infant colonies could send into the field 1000 mounted men. The white population continued to increase so rapidly, that in less than ten years from the date

---

* See, for a more detailed account of this battle, Butler, p. 125. seqq.   † Id. p. 131. seqq.

INTRODUCTION.

of the battle of the Blue Licks, Kentucky, which had hitherto been a mere county dependent on Virginia, was strong enough to claim admission into the Union, as a separate State. The application was first made in 1790; but the convention of deligates for framing the new State Constitution was able to close its labours only on the first of June, 1792. At this latter date Kentucky was recognized as an independent Commonwealth.* She was the first addition to the venerable *thirteen*, who had gloriously fought the battles of Independence.

This war had come to a triumphant termination in 1782—the same year that the battle of the Blue Licks was fought. The United States, now freed from all apprehensions from a foreign foe, had time to breathe, and to devise measures for the protection of the west from Indian invasion. In the year 1790, the United States government commissioned General Harmar, with 320 regular troops under his command, to prosecute the Indian war in the northwest. In the west, his army was joined by a much larger body of militia and volunteers; and the expedition marched from Fort Washington—the site of the present city of Cincinnati—on the 30th of Sept. 1790. The Miamis were the first objects of attack.

But General Harmar was unskilled in the tactics of Indian warfare; and he was too confident in his own opinions to listen to the advice of his western subalterns in command. He proceeded against the Indians according to the rules of regular warfare. The savages outgeneralled him, and his expedition turned out a complete failure. After a few month's campaign, the troops under

* Butler, p. 211.

his comand returned to Fort Washington, without having effected anything, except the destruction of the Indian towns and provisions!* In this expedition Col. Hardin from Kentucky signalized his bravery in many sharp skirmishes with parties of the Indians.

On the failure of Gen'l. Harmar's expedition, the veteran, Gen'l. Arthur St. Clair, was appointed to the command of the American army of operations against the Indians. He had fought bravely in the war of the Revolution; but was now old and infirm. So far was he disabled, in fact, that he was carried on the march in a litter. He had under his command about 3000 men, nearly half of whom were regulars. He marched in good order to the Indian towns: but on the memorable 4th of November, 1791, his army was suddenly attacked and defeated, with dreadful slaughter, by the Miamis. His troops were completely routed, and the retreat was a precipitate flight. Many of the soldiers threw away their arms; and the army left in the hands of the Indians their baggage, artillery, and munitions of war. So disastrous a defeat had never yet occurred in the annals of Indian warfare in the west.†

So far the Indians had triumphed, even over the regular forces of the United States. They clung with tenacity to the cherished tombs of their fathers; and were prepared to resist to the utmost all attempts of the white man to encroach on their territory. Can any one blame them for thus gallantly defending their own lands and firesides?

A deep gloom overspread the frontier settlements of the west. All were alarmed at the prospect of a dreadful Indian invasion, with its attendant hor-

* Butler, p. 191. seqq. † Id. p. 203. seqq.

rors. The terrible war-whoop seemed already to ring in their ears: and the fond mother pressed her infant more warmly to her bosom, as she reflected that perhaps on the morrow its brains might be dashed out by the ruthless savage, and her own head scalped or riven by the knife or tomahawk. The long years of bitter struggle with the Indians had proved, that these terrors were not wholly without foundation.

In this emergency, the United States government at length selected a man who was adequate to the undertaking of putting an end to the Indian War, and of thus effectually protecting the western settlements. Gen'l. Anthony Wayne, an officer of the Revolution, combined great coolness of purpose with that impetuosity of bravery, which had already obtained for him the *soubriquet* of "*Mad Anthony.*"

This brave and experienced officer marched, during the winter of 1793, to the scene of Gen'l. St. Clair's disastrous defeat. He re-occupied it, and on its site erected a fort, which he called Fort Recovery. In the summer of 1794 he was joined by about 1600 Kentucky volunteers, under Gen'l. Scott: and he then found himself in command of about 3200 troops, one half of whom were regulars. He was unremitting in his labors, to train his army to all the subtle tactics of Indian warfare. He caused them to sleep on their arms; and during the night, he often had them aroused by feigned surprises from the Indians. The troops were thus schooled to the vicissitudes of an Indian campaign.

After having sufficiently trained his men, and engaged in several skirmishes with the savages, he marched his forces to the principal Indian settlements, at the confluence of the Au Glaize and

HISTORICAL SUMMARY.

Maumee rivers. Here he attempted a surprise, but without effect, the Indians having already fled. He continued his march to the Rapids of the Maumee, where, on the 20th of August, 1794, he encountered the whole Indian force. A great and decisive engagement ensued, which, after a short contest, resulted in a complete victory for the Americans. The power of the Indians was broken overwhelmingly, and, as the event proved, for ever.*

In the following year, 1795, the great Treaty of Greenville secured a permanent peace between the Indians and the white men, and protected the latter from all fear of further invasion. After this treaty, the Indians made few more struggles for their territory, which they beheld fast escaping from their hands. They sullenly yielded to their fate, and gradually melted away, before the march of *civilization*,(!) leaving the graves of their fathers behind them. Thus terminated the Indian border wars of the northwest.

*Butler, p. 235. seqq.

CHAPTER II.

The Early Catholic Emigrants to Kentucky.

Glowing reports of the Pioneers—Virginia and Maryland in motion towards the West—The first Catholic Emigrants to Kentucky—Dr. Hart—Wm. Coomes—The first Physician and the first School—The Successive Catholic colonies—Dangers on the way—Running the gauntlet—Indian attacks—Death of McManus, of Cox, and of Buckman—The Savages and the Cross—Thrilling incident of the Late War—Mode of procuring salt—Domestic manners of the Early Emigrants to Kentucky—Furniture, food, and apparel—Hospitality—Singular adventures and hair-breadth escapes of William Coomes—Incidents in the early history of Harrod's Town.

THE reports carried back to Virginia and Maryland, by the first adventurers who had visited Kentucky, were of so glowing a character as to stimulate many others to emigrate thither. The new country was represented as a sort of promised land, with an exuberant and fertile soil; and, if not flowing with milk and honey, at least teeming with all kinds of wild game. This rich country now lay open to the enterprising activity of the white man; its fertile lands could be obtained by occupation, or purchased for a mere trifle; and the emigrants might subsist, like the Indians, by hunting, until the soil could be prepared for cultivation.

To be sure, dangers were to be encountered on the way to this beautiful region; and these dangers would perhaps increase, after the emigrant should be able to settle down at his new home. The reports of the first pioneers were interspersed with tales of horror concerning those who had been killed and scalped by the Indians, or who had been dragged into captivity and mercilessly burnt at the stake. But these frightful narratives, however much they grated on the ear, could not quench, or even check to any great extent, the growing spirit of adventure. Men and women, young and old, caught up this spirit; and soon nearly half of Virginia and Maryland was in motion for the west. In the brief space of seventeen years—between 1775 and 1792—Kentucky, from being a vast unreclaimed wilderness, became a state of the Union!

The Catholic population of Kentucky emigrated almost entirely from Maryland; chiefly from St. Mary's Charles', and Prince George's Counties. They were descendents of the good old Colonists of Lord Baltimore. Maryland was, in every respect, the great *alma mater* of the Catholics of Kentucky. She supplied them with people from her superabundant population; and she too sent out the first missionaries who broke to them the bread of life.

The first Catholics who are known to have emigrated to our State, were Wm. Coomes and family, and Dr. Hart. They both came out in the spring of 1775, among the very first white people who removed to Kentucky. They settled in Harrod's station, at that time the only place in Kentucky, except Boonesborough and perhaps Logan's station, where emigrants could enjoy any degree of security from the attacks of the Indians.

Dr. Hart was an exemplary Irish Catholic. He was one of the first physicians, if not the very first of the profession, who settled in Kentucky. He lived for many years in Harrod's Town, where he was engaged in the practice of medicine. After the great body of the Catholics had located themselves in the vicinity of Bardstown, he too removed thither, in order to enjoy the blessings of his religion. He purchased a farm about a mile from Bardstown, embracing the site of the present burial-ground of St. Joseph's congregation. It was he who made a present to the church of this lot of ground, upon which old St. Joseph's church was erected. Towards the building of this, one among the oldest Catholic churches of Kentucky, he also liberally contributed. He was the first Catholic who died in Kentucky, and the first that was buried in the cemetery which himself had bestowed.

William Coomes was originally from Charles co., Maryland, whence he had removed to the south branch of the Potomac river, in Virginia. He emigrated to Kentucky, with his family, together with Abraham and Isaac Hite. On their way through Kentucky to Harrod's Station, the party encamped for seven weeks at Drilling's Lick, in the neighbourhood of the present city of Frankfort. Here Mrs. Coomes, aided by those of the party who were not engaged in hunting, employed herself in making salt—for the first time, perhaps, that this article was manufactured in our State.

Some time after the party had reached Harrod's Town, the men of the station being all otherwise busily engaged, Mrs. Coomes, at the urgent request of the citizens, opened a school for the education of children. This was, in all probability, the first elementary school established in Kentucky. Thus the first school-teacher, and probably the first physician of our Commonwealth, were both Catholics.

Of the remarkable adventures of Wm. Coomes, we intend to speak more in detail at the close of the present chapter. We will here rapidly glance at the chief colonies of Catholics, who successively removed to the State, and of the dangers they severally encountered on the way. Our information has been carefully gleaned from the oral statements of many of the old emigrants, who are now fast disappearing from the stage of life.

The first Catholic colony which emigrated to Kentucky, after those already named, was the one which accompanied the Haydons and Lancasters. They reached the new country some time in the year 1785; and located themselves chiefly on Pottinger's Creek, at the distance of from ten to fifteen miles from Bardstown. A few of them, however, settled in the more immediate vicinity of Bardstown. The selection of Pottinger's Creek as the location of the new Catholic colony, was unfortunate. The land was poor, and the situation uninviting. Yet the nucleus of the new colony having been formed, these disadvantages were subsequently disregarded. The new Catholic emigrants from Maryland, continued to flock to the same neighbourhood. They preferred being near their brethren, and enjoying with them the advantages of their holy religion, to all other mere worldly considerations. They could not brook the idea of straggling off in different directions, where, though they might better their earthly condition, they and their children would, in all probability, be deprived of the consolations of religion.

The Protestant emigrants to our State seem to have been guided by no such principle: and this may serve to explain to us their general superior advantages, in a worldly point of view. The all-pervading principle of Catholicity is union; while disunion, on the contrary, is the distinctive feature of Protestantism. And while on this subject, we may remark, in general, that, with two or three exceptions, the Catholic emigrants to Kentucky selected poor and unproductive land for their settlements. They followed each other like a flock of sheep: nor is this a disparaging comparison; for our Blessed Lord often adopted it as a favorite illustration of the distinctive qualities of His disciples.

A much larger colony of Catholics than that just named emigrated to Kentucky in the spring of the year 1786, with Captain Jas. Rapier. They settled in the same neighborhoods with those who had preceded them, in the previous year. In the following year, 1787, another colony came out with Philip Miles and Thomas Hill. Catholic emigrants continued to pour into Kentucky, during the following years. In 1788, Robert Abell emigrated thither with some of his friends.* In the year 1790, a

* Robert Abell was one of the Delegates to the Convention which framed our State Constitution; and he was the only Catholic in that body. The following incident may not be here inappropriate. The Convention had agreed that each of the delegates might draw up a draught of the new Constitution; and that, on the debate in regard to each provision, those should be selected from the respective draughts which should be deemed best by the majority of delegates. Robert Abell had two room-mates: the late distinguished Felix Grundy of Nashville, and a lawyer, who had been a Presbyterian preacher. The last named, one day called the attention of his two companions to a provision which he had inserted in his draught of the Constitution, which ran about as follows: "And be it further provided, that no papist or Roman Catholic shall hold any office of profit or trust in this Commonwealth." Immediately, Felix Grundy seized his pen, and indited the following clause in *his* draught: "And be it also provided, that no broken-down Presbyterian preacher shall be eligible to any office in this Commonwealth." This clause he read to the lawyer-preacher, whom he further assured that he would lay it before the Convention, and advocate its adoption, the very moment the provision excluding Roman Catholics should be read before that body. The "broken-down" preacher looked blank, and no more was heard of his famous clause. This incident was related to a son of Robert Abell, by Felix Grundy himself.

colony came out with Benedict Spalding, from St. Mary's county, Maryland. This was followed, in the ensuing year, by other emigrants who accompanied Leonard Hamilton. The greater portion of these three last named colonies located themselves on the Rolling Fork of Salt river, in the present county of Marion. After the cessation of Indian hostilities, and the treaty of Greenville, in 1795, emigration to the west was not attended with so much difficulty or danger, as before; and the number of Catholics who removed to Kentucky proportionably increased.

But before this period, the hardships and dangers which the emigrant had to encounter, both on the way and after he had reached his destination, are almost incredible at the present day. The new comers generally descended the Ohio river in flat boats from Pittsburgh. The Indians lurked in the forests, on both sides of the river, awaiting the first favorable opportunity to pounce upon their prey; to seize the boats, and to capture or butcher the occupants. The boats of Miles and Hill, in 1787, were fired on by the Indians, about twenty miles above Louisville: all the horses were killed, and likewise one man, by the name of Hall, who was acting as stearsman; but the boats fortunately escaped. We may also mention that one of the Haydons lost seven, and the other, three members of his family, from hardship and sickness, while on their way to Kentucky.

Descending the Ohio river, at that time, was like running the gauntlet between two files of savages. After the failure of General Harmar's expedition, in 1790, the Indians, elated with their success, became still more troublesome to those who were travelling westward. They lay in wait, in large and formidable parties, for the boats floating down the Ohio; and many a death-struggle took place between them and the boatmen. In that, or the following year, the boat of Captain Hubbell, with nine men on board, was attacked by the Indians, who approached it in canoes. A desperate contest ensued, in which Capt. Hubbell had three of his men killed, and three wounded, himself having been shot through the arm. At length, however, the Indians were beaten off with handspikes from the gunwales of the boat, upon which they had seized, in the desperate attempt to board it. The boat escaped.*

The boat of Greathouse, which was descending the Ohio about the same time, was less fortunate. It was captured almost without resistance, and the miserable crew were hurried off into a dreadful captivity. In the same year, another boat, with some Catholic families on board, was likewise attacked, but it succeeded in effecting its escape. Some of the men were, however, killed, and among them, Mr. McManus, the father of the late estimable Charles McManus of Bardstown. His bereaved widow continued her journey to Kentucky, with the family, and settled in Bardstown. During the rest of her life she edified all by her exemplary piety, and died a most edifying death, on the 5th of October, 1825.

The following testimony of a distinguished cotemporary, Judge Innes of Kentucky, may serve to show us how great were the dangers encountered by those who attempted to emigrate to Kentucky, during the time of which we are speaking. In a letter to Secretary Knox, written on the 7th July, 1790, he says: "He had been intimately acquainted with this district (Kentucky) from November 1783, to the time of writing; and that *fif-*

* See Hubbell's Narrative—and Butler, p. 195.

teen hundred souls had been killed and taken in the district, and migrating to it; that upwards of twenty thousand horses had been taken and carried off; and other property, to the amount of at least fifteen thousand pounds."*

Nor were the emigrants more safe after they had reached their destination in Kentucky. The Indians continually prowled about in the vicinity of the new settlements, attacking them if they seemed left defenceless, and murdering women and children, or dragging them into captivity. In the spring of 1788, the house of Col. Isaac Cox, about eleven miles from Bardstown, was attacked by them, and he was slain, his body being left in a dreadfully mutilated and mangled condition. In the year 1794, a Catholic man, named Buckman, was likewise killed, on Cloyd's creek, near the Rolling Fork. In the panic which followed this murder, many Catholics left that settlement, and removed for a time to Bardstown, around which the people were more densely settled. One who remained at his home, is said to have made a large cross with charcoal, on the outside of his cabin door; and it is farther reported, that the Indians, seeing this sign, passed the house by unharmed. They probably belonged to those tribes of the northwest, which, many years before, had been taught Christianity by the Jesuit missionaries; and they may have still retained some remembrance of the principles they or their fathers had then imbibed. This may explain to us their respect for the cross; if indeed the story be thought worthy of credit.

This reminds us of another anecdote of a similar nature, which rests on the most respectable authority, and which we will briefly relate, though

* Political Transactions, p. 58—and Butler, p. 195.

it does not properly belong to the history which we are attempting to sketch.

In the late war, an Irish Catholic, a deserter from the British army, had enlisted in the American service. The regiment to which he was attached marched to the northern frontier, near which, about the year 1812 or 1813, it encountered a formidable body of British and Indians. The Americans were defeated and fled precipitately, the Irishman flying with the rest. The Indians pursued with the deafening war-whoop, and with uplifted tomahawks. The Irishman finding that he was about to be overtaken by a stout warrior, fell on his knees, and made the sign of the cross, and endeavored, as well as he could, to prepare himself for death. The warrior suddenly stopped, dropped his tomahawk, and falling likewise on his knees, embraced the white man, exclaiming: "You are my brother!" Meantime, other Indians came up and witnessed the affecting scene. The warrior told them of the treasure of a brother he had been so fortunate as to find; and, after a brief consultation, they determined to take the Irishman to their camp, and to constitute him their "father prayer." The Irish Catholic gladly accepted the proposition, and remained with them for a few days, saying prayers for them, and teaching them the principles of the Catholic faith, as best he could. But knowing the fate which awaited him, if he should fall into the hands of the British, he told his Indian brethren that he was not a real "father prayer;" but that if they would permit him to go to New York, he would exert himself to procure for them a Catholic priest, who would teach them their prayers. The Indians assented to the proposal; and, on his arrival in New York, the Irishman related the whole adventure to the Rev

Benedict Fenwick, S. J.—the present distinguished Bishop of Boston—who was then stationed in New York.*

These Indians probably belonged to the tribe of the Penobscotts or the Abenakis of Maine, whose forefathers had learned the Catholic faith from the Franciscan and Jesuit missionaries. This incident, and that previously mentioned, in which the sign of the cross was the means of warding off danger and saving life, remind us of the blood of the lamb, sprinkled on the lintels of the doors, by the Israelites in Egypt, to avert the scourge of the destroying angel.

The early Catholic emigrants to Kentucky, in common with their brethren of other denominations, had to endure many privations and hardships. As we may well conceive, there were few luxuries to be found in the wilderness, in the midst of which they had fixed their new habitations. They often suffered even for the most indispensable necessaries of life. To obtain salt, they had to travel for many miles to the licks, through a country infested with savages; and they were often obliged to remain there for several days, until they could procure a supply.

There were then no regular roads in Kentucky. The forests were filled with a luxuriant undergrowth, thickly interspersed with the cane, and the whole closely interlaced with the wild pea-vine. These circumstances rendered them nearly impassable; and almost the only chance of effecting a passage through this vegetable wilderness, was by following the paths, or *traces*, made by the herds of buffalo and other wild beasts. Luckily, these *traces* were numerous, especially in the vicinity of

* We are indebted for this anecdote, to the Very Rev. Stephen Theodore Badin.

the licks, which the buffalo were in the habit of frequenting, to drink the salt water, or *lick* the earth impregnated with salt.*

The new colonists resided in log cabins, rudely constructed, with no glass in the windows, with floors of dirt, or, in the better sort of dwellings, of puncheons of split timber, roughly hewn with the axe. After they had worn out the clothing brought with them from the old settlements, both men and women were under the necessity of wearing buckskin or homespun apparel. Such a thing as a store was not known in Kentucky for many years: and the names of broadcloth, ginghams and calicoes, were never even so much as breathed. Moccasins made of buckskin, supplied the place of our modern shoes; blankets thrown over the shoulder answered the purpose of our present fashionable coats and cloaks; and handkerchiefs tied around the head served instead of hats and bonnets. A modern fashionable bonnet would have been a matter of real wonderment in those days of unaffected simplicity.

The furniture of the cabins was of the same primitive character. Stools were used instead of chairs; the table was made of slabs of timber, rudely put together; wooden vessels and platters supplied the place of our modern plates and chinaware; and "a tin cup was an article of delicate furniture, almost as rare as an iron fork."† The beds were either placed on the floor, or on bedsteads of puncheons, supported by forked pieces of timber, driven into the ground, or resting on pins let into *auger* holes in the sides of the cabin.

---

* This circumstance, as every body knows, caused those places to be called *licks*.

† Marshall—History of Kentucky—vol. 1. p. 123. Edit. *Sup. cit.*

Blankets, and bear and buffalo skins, constituted often the principal bed covering.

One of the chief resources for food was the chase. All kinds of game were then very abundant; and when the hunter chanced to have a goodly supply of ammunition, his fortune was made for the year. The game was plainly dressed, and served up on wooden platters, with corn bread, and the Indian dish—the well known *homeny*. The corn was ground with great difficulty, on the laborious hand-mills; for mills of other descriptions were then, and for many years afterwards, unknown in Kentucky.

Such was the simple manner of life led by *our* "pilgrim fathers." They had fewer luxuries, but perhaps were, withal, more happy than their more fastidious descendants. Hospitality was not then an empty name; every log cabin was freely thrown open to all who chose to share in the best cheer its inmates could afford. The early settlers of Kentucky were bound together by the strong ties of common hardships and dangers—to say nothing of other bonds of union—and they clung together with great tenacity. On the slightest alarm of Indian invasion, they all made common cause, and flew together to the rescue. There was less selfishness, and more generous chivalry; less bickering, and more cordial charity, then, than at present; notwithstanding all our boasted refinement.

We will close this chapter with a brief account of the singular adventures and hair-breadth escapes of William Coomes, who, as we have already seen, was, with Dr. Hart, the first Catholic that came to Kentucky.* He settled with his family

* We have derived our information from Mr. Walter A. Coomes, the son of Wm. Coomes. He was a lad of about six-

in Harrod's Town, in the spring of 1775, and remained there for about nine years, sharing in all the dangers and hardships of his fellow-townsmen. Early in March, 1777, the Indians appeared in the vicinity of Harrod's Town, to begin the memorable siege which was to last, with little intermission, for nearly four years. Mr. Butler, the historian of Kentucky, thus introduces the account of this attack; in which, as elsewhere, he follows Marshall. *

"On the 29th of December (1776,) a large body of Indians attacked McClellan's fort, on Elkhorn, killed McClellan, his wife, and two others, which drove the residue of the people to Harrod's Town. This necessarily produced great alarm; it was soon much increased by an attack of the Indians on James Ray, his brother, and *another* man, who were clearing some land about four miles from Harrod's Town, at the present residence of this venerable and distinguished pioneer. (*Ray*) The hostile party, consisting of forty-seven warriors, under command of Blackfish, a celebrated chief, attracted by the noise of the axes, rushed upon the little party of choppers, killed the younger Ray, and took the *third man* prisoner. The elder Ray escaped by his uncommon swiftness of foot."

The *third man* here referred to was William Coomes; but there was yet a *fourth* man, named Thomas Shores, whom Mr. Butler does not men-

---

teen, when he emigrated to Kentucky, with his father; and he is now in his 74th year. He states that his father reached Harrod's Town in the spring of 1774; but as this date does not seem to tally with those of corresponding facts stated by Butler, who follows Marshall, we have preferred the statement, that Wm. Coomes emigrated a year later. This throws back, by one year, each of the dates mentioned in the original statement of Mr. Coomes.

Butler, p. 42—Marshall, vol. 1, p. 48.

tion. He, and not William Coomes, as we shall presently see, was taken prisoner by the Indians, at the Shawnee Springs. The historian's statement does not tally with that of Mr. Coomes in many other important particulars. The statement of the latter* is briefly as follows; and we have not a doubt of its substantial accuracy.

The party of choppers alluded to, consisted of the two Rays, Wm. Coomes, and Thomas Shores, who were engaged in clearing land, at the Shawnee Springs, for Hugh M'Gary, the father-in-law of the two Rays. On the 6th of March, 1777, the two Rays and Shores visited a neighbouring sugar-camp, to slake their thirst, leaving Mr. Coomes alone at the clearing. Wm. Coomes, alarmed at their protracted absence, had suspended his work, and was about to start in search of them; when he suddenly spied a body of Indians—fifteen in number—coming directly towards him from the direction of the sugar-camp. He instantly concealed himself behind the trunk of the three which he had just felled, at the same time seizing and cocking his rifle. Fortunately, the Indians had not observed him, owing to the thick canebrake and undergrowth: they passed by him in Indian file, to a temporary log cabin, which the woodmen had erected for their accommodation.

So soon as they were out of sight, Coomes escaped towards the sugar-camp, to find out what had become of his companions. Discovering no trace of them, he concealed himself amidst the boughs of a fallen hickory tree, the yellow leaves of which were of nearly the same colour as his garments. From his hiding place he had a full view of the sugar-camp; and after a short time he

* Furnished us, as we have said, by his son, who was at the time in Harrod's Station, a youth then about 18 years of age.

observed a party of forty Indians halt there, where they were soon rejoined by the fifteen whom he had previously seen. They tarried there for a long time, drinking the syrup, singing their war-songs, and dancing their war-dance. Coomes was a breathless spectator of this scene of revelry, from the distance of only fifty or sixty yards. Other straggling parties of savages also came in, and the whole number amounted to about seventy, instead of forty seven, as stated by Butler and Marshall.

Meantime, James Ray had escaped and communicated the alarm to the people at Harrod's Town. Great was the terror and confusion which ensued there. The hot-headed McGary openly charged James Harrod with having been wanting in the precautions and courage necessary for the defence of the fort. These two men, who had a personal enmity against each other, quarrelled and levelled their fatal rifles at each other's bosoms. In this conjuncture, the wife of McGary rushed in, and turned aside the rifle of her husband, when Harrod immediately withdrew his, and the difficulty was temporarily adjusted.

McGary insisted that a party of thirty should be immediately despatched with him in search of Coomes, Shores, and his son-in-law, Wm. Ray: Harrod, the commandant of the station, and Col. James Rogers Clark, thought this measure rash and imprudent, as all the men were necessary for the defence of the place, which might be attacked by the Indians at any moment. At length, however, chiefly at the urgent instance of a Mr. Pendergrast,* the request of McGary was granted; and thirty mounted men were placed under his command for the expedition.

* Who subsequently removed to Louisville.

The detachment moved with great rapidity, and soon reached the neighbourhood of the sugar-camp, which the Indians had already abandoned. Near it they discovered the mangled remains of Wm. Ray, at the sight of which McGary turned pale, and was near falling from his horse, in a fainting fit. As soon as the body was discovered, one of the men shouted out: "See there! they have killed poor Coomes!" Coomes, who had hitherto lurked in his hiding place, now sallied forth, and ran towards the men, exclaiming: "No, they haven't killed me, by Job! I'm safe!"

The party having buried Ray, and rescued Coomes, returned in safety to Harrod's Town, which they reached about sunset. All hands then set to work to put the place in a state of defence; and on the next morning, the memorable seige commenced, which was destined to keep Harrod's Town in danger, and in constant alarm, for several years. During this whole time the gallant little garrison was harrassed day and night. Ten sentinels mounted guard during the day, and double that number at night. The whole number of fighting men in the station scarcely exceeded sixty. Their provisions and ammunition were often exhausted; and the obtaining of a new supply was attended with great danger. Yet it was frequently accomplished, in the very face of the besiegers. Small parties escaped from the fort in the night, and after having secured an abundant supply of game, in a distant hunting-ground, or obtained ammunition from a neighbouring station, returned with the same caution to the fort. James Ray was often a leader of these foraging parties.

The people in the station received their daily supply of provisions from a common store: there was an officer appointed to distribute the rations to each

E

family, in proportion to the number of its members. Things were conducted pretty much on the same plan as in a regular army, or in a man of war at sea. The women and children shared in the gallantry of their husbands and fathers for the defence of the fort.

We find no mention, by either of the historians of Kentucky, of the following stirring adventure, in which Wm. Coomes was likewise an actor. In the spring of 1778, he was one of a party of thirty men, sent out under Col. Bowman, for the purpose of shelling corn at a plantation about seven miles distant from Harrod's Town. The men were divided into pairs, each of which had a large sack, which was to be filled and brought back to the fort. While engaged in filling the sacks, they were fired on by a party of about forty Indians, who had lain concealed in the neighbouring canebrake. At the first fire seven of the white men were shot down, and among them a Mr. H. Berry, the person standing by the side of Wm. Coomes, whose face was bespattered with the blood from the wounds of his fallen comrade. Eight others of the white men fled for shelter to the canebrake; but the rest of them, rallied by the loud cries of Col. Bowman, seized their rifles, and, sheltering themselves in an adjoining cabin, or behind the trees, prepared to defend themselves to the last. One of the men, observing the face of Coomes reddened with blood, mistook him for an Indian, and was levelling his rifle at him, when the latter, fortunately remarking his movement, cried out, and thus saved his life.

Meantime, Col. Bowman despatched a courier on horseback to Harrod's Town, to carry the alarm, and to obtain a reinforcement. The messenger sped his way unharmed to the fort, though many a rifle was aimed at him, and though another strong party of savages were lying in ambush on the way he had to travel. In a few hours, the expected reinforcement arrived; when the Indians, baffled in their object, betook themselves to flight. The white men, after burying their dead, returned to Harrod's Town in the evening, with their replenished sacks of corn.

This adventure was but one out of a hundred of a similar character which occurred in the vicinity of Harrod's Town, during the four years' siege of that station.* So fully resolved were the Indians to break up this fort, that they had erected a counter fort in the neighbourhood of the place. This Indian station was discovered by one of the small foraging parties from Harrod's Town. A detachment was immediately sent out, which, after a short contest, succeeded in dislodging the Indians from this stronghold, which was reduced to ashes.

We have entered into all these details, because they appear to us to throw some additional light on the early history of Harrod's Town: and because they also serve to show us what dangers the first Catholic emigrants to Kentucky shared, in common with their brethren of other denominations. The siege of Harrod's Station continued, till the year 1781, when about a hundred additional emigrants, chiefly from Virginia, took up their

* The Indians had a great dislike for McGary, whom they often endeavoured to kill. On one occasion they left a fine moccasin in a road near Harrod's Town, over which they expected him to pass. They intended to shoot him as he stopped to pick up the moccasin. But McGary, suspecting their plan, put spurs to his horse, and escaped, though more than one rifle ball whistled by his head.

residence in the place. The Indians then gave up the siege in despair, and returned to their own wigwams in the northwest.

William Coomes, after residing for nearly nine years in Harrod's Town,* removed, in 1783, to the vicinity of Bardstown, in order to be near his Catholic brethren, and to enjoy the advantages of his holy religion. He lived here for many years, and died in a good old age.

* Wm. Coomes had a son, who fought in the battle of the Blue Licks, from which he very narrowly escaped with his life.

CHAPTER III.

The First Catholic Missionary in Kentucky—His Life and Times.—From 1787, *to* 1793.

Father Whelan—His early history—His appointment to the Mission of Kentucky—His arrival and missionary labors—Promiscuous meetings and dancing—Prejudices of Sectarians—Anecdotes—Father Whelan's trials and difficulties—His return to Maryland and subsequent life—Rev. Wm. De Rohan—Remarkable adventures of John Lancaster.

As we have already seen in the preceding chapter, considerable colonies of Catholics had emigrated from Maryland to Kentucky, in the years 1785 and 1786, especially in the latter. We have also seen what difficulties and dangers they had to encounter, both on their journey westward, and after they had reached their new home in the wilderness. But the privation which they felt most keenly was, that they were without the consolations of their Holy Religion. They formed a flock without a shepherd. No Catholic priest had as yet penetrated those remote wilds: the clean oblation of the New Law had never yet been offered up on the " dark and bloody ground !"

Ireland had the honor of sending one of her sons as the first missionary to Kentucky. One of the principal Catholic emigrants to Kentucky, on his return to Maryland in the spring of 1787, represented the bereaved condition of the Catholic colonists to the Very Rev. John Carroll, then Vicar General of the Bishop or Vicar Apostolic of the London District. He represented, that there were already in Kentucky about fifty Catholic families —the number of which was yearly increasing— and that all of these were totally deprived of every religious succour, which they, however, greatly needed amidst the difficulties and perils that daily encompassed them.

The paternal heart of the zealous Vicar General was moved at this picture of spiritual bereavement; and he determined immediately to supply the pressing wants of so distant a branch of his extensive charge.* After mature deliberation, he selected for this difficult and dangerous mission the Rev. Mr. Whelan, an Irish Franciscan, who had been already for some years employed on the American missions.

F. Whelan, it appears, had received his theological education in France, and he had served as Chaplain in one of the French ships of war sent out to the aid of the American colonies in their struggle for Independence. At the happy close of the revolutionary war, in 1782, being pleased with the new American Government, and strongly impressed with the wants of the American Catholic Church, he determined to select America as the land of his adoption, and to devote the rest of his life to its infant missions. Accordingly, he offered his services to the Very Rev. Dr. Carroll, who cheerfully accepted them. At the time that he was selected for the mission of Kentucky, he was residing with the Jesuits at New Town, in Maryland.

He did not hesitate long ere he accepted the appointment tendered him by his superior. Though past the flower of age, and though he had been

* His jurisdiction extended over the whole territory owned by the United States at the peace of 1782.

trained up amidst the refinements of one of the most highly civilized nations in the world, yet he cheerfully responded to the call, regardless of the hardships and dangers which stared him in the face, on the distant field of his future labours. He immediately took his departure with a new Catholic colony which was emigrating to Kentucky in the spring of 1787; and, after sharing with them in all the privations and perils of their long journey, he happily reached his destination in the fall of the same year. Those who have read the two preceding chapters will be able to estimate the dangers through which he had to pass on his journey westward. The whole country which he traversed from the frontier settlements of Maryland and Pennsylvania to the heart of the wilderness, was infested with savages thirsting for the blood of the white man.

On his arrival, F. Whelan found an ample field for the exercise of his zeal. The Catholics of the infant colonies received him with open arms; many of them had not seen a priest for two years. They were poor, were scattered over an extensive territory, and had no church in which the divine mysteries might be offered up. They were in too destitute a condition to be able to erect even a temporary place of worship. F. Whelan visited the different neighbourhoods in which the Catholics were located, offered up the Holy Sacrifice in the rude log cabins of the country, and laboured indefatigably to stir up in the people proper sentiments of piety. He laboured day and night, preaching, catechizing, administering the sacraments, and making himself "all to all in order to gain all" to Christ.

He was assiduous in the discharge of his duties. He was never known to miss an appointment, no matter how inclement the season, or how greatly he had been exhausted by previous labours. Often was he known to swim rivers, even in the dead of winter, in order to reach a distant station on the appointed day.* On these occasions, the vestments, Missal, and ornaments of the altar, which he was compelled always to carry with him, were immersed in the water; and he was under the necessity of delaying divine service until they could be dried at the fire.

During their brief sojourn in the wilderness, his little flock had gradually fallen into many practices which were dangerous to piety. They were in the habit of gathering promiscuously on Saturday evenings and Sundays, and of dancing to a late hour. In the rude state of society at that time, these meetings were often attended with great disorders. F. Whelan was uncompromising in his opposition to such assemblages, and he made every effort to put a stop to them; nor did he relax in his exertions until he had, in a great measure, succeeded in his purpose. He thus had the satisfaction of seeing that his labours were not without fruit; though, with all his exertions, he was unable to have even one Catholic church erected during his short stay in Kentucky.

Besides these difficulties with his own flock, he had to encounter the fierce opposition of the sectarians, whose prejudices against the Catholic church were of the grossest character. Misled by the erroneous opinions which their forefathers had inherited from England, they were in the habit of viewing Catholics as idolaters, and the priests as a

* These particulars, as well as those preceding and following, have been carefully gleaned from the oral statements of the Very Rev. M. Badin, and of some of the oldest Catholic emigrants to Kentucky.

species of jugglers. Nor were they at all reserved in the manner of exhibiting this prejudice.

F. Whelan was often rudely interrupted in the midst of his sermons, which he delivered with the warmth and eloquence not uncommon to his countrymen. On one of these occasions, while he was preaching in the open air, near the site of the present church of Holy Cross, an ignorant man, a tailor, stopped him in the middle of his discourse. F. Whelan paused, and remarking with a smile, that he supposed every one should know his own trade best, asked the interlocuter—"What was his profession?" The man, somewhat abashed, answered that he was "a tailor." "Well then," resumed F. Whelan, "will you be so good as to inform me how many yards of cloth would be required to make a suit of clothes for a man who should stand with one foot on the court-house at Bardstown, and the other on the *knob*,* or eminence near which we are now assembled?" The distance was about ten miles. The tailor was silent. "Do you see," continued F. Whelan, "this man is wholly ignorant of his own trade, and yet he ventures to instruct me in mine." The man was non-plussed, and the priest resumed his discourse, amidst the smiles of the audience.

On another occasion, he was attacked by a sort of preacher, who professed to understand every thing that was contained in the Bible. F. Whelan so effectually exposed his ignorance, that the man lodged a complaint against him, stating, among other things, that the priest had called him an *ignoramus*. F. Whelan called for a New Testament, and pledged himself to prove the truth of the allegation, to the satisfaction of all present.

* Now called "Rohan's Knob."

He read aloud the first verse of St. Mathew's Gospel, in which Jesus Christ is styled "the Son of David, the Son of Abraham;" and asked the preacher "how Christ could be the son of David, who had lived about a thousand years before him, and of Abraham, who had lived at a much earlier period; and how, even if this difficulty were removed, Christ could have two fathers?" The man put on his spectacles, read the passage attentively; and after remaining silent for some time, remarked, with evident embarrassment, that he supposed there must be some mistake in the text!!

But F. Whelan was destined to encounter difficulties of a much more painful nature, with some members of his own flock. And though it is not deemed necessary to dwell upon these painful occurrences at any great length, yet this sketch would be incomplete without a brief explanation of their origin, progress, and results. The early missions of every country have been beset with similar difficulties.

Previous to his departure from Maryland, the Very Rev. Dr. Carroll had thought it prudent to adopt such measures as would secure to him a competent support in the new mission in which he was to labour. Accordingly, an instrument of writing was drawn up, by which six of the principal emigrants to Kentucky had bound themselves to pay him annually the sum of one hundred pounds in currency—a sum about equal to $280 of our present money. Yet F. Whelen had not been more than six months in Kentucky, when an effort was made by one or two of the principal contractors to have this instrument set aside and declared illegal by the courts of law. The jury decided for the validity of the contract, but, singularly enough, subjoined to their verdict the clause, that the amount called for should be paid in the produce of the country, and not in money.

The prosecutors were foiled, but still resolved to use every effort to be freed from their engagement. For speaking with some vivacity of their conduct at the trial, in the presence of a person who reported his words, probably with exaggerations, to those concerned, F. Whelan was sued for slander, before the same court; and the jury brought in a verdict of five hundred pounds fine, or imprisonment until the payment of this large amount could be secured. At that time, there was not, in all probability, that amount of money in the whole district of Kentucky. F. Whelan was, in fact, about to be taken to prison, whither he cheerfully offered to go, when the principal prosecutor, a nominal Catholic, offered to go his bail. This man was afterwards heard to boast, that, in the fine thus imposed, he had an abundant off-set to the amount called for in the article of agreement.

The following incident may serve to show what spirit actuated the jury which gave this strange verdict; and also, what likelihood there was that a Catholic priest could then expect a fair and impartial trial. About ten years afterwards, the Rev. M. Badin was travelling somewhere in what is at present Shelby county; and he stopped for the night with a man by the name of Ferguson. The conversation turned on Catholics; .or the *Romans*, as they were called by ignorant Protestants; and the man, not suspecting that his guest was a Catholic priest, related the whole affair of priest Whelan's trial. He stated exultingly that he was one of the jury, and that "they had tried very hard to have the priest hanged, but were sorry that they could find no law for it!!"

It is not at all surprising, that all these difficulties combined should have discouraged F. Whelan, and hastened his departure from a mission beset with so many hardships, and where his services did not appear to be properly appreciated. Accordingly, he left Kentucky early in the spring of 1790, and returned to Maryland, by the way of New Orleans. He had laboured on this rude mission for two years and a half, with a zeal worthy of better success. Faults he may have had; but those who are just will be disposed to make great allowances for the peculiar difficulties of his position. He was alone in the heart of a vast wilderness, with no brother clergyman to assist him with his advice, or to comfort him in his troubles. He was the only Catholic clergyman west of the Alleghany Mountains, except, perhaps, one or two at the French stations on the Wabash and the Mississippi;* and owing to the circumstance, that the intervening wilderness was infested with hostile savages, the communication with these was perhaps equally as difficult as that with his brethren beyond the mountains. After his return to Maryland, he resumed his missionary labours with his wonted zeal. He seems to have been stationed on the eastern shore, where he continued to discharge his duties until his death, which occurred in 1805 or 1806.

After the departure of F. Whelan, the Catholics of Kentucky were again left without a pastor. In

---

* We have not been able, from any sources of information within our reach, to ascertain with precision the names and number of these missionaries at that time. In 1779, and probably for some years afterwards, M. Gibault was the priest stationed at Post Vincennes. (See Judge Law's Speech, *sup. cit.*) In 1792, M. Flaget, the present venerable Bishop of Louisville, was engaged in this same mission, where he laboured for more than two years.

the following summer, however, there arrived among them, in company with a caravan of emigrants from North Carolina and East Tennessee, the Rev. Wm. de Rohan. He seems to have been born in France, of Irish parentage, and was a reputed doctor of the Sorbonne. Some chance had thrown him on the American shores; and a few years previous to his arrival in Kentucky, he had received faculties for a mission in Virginia, from the Very Rev. Dr. Carroll. Shortly afterwards he had travelled to Tennessee, where he remained for more than a year. In Kentucky, he said Mass for the Catholics, visited the sick, and administered the sacraments of Baptism and Matrimony; but he abstained from hearing confessions, as he did not at first believe that his powers extended to this distant mission. He subsequently changed his opinion on this subject, on the ground that Kentucky was a county of Virginia at the date of his faculties, which had been given for the latter State, or a portion of it. On being informed of this fact, the Rt. Rev. Dr. Carroll, lately consecrated Bishop of Baltimore, disapproved of his proceedings. Mr. de Rohan cheerfully submitted to the decision of his superior..*

We will close this chapter with a brief account of the remarkable adventures of John Lancaster, which occurred during the period of which we have been treating.† The recital will show us to what dangers the early Catholic settlers in Kentucky were constantly exposed.

* He passed the last years of his life at the Theological Seminary of St. Thomas, where he died piously, abut the year 1832.

† Our information is derived partly from the journal which Mr. Lancaster has left of what happened to him during the first two days of his captivity among the Indians; and partly from the statement of his respectable widow, to whose clear and retentive memory we are also indebted for much other valuable information.

John Lancaster was descending the Ohio river in a flat boat, bound from Maysville to Louisville. His companions on the boat were Col. Joseph Mitchell and son, and Alexander Brown. When they had reached the mouth of the Miami river, on the 8th of May, 1788, the boatmen discovered a large party of Indians lying in wait for them. They did not make this fearful discovery until they were very near the party; and unfortunately the current bore the boat directly towards them. Escape was hopeless. The savages displayed a white flag, in token of friendship: but at the same time levelled their muskets at the man who was at the oar, and would have shot him down, had not the chief interposed. This man was called Captain Jim, or *Shawnese* Jim, and he spoke a little broken English, which he had probably learned at some of the British military posts in the northwest. He assured the white men that his people meant them no harm, and that they merely wished to trade with them.

Meantime, a skiff manned by four Indians, was seen to put off from the shore, and was rowed rapidly towards the boat, which it struck with so much violence as to upset the skiff, and to precipitate three of the Indians into the river. John Lancaster here showed great presence of mind, by leaping promptly into the river, and aiding the struggling Indians in their efforts to escape from a watery grave. He succeeded, and had reason to hope that he had done much to conciliate their good will—a hope which the event did not however justify. On entering the boat, the Indians seized on the white men, and made them prisoners, two of them struggling violently for the possession of Mr. Lancaster. Some time after they had reached the shore, these same two savages came to blows, and had a desperate fight on the same ground of quarrel, when Captain Jim interposed, and decided in favour of the first who had seized the person of the captive.

The boat was soon rowed to the shore and robbed of all its effects. The Indians then decamped with the booty, and the four prisoners whom they had taken. The first night was devoted to revelry and drunkenness; the savages having carried with them the whiskey with which the boat was partly laden. The prisoners were bound down on their backs to the earth, with cords which were passed around their limbs and bodies, and tied closely to stakes driven in the ground. During the whole night, the rain poured down in torrents, on their faces and bodies; while their only covering was a blanket, their Indian captors having already stripped them of their clothing and money. They passed a sleepless night, witnessing the wild revelry of the Indians, and musing sorrowfully on the dreadful fate which probably awaited them on the morrow.

On the next morning they were released from their confinement, and were hurried on towards the Indian village in the interior, which Mr. Lancaster estimates was about sixty-five miles from the mouth of the Miami, and twenty-five miles lower down the Ohio river. After they had reached their encampment, which was probably one of the Shawnese towns, they were made to witness new scenes of stirring interest. While the captives were gloomily meditating on their probable doom to the stake, the Indian master of John Lancaster suddenly came up to him, and embraced him, shedding tears, and exclaiming, amidst sobs and lamentations, that "he was his brother, who should take the place of one who had been slain during the previous year!" Immediately the Indian ceremony of adoption took place. Mr. Lancaster was stripped of his blanket, and had his body greased with bear's oil, and painted of a vermillion colour. He was then taught some scraps of Indian song, and was made to join in the savage festival which ensued. This consisted of songs and the war-dance, one Indian beating time with a stick, the head of which was curiously wrought and trimmed with the hoofs of deer. After the performance of this singular ceremony, he was viewed as having been regularly adopted into the Indian tribe.

Mr. Lancaster continued a captive in the Indian camp for eight days, during which he made great proficiency in the knowledge of Indian manners and customs. He was called *Kiohba*, or the *Running Buck*, from his remarkable activity and fleetness of foot. He was placed on an equal footing with the Indians, and his new brother treated him with great kindness. After some days, however, this foster brother was sent off from the camp, and then he experienced rougher treatment. Captain Jim, under whose charge he was now left, became sullen and vindictive. He quarrelled with his wife, who, fearing his vengeance, fled from the camp. Jim immediately pursued her, threatening vengeance, and was soon perceived returning to the camp, after having, in all probability, been her murderer. As he was returning, his daughter, who was well acquainted with her father's moods, and who had entertained a partiality for *Kiohba*, said to the latter: *puckete—run!* He took her advice, and instantly darted from the camp.

On casting a glance backward, from a neighbouring eminence, he perceived Captain Jim beating the elder Mitchell with a tent pole. After his final escape from the Indians, he learned that, soon after his departure, young Mitchell was painted black and burned at the stake ; but that his father and Alexander Brown, after suffering almost incredable hardships and privations, were finally ransomed by their friends, and returned to Pittsburgh.

John Lancaster was soon out of sight of the Indian encampment. He took the direction of the Ohio river, but ran in different directions, and crossed repeatedly the various Indian trails, in order the more easily to elude pursuit. He was particularly fearful of about fifty Indian dogs who had been trained to following the footsteps of man. He was however fortunate enough to escape all these multiplied dangers; and after running for six days, during which his only subsistence was four turkey eggs, which he had found in the hollow of a fallen tree, he safely reached the Ohio river. Exhausted as he was, he immediately tied himself with bark to the trunk of a box-elder tree, and after four hours' unremitting toil, succeeded in crossing to the Kentucky side. While crossing he had swallowed much water; and he now perceived that his strength had almost entirely failed.

After resting a short time, he determined to float down the river, to the station at the Falls, which he estimated was between twenty and thirty miles distant. Accordingly, he made a small raft, by tying two trees together with bark, on which he placed himself, with a pole for an oar. When a little above eighteen mile Island, he heard the sharp report of a rifle, when, thinking that his pursuers had overtaken him, he crouched down on his little raft, and concealed himself as best he could. Hearing no other noise, however, he concluded that his alarm was without foundation. But shortly after, a dreadful storm broke upon the river; night had already closed in, and he sank exhausted and almost lifeless on his treacherous raft, drenched with the rain, benumbed with cold, and with the terrible apprehension on his mind, that he might be precipitated over the Falls during the night.

At break of day, he was aroused from his death-like lethargy, by one of the most cheering sounds that ever fell on the ears of a forlorn and lost wanderer—the crowing of a cock—which announced the immediate vicinity of a white settlement. The sound revived him; he collected all his energies for one last effort, and sat upright on his little raft. Soon, in the grey light of the morning, he discovered the cabins of his countrymen, and was enabled to effect a landing at the mouth of Beargrass—the site of the present city of Louisville. He immediately rejoined his friends, and their warm welcome soon made him forget all his past sufferings. He lived for many years to recount his adventures; and died a few years ago of a good old age, surrounded by his children and his children's children.

CHAPTER IV.

Reverend M. Badin in Kentucky.—
From 1793 *to* 1797.

The French Revolution—Virtues of the exiled French Clergy—M. Badin—His early studies—Anecdote—His firm attachment to the faith—He sails for America—Singular coincidence—Anecdote of Bishop Carroll—M. Badin appointed to the missions of Kentucky—Characteristic conversation between him and Bishop Carroll—Departure for Kentucky—Delay at Gallipolis—Arrival—M. Barrieres—M. Badin alone in Kentucky—His troubles—Christian friendship—M. Rivet—M. Badin's labours in Kentucky—His missionary stations—Teaching Catechism—Morning and evening prayer—His Maxims—Curious anecdote—Hearing confessions—Dancing—Anecdotes—Strange notions respecting Catholic priests—M. Badin's privations—His disinterested zeal—His dangers and adventures—How to cure the pleurisy—St. Paul.

The tide of emigration had continued to set so strongly towards Kentucky, that, on its admission into the Union, in 1792, the population amounted to about 70,000. The Catholic portion of this large population had been, in a great measure, deprived of all pastoral succor, since the departure of F. Whelan, in 1790. The next mission to this

* For almost all the facts contained in this chapter, we are indebted to the Very Rev. S. T. Badin, whose tenacious memory of facts and dates is really astonishing, considering his advanced age and the hardships through which he has passed. Like most old persons, he remembers events long passed much better than those of more recent occurrence.

F

remote part of the vast Diocess of Baltimore, was commenced under better auspices, and was destined to be more permanent.

The French Revolution had declared a war of extermination against the Catholic religion and clergy. Many of the latter had been driven from France, and compelled to seek shelter in England, Spain, and the United States. The ways of Divine Providence are truly admirable: God often draws the greatest good out of the greatest evil. Many of the most zealous of the French clergy, expelled from their native country, transferred their labours to other lands, and scattered the good seed of the Gospel on the soil of distant regions. Thus persecution, instead of destroying religion, served rather to diffuse it over the world. The exiled clergy of France, in conformity with the advice of our Blessed Lord, when persecuted in one city, fled to another; spreading wherever they went the good odour of Christ. By the fruits which their zeal every where produced, God proclaimed the virtues of his persecuted servants, and confirmed the divinity of a religion, the spirit of which persecution could not quench, or even diminish.

The Catholic Church in the United States is deeply indebted to the zeal of the exiled French clergy; no portion of the American church owes more to them than that of Kentucky. They supplied our infant missions with most of their earliest and most zealous labourers; and they likewise gave to us our first Bishops. There is something in the elasticity and bouyancy of character of the French, which adapts them in a peculiar manner to foreign missions. They have always been the best missionaries among the North American Indians; they can mould their character to suit every circumstance and emergency. They can be at home and cheerful every where. The French clergy who landed on our shores, though many of them had been trained up amidst all the refinements of polished France, could yet submit without a murmur to all the hardships and privations of a mission on the frontiers of civilization, or in the very heart of the wilderness. They could adapt themselves to the climate, and mould themselves to the feelings and habits of a people congenial to them in temperament and character.

One of these French clerical refugees, the Rev. Stephen Theodore Badin, was the man appointed by Divine Providence to succeed the Rev. F. Whelan in the missions of Kentucky, and to become one of the chief religious pioneers of the west. This indefatigable and venerable missionary, still lingering above the horizon of life, celebrated, during the last year, the *fiftieth* anniversary of his arrival in Kentucky, by offering up the Holy Sacrifice in Lexington, the first place at which he had said Mass on his reaching the State. Before we speak of his missionary labours among us, a few incidents of his early life will not, perhaps, be out of place.

M. Badin was born of pious parents, at Orleans, in France, on the 17th of July, 1768. He was the third of fifteen children, and the oldest son. His parents, pleased with the sprightliness of his mind, determined to give him a finished classical education. They accordingly sent him to the College Montagu in Paris, where he remained for three years. He distinguished himself among his fellow students, and soon mastered the ancient classical writers so thoroughly, that he can quote them with facility even to this day. While at this college, he gave frequent evidences of that ready wit for which he was so conspicuous in after life. We will give one little incident of this kind.

His professor of Greek was as remarkable for his penuriousness as he was for his ardent attachment to the ancient Greek authors. He often gave his lessons to youths trembling with cold, though it was his place to have the lecture-room warmed at his own expense. One day, he was lecturing on the beauties of Homer, and in his enthusiasm remarked to his shivering hearers, that reading Homer was enough to *warm* any one. "It is at least very *cheap* fuel"—remarked M. Badin, looking significantly at the two little sticks of wood on the fire. All the students smiled, and the professor had a blazing fire in the room the next day.

Having determined to study for the church, he, in the year 1789, entered the flourishing Theological Seminary conducted by the Sulpicians, at Orleans. Here he remained for two years, until the Seminary was dissolved, in 1791. The circumstances which attended its dissolution served to set forth, in the strongest light, the unalterable attachment of M. Badin to the Catholic faith, and that unyielding firmness of purpose, which was a principal feature in his character throughout life. The Bishop of Orleans had unhappily taken the odious constitutional oath; and M. Badin, with the great body of the seminarians, determined that he would not be ordained by such a prelate. Accordingly, early in July, 1791, about a week before the great anniversary of the taking of the Bastile, he and the majority of his companions left the seminary, fearing, also, that on that day they might be involved in difficulties about the oath.

Not being as yet in Holy Orders, he returned to his parents, with whom he remained until the 3rd of November, 1791; at which time he left his father's house for Bordeaux, where he had determined to embark for America. Here he met with the Rev. MM. Flaget and David, whose company he enjoyed on the voyage. Divine Providence thus caused the three men, who were afterwards destined most to signalize their zeal on the missions of Kentucky, to meet together from different parts of France, without any previous concert, and to sail on the same ship for America. After many years of arduous missionary duty, in different parts of the United States, these same three devoted missionaries met again amidst the waving forests of our State, where two of them are yet living.

These distinguished exiles from France reached Philadelphia on the 26th, and Baltimore on the 28th of March, 1792. They found that another illustrious colony of French priests had already arrived in Baltimore, six months before.*

Early on the morning following their arrival in Baltimore, the exiles went to pay their respects to Bishop Carroll. They met him on the way hastening to pay them the first visit; and they apologized to him for the tardiness which had prevented them from visiting him first. Bishop Carroll, smiling and bowing to them, said, with ineffable grace and dignity: it is surely little enough, gentlemen, that I should be the first to visit you, seeing that you have come 1500 leagues to see me."

M. Badin was ordained priest by Bishop Carroll, in the old cathedral of St. Peter's, on the 25th of May, 1793. He was the first priest that was ever ordained in the United States. He shortly afterwards went to Georgetown College, to perfect

* On the breaking up of the seminary at Orleans, M. Chicoigneau, the superior, had also proposed to emigrate to America; but some cause detained him in France.

himself in the knowledge of the English. To show the rapid increase of Catholic clergymen in the United States, at that time, we may here mention the fact, that when F. Whelan was sent to Kentucky, in 1787, there were scarcely twenty in the whole Union; whereas, there were twenty-four who attended the first Synod held in Baltimore by Bishop Carroll, in 1791, besides a great number employed on the distant missions.

The mission of Kentucky still continued in a destitute condition; and Bishop Carroll's zeal for all portions of his extensive flock was quickened by frequent and urgent applications for a pastor from the Catholics of that distant region. He selected M. Badin for this arduous mission, and soon communicated his wishes to him. M. Badin manifested great reluctance to undertake so difficult a task; he represented his youth—he was but twenty-five years of age—his slight acquaintance with the English language, and his inexperience. He earnestly requested that some one of more mature age, and better qualified, might be appointed. Bishop Carroll listened to his reasons with great meekness; and finally proposed that no decisive step should be taken for nine days, during which both should unite in prayer, and recommend the matter to God, by performing a *novena* in unison. M. Badin acceded to the proposal, and departed. On the ninth day he returned according to appointment, when the following characteristic conversation took place.

Bishop Carroll. "Well, M. Badin, I have prayed, and I continue still in the same mind."

M. Badin, smiling: "I have also prayed; and I am likewise of the same mind as before. Of what utility, then, has been our nine days' prayer?"

HIS LIFE AND EARLY LABOURS. 61

Bishop Carroll smiled too; and after a pause, resumed with great dignity and sweetness: "I lay no command; but I think it is the will of God that you should go."

M. Badin instantly answered with great earnestness: "I will go, then," and he immediately set about making the necessary preparations for the journey.

The event justified Bishop Carroll's choice. The buoyant elasticity, the persevering zeal, and the indomitable energy of M. Badin's character, had not escaped his quick eye; and his great forecast and wonderful power of discriminating character, were not, at least in the present instance, at fault. Perhaps, among all the clergy attached to the vast Diocess of Baltimore, at that time, there was not one better suited to the rugged mission of Kentucky, than M. Badin.

Bishop Carroll, in consideration of M. Badin's youth, assigned to him as a companion a more aged clergyman—the Rev. M. Barrieres, who was constituted Vicar General in the distant missionary district. The two missionaries left Baltimore on the 6th of September, 1793, and travelled, like the Apostles, on foot to Pittsburgh, over bad roads, and a rugged wilderness country. On the 3rd of November, they embarked on a flat boat, which was descending the Ohio, in company with six others. These boats were all well armed, for fear of an attack from the Indians. About that time, however, Gen'l. Wayne was preparing his great expedition against them; and they had enough to do to defend their own wigwams, without prowling about near the frontier settlements.

The boats were seven days in going down to Gallipolis; and between this place and Pittsburgh, the travellers saw but two small towns—Wheeling and Marietta. The two priests remained for three days at Gallipolis, the inhabitants of which place were French Catholics, who had been long without a pastor. They heartily welcomed the missionaries, who, during their brief stay, sang High Mass in the garrison, and baptized forty children. The good French colonists were delighted; and shed tears on their departure. They were but a remnant of a large French colony of about 7,000, who had emigrated to America four or five years previously. A French land company had purchased for them a large territory on the Scioto river: but the title to these lands proved defective; the colonists were defrauded, and many of them returned in disgust to France, bitterly inveighing against Yankee shrewdness in bargaining.

The two missionaries landed at Limestone, or Maysville, where there were at that time about twenty families. They proceeded on foot to Lexington, a distance of about 65 miles. They passed the first night in an open mill, six miles from Limestone, lodging on the mill-bags, without any covering, during a cold night, late in November. On the next day, they passed the battle-ground of the Blue Licks, where M. Barrieres picked up the skull of one of those who had fallen there eleven years before. He carried it with him, and retained it, as a relic of the disastrous battle, and as a *memento* of death. On the first Sunday of Advent, M. Badin said Mass, for the first time in Kentucky, at Lexington, in the house of Dennis M'Carthy, an Irish Catholic, who acted as clerk in the commercial house of Col. Moyland, brother of the then Bishop of Cork.

The missionaries had with then but one chalice; and after having offered up the Holy Sacrifice, M. Badin travelled sixteen miles, to the Catholic settlement in Scott county, where M. Barrieres said Mass on the same day. Preparations were then in progress to erect in this place a frame church. M. Badin remained in Scott county for about eighteen months, occasionally visiting the other Catholic settlements in Kentucky; M. Barrieres proceeded immediately to take charge of the Catholic families in the vicinity of Bardstown.

The difficulties of the times, and the rude state of society in the infant colonies, soon determined M. Barrieres to leave the country. His habits had been already formed, and he thought that he could not adapt himself to the new state of things in the wilderness. Accordingly, about four months after his arrival in Kentucky, he left the State. In April, 1794, he departed from Louisville, in a pirogue* for New Orleans, which, with all Louisiana and Missouri, was then in possession of the Spaniards.

The Spanish government was at that time apprehending an attack on Louisiana from the French Republic; and M. Barrieres, being a Frenchman, was arrested and detained for some time at New Madrid. He immediately wrote to Baron Carandolet, the Spanish Governor of Louisiana, representing the objects of his visit: and the Baron soon liberated him, and permitted him to proceed without farther molestation, to New Orleans. Shortly after his arrival in this city, he went to Attakapas, where he laboured zealously in the missions for nearly twenty years. In 1814, he sailed for Bordeaux, where he died eight days after his arrival. About twenty-three years before, he had escaped from a prison of this city, and from the

* A large species of canoe, then much used on the Ohio and Mississippi.

death which probably awaited him at the hands of the French Jacobins; and he had sailed from this port for America: and now he returned to the same place, but to breathe his last.

M. Badin was now left alone in the heart of the wilderness. Keenly as he felt the desolation of heart which this state of isolation brought with it, he yet reposed his whole trust in God, who abundantly consoled him in all his tribulations. He remained alone for nearly three years, and was at one time twenty-one months without an opportunity of going to confession. He had to form the new congregations, to erect churches at suitable places, and to attend to the spiritual wants of the Catholic settlements scattered over Kentucky; and he had to do all this alone, and without any advice or assistance. Well might he exclaim: "Oh! how much anguish of heart, how many sighs, and how many tears, grow out of a condition so desolate!"* Still he was not cast down, notwithstanding all his perplexities.

His mind was also soothed by the cheering voice of friendship. The nearest Catholic priest was M. Rivet, who was stationed at Post Vincennes in 1795, shortly after the departure from that station of that illustrious missionary pioneer, the Rev. M. Flaget. In France, he had been professor of Rhetoric in the College of Limoges: and he still continued to write Latin poetry with ease and elegance. He occasionally sent his Latin poems to M. Badin, who also, as we shall see, excelled in this species of composition. When the French Revolution burst over Europe, M. Ri-

* From a brief statement of the missions of Kentucky drawn up by M. Badin, while in France in the year 1822, and published in the "Annales de la Propagation de la Foy," for 1823, No. 2. This statement is very condensed, but admirably written.

vet took refuge in Spain, where the Archbishop of Cordova made him his Vicar General, for the benefit of the numerous French refugees who had taken shelter beyond the Pirrenees.

He and M. Badin mutually consoled each other, by carrying on as brisk a correspondence as the difficulties of the times would permit. There were then, however, no post offices in the west; and the frowning wilderness which interposed between these two friends rendered the exchange of letters extremely difficult; and wholly precluded the possibility of their visiting each other; even if this had been permitted by the onerous duties with which each was charged. M. Rivet had discovered at Vincennes a precious document of the old Jesuit missions among the Indians of the northwest. It consisted of two large folio volumes in manuscript, containing the Mass, with musical notes, and explanations of it, together with catechetical instructions, in the Indian language. This document has probably since disappeared.

When M. Badin first came to Kentucky, he estimated the number of Catholic families in the State at three hundred. These were much scattered; and the number was constantly on the increase, especially after Wayne's victory in 1794, and the treaty of Greenville in the following year. There was then but one Catholic in Bardstown—Mr. A. Sanders, to whose liberality and generous hospitality the clergy of the early church in Kentucky were so much indebted.

He found the Catholics suffering greatly from previous neglect, and in a wretched state of discipline. Left alone with this extensive charge, he had to exert himself to the utmost, and, as it were, to multiply himself, in order to be able to meet every spiritual want of his numerous flock. As the Ca tholics were then almost wholly without churches or chapels, he was under the necessity of establishing stations at suitable points, in private houses. These stations extended from Madison to Hardin county—a distance of more than a hundred and twenty miles; and to visit them all with regularity, he was compelled almost to live on horseback. He estimates that, during his sojourn in Kentucky, he must have rode on horseback at least 100,000 miles. Often was he exhausted with his labours, and weighed down with the "solicitude of all the churches."

His chief stations during this time were those at Lexington, in Scott county, in Madison county, in Mercer county—where there were then about ten families—at Holy Cross, at Bardstown, on Cartwright's Creek—two miles from the present church of St. Rose—on Hardin's Creek, on the Rolling Fork, in Hardin county, and at Poplar Neck on the Beech Fork.

In all these places, except Madison and Mercer counties,* there are now fine brick churches; but at the period of which we are speaking, there was not one of any kind, except a miserable log chapel, on the site of the present church of Holy Cross; and this had been erected at the instance of M. De Rohan, before the arrival of M. Badin in Kentucky. This temporary hut was covered with clapboards, and was unprovided with glass in the windows. A slab of wood roughly hewed, served for an altar. Such was the first Catholic church in Kentucky! As it was situated near the centre of the Catholic settlements, M. Badin soon took

* The Catholics have since, in a great measure, removed from both of these counties; and, in consequence, the brick church formerly erected in Danville, Mercer county, has been disposed of.

up his residence near it; and it then became the central point of his mission, and the *alma mater* of Catholic churches in Kentucky. He subsequently erected a temporary chapel at his own residence, three miles from Holy Cross: this he called St. Stephen's, after his patron Saint.

M. Badin was indefatigable in his efforts to awake piety, and to restore a proper discipline among his flock. He insisted particularly on having servants and children taught the catechism. At every station he had regular catechists, whose duty it was to teach them the elements of the faith. He displayed on all occasions particular zeal in the instruction of poor servants of colour. Whenever he visited a Catholic family, it was his invariable custom to have public prayers, followed by catechetical instructions. He every where inculcated by word and example the pious practice of having morning and evening prayer in families. He was in the habit of repeating to children, in his usual emphatic and pointed manner, the following maxims: "My children, mind this; no morning prayer, no breakfast; no evening prayer, no supper:" and, "my children, be good, and you will never be sorry for it."

His zeal for promoting the regular practice of morning and evening prayers, occasionally betrayed him into some eccentricities. Once, a man travelling to the Green river country, called at his residence at St. Stephen's, at a late hour in the evening, requesting permission to stay during the night. M. Badin cheerfully granted the request, telling him at the same time, that he was a Catholic priest, and could charge nothing for his hospitality. The man looked a little shy, but thanked him for his kindness. When, after supper, he was about to retire to rest, M. Badin asked him, whether he had said his night prayers? The man looked blank, and answered in the negative. "Well," rejoined M. Badin, "I have already said *my* prayers, but I will cheerfully say them again to accommodate you, and to bear you company." Then he immediately fell on his knees, the man following his example, and said aloud the usual prayers. As he was lighting his guest to his room, he told him, "that he might die before morning, and that he should never retire to rest without preparing himself for death." On the next morning, M. Badin went to awake the stranger, but he had, it seems, said prayers enough already, and had escaped before the dawn of day.

On reaching a station, M. Badin would generally hear confessions till about one o'clock. Meantime, the people recited the Rosary at intervals, and the boys, girls, and servants, were taught catechism by the regular catechists. Hearing confessions was the most burdensome duty he had to discharge; and he was fully aware of its deep and awful responsibility. He spared no labour nor pains to impart full instructions to his penitents, who thronged his confessional from an early hour. So great, in fact, was their number, that he found it expedient to distribute among them tickets, fixing the order in which they should approach the holy tribunal, according to priority of arrival at the church. He was a thorough tactician, and was inflexible in maintaining this order. Frequently, persons would be obliged to make several attempts before they could succeed in going to confession.

He was always an implacable enemy of dancing, which, in the rude state of society at that early period, was often attended with great disorders.

The following amusing anecdotes will illustrate the manner in which he warred against the practice.

Some time in the year 1795, or 1796, the Catholics on Pottinger's Creek got up a dancing-school, and employed an Irish Catholic as dancing-master. In his regular visit to the neighbourhood, M. Badin repaired as usual to the station on Saturday evening, to hear confessions and to teach catechism to the children. He found very few in attendance, and soon learned that they were all gone to the dancing-school, at a neighbouring school-house. He immediately went thither himself, and his appearance disturbed, in no slight degree, the proceedings of the merry assemblage: "My children," said he, smiling, as he stood in the middle of the room, "it is all very well: but where the children are, there the father must also be; and where the flock is, there the pastor must attend." He caused them all to sit down, and he gave them a *long* lesson in their catechism. On the following morning, he said Mass for them in the same apartment, and caused the dancing-master himself to attend.

He sometimes arrived unexpectedly at a house, in the evening, while dancing was going on, glided into the room before any one perceived it, and told them smiling, "that it was time for night prayers." The action was suited to the word, and most of the merry dancers generally effected their escape before the close of the evening devotions. He managed all this with so much tact and good humour, that the people, acquainted with his eccentricity, and respecting his zeal, were not usually offended at his conduct.

It is indeed strange, what ideas many Protestants then had of a Catholic Priest. They viewed him as something singular and unearthly, wholly different from any other mortal. Often, when M. Badin was travelling, he observed people peeping timidly at him from behind the corners of houses: and once, in particular, when it was rumoured through a neighborhood, that the priest was coming to a certain house, a party concealed themselves in the woods near the road, in order to have a peep at him as he was passing. They were afterwards heard to wonder that the priest was like any other man, and that he was no great show after all! And yet these people lived in an age of "open Bibles," and of boasted enlightenment! And yet the preachers, who are mainly chargeable with keeping up this absurd prejudice, have still the assurance to charge the Catholic priests with keeping the people in ignorance!! This bigotry has indeed abated, but it is not yet wholly extinct.

In his solitary and forlorn condition, M. Badin was wholly deprived of the luxuries, and often suffered for the very necessaries of life. His clothing was made of cloth manufactured in the country:* and his food, besides being often scanty enough, was of the coarsest kind. For several years, he was often compelled to grind his own corn on the hand-mill. He asked for his support the hundredth bushel of grain that was raised by the members of his congregation; but for various reasons he did not usually receive the thousandth. Once, he was for many days without bread, at his own residence of St. Stephen's; until the good Mr. Sanders, who became accidently apprised of the fact, sent him the necessary supply.

* Judge Broadanax used to compliment him for his patriotism, in thus encouraging domestic manufactures: but there was evidently more of necessity than of virtue in the matter.

The following incident will serve to show how disinterested was his zeal, in the midst of all these privations. In the year 1796, when his sufferings and hardships were the greatest, he received a letter from the Spanish Governor of St. Genevieve, earnestly pressing him to leave Kentucky, and come to reside in St. Genevieve, where he was offered an annual salary of $500, besides valuable perquisites. The situation was easy and inviting, and the offer was tempting. M. Badin, in fact, viewed the whole matter in the light of an evil temptation to abandon the field of labour which Divine Providence had assigned him; and he accordingly threw the Governor's letter into the fire, and did not even return any answer. His motto was: *follow Providence.*

This chapter would swell to an unwarrantable length, should we attempt to describe all the dangers through which M. Badin passed, or to relate a tenth part of the strange adventures with which he met. The subject will probably come up again in the sequel. We will here state, that he was often called to a distance of fifty, and even eighty miles, to visit the sick,[*] on which occasions he had often to strain every nerve, and to ride day and night, in order to be able to meet his other pressing engagements. He made it an invariable rule never to miss an appointment, no matter what obstacles interposed.

He often missed his way, and was compelled to pass the night in the woods, where he kindled a fire, by the light of which he said his office. On one of these occasions, a heavy rain set in and continued during the whole night: the leaves were

---

[*] After one of these long rides, he found the sick man sitting on a stool, eating hard boiled eggs, to cure the pleurisy.

so wet, that his companion had to climb some neighbouring trees, in order to collect dry fuel for lighting the fire, an operation which consumed three hours. Yet they passed the night merrily, singing and praying alternately; and at break of day had the satisfaction to find that they were but five feet from the road.

Once, he lost his hat in the night, and being unable to find it in the darkness, was compelled to ride many miles bareheaded, to the distant station which he was on his way to visit. On another occasion, while about to cross Salt river, near the mouth of Ashe's creek, his horse missed his footing in the darkness, and rolled down the elevated cliffs with his rider. M. Badin found himself in a deep fish-pot, with one foot in the stirrup and the other immersed in the water. The horse, usually spirited and restive, stood perfectly quiet, and the rider was unhurt. He had the Blessed Sacrament with him, and he returned thanks to God for his preservation from a danger so imminent.

In short, he passed through almost as many hardships and dangers as St. Paul so graphically describes in his Second Epistle to the Corinthians.* Yet he was not discouraged, nor was his health impaired. His strength seemed even to increase with the hardships he had to endure. And he was consoled by the abundant fruits with which God was pleased to bless his ministry. Of these we purpose to treat more at length in a subsequent chapter.

---

* Chap. xi. 26 seqq. "In journeys often, in perils of rivers, in perils of robbers, in perils from my own nation, in perils from the Gentiles, in perils in the city, in perils in the wilderness, ... in labour and painfulness, in watchings often, in hunger and thirst, in many fastings, in cold and nakedness," &c.

CHAPTER V.

Arrival of other Missionaries—From 1797 *to* 1803.

Rev. M. Fournier—Traits and facts of his early life—His arrival in Kentucky—His stations and labours—His character—his sudden death—Rev. M. Salmon—His zeal and labours—Humorous incident—His tragical death—His Epitaph—Rev. Mr. Thayer—Anecdote of Franklin—Mr. Thayer's conversion—His labours in Boston—In Kentucky—And in Limerick—His death.

For about three years M. Badin had been alone, desolate in heart, and weighed down with labours. At length, Divine Providence took compassion on his loneliness, and sent other labourers into a harvest now become much too extensive to be cultivated by one man. The new missionary recruits were from among those illustrious clerical exiles from France, to whose apostolic zeal America is so greatly indebted, and without whose generous aid our infant missions could scarcely have been sustained.

The first of these who arrived in Kentucky, was the Rev. M. Fournier, in the year 1797. He was a native of the Diocess of Blois in France; and, when driven from his native country, by the French Revolution, he took refuge in England. In London he taught the French language for about four years, in order to obtain a subsistence. Weary of this manner of life, and panting for a field of action more congenial to his zeal for the salvation of souls, he sailed for America, which he reached towards the close of the year 1796. He immediately offered his services to Bishop Carroll, who gratefully accepted them, and immediately sent him to Kentucky to the assistance of M. Badin, of whose melancholy condition he had been already well apprised.

M. Fournier, after a long and painful journey, in the dead of winter, reached Kentucky in February, 1797. M. Badin received him with open arms, and extended to him for several months the hospitality of his own log cabin of St. Stephen's. M. Fournier soon purchased one hundred acres of ground, on the Rolling Fork—the site of the present Holy Mary's—and, after having erected a temporary hut, removed thither in 1798. He then took charge of a portion of M. Badin's stations. He attended the congregations situated on the Rolling Fork, on Hardin's Creek, on Cartwright's Creek, on Rough Creek in Hardin county, with those at Danville, and in Madison county. When we reflect that a distance of at least one hundred and twenty miles intervened between the two extreme points of this circuit, we will probably come to the conclusion, that, like his fellow-labourer in the same field, he was certainly in no lack of employment.

He was an excellent priest; pious, zealous, laborious, and punctual to all his appointments. He was of the ordinary size, and had a thin visage, furrowed with care, but still beaming with habitual cheerfulness. His manners were extremely popular; he soon caught the spirit, and adapted himself to the manners of the country; and he had not one personal enemy. He spoke English remarkably well, and preached sermons which had the triple merit of being solid, short, and intelligible to the meanest capacity.

OTHER MISSIONARIES. 75

When not engaged in his missions, he was almost constantly labouring on the little farm adjoining his residence. His death was caused by the rupture of a blood-vessel through over exertion in raising large beams of wood, to be sawed into plank. It was so sudden, that his friend, M. Badin, arrived only in time to assist at his funeral. His body was interred at the church of Holy Cross. He had not yet reached his fiftieth year.

Another French priest, M. Salmon, reached Kentucky in February, 1799. He was from the same Diocess of Blois, and was an old and long tried friend of M. Fournier, with whom he had been a fellow student in the Diocesan Seminary of Blois,* as well as his associate in exile from his country. The two friends had met and passed some years together in London. After the arrival of M. Fournier in Kentucky, he wrote to his friend in London, who followed him as soon as he could make the necessary arrangements. He was about forty-two years of age, was of a delicate frame, and, like M. Fournier, was well versed in the English language.

M. Badin, who was Vicar General, assigned him the stations at Hardin's Creek, Poplar Neck, Mr. Gardiner's, and Bardstown. He was zealous and indefatigable in the discharge of all his missionary duties. Especially did he labour without intermission for the instruction of children and servants in their catechism. In whatever Catholic house he visited, he made it an invariable rule to examine the children on their knowledge of their Christian duties. And, as we shall soon see, his premature death was the consequence of his burning zeal for the salvation of souls.

* Conducted by the Lazarists.

The following humorous incident is, perhaps, not worth recording, though it may serve to illustrate his zeal for the instruction of poor servants. When he was at the house of Mr. Thomas Gwynn, near Bardstown, he undertook as usual to instruct the servants in their religion. He had them all assembled, and was struck by the readiness of their answers. His gravity was, however, not a little disturbed, when, on his asking a servant girl of sixteen—"which is the last sacrament you would wish to receive were you on the point of death?" she answered immediately—thinking of the last one on the list—"Matrimony."

His zeal was rewarded with abundant fruits; though it pleased God, in the unsearchable ways of His Providence, speedily to put an end to his labours and sufferings on this mission. He had been in Kentucky but nine months, when his career was suddenly cut short by death. He was the first priest who died on this laborious mission—and he fell a martyr to his zeal.

In the discharge of his duties, he had caught a violent cold, which confined him to his bed for six weeks, in the house of M. Badin. When convalescent, he determined to visit the station at Mr. Gwynn's, where he had an appointment to meet a Protestant lady whom he was instructing and preparing for Baptism.* He was a bad horseman, and was still very feeble from his previous sickness. It was the 9th day of November, 1799; and the snow covered the ground, concealing a road which was rugged and difficult. M. Badin endeavoured to dissuade him from undertaking the journey, in his debilitated condition; but he

* This lady afterwards became an exemplary member of the Catholic church.

OTHER MISSIONARIES.

was firm in his resolution, and departed at an early hour in the morning.

About a mile from Bardstown, on the road to Mr. Gwynn's, he was thrown violently from his horse, and was dashed against a tree. He was stunned and mortally wounded, in the breast and head. In his struggles, he succeeded in dragging himself to a tree, against which he leaned his head and shoulders, and thus sat upright, near the road side. From 12 o'clock until night, he remained in this dreadful situation, surrounded by the snow, benumbed with the cold, and in the very agonies of death. A lad, who was cutting wood in the neighbouring forest, soon discovered him in this condition, and requested permission from his employer, to repair to his assistance. But the overseer* brutally replied, that it was "only a—priest, who was probably drunk!" Near sunset, this man saw Mr. Gwynn passing, and shouted out to him, that "his priest was lying in a certain spot, perhaps dying."

The Good Mr. Gwynn, deeply affected, flew to the spot, where he discovered that his worst anticipations were more than realized. M. Salmon seemed on the very point of death. He was immediately placed on horseback, and conveyed, with as much tenderness as possible, to the residence of Mr. Gwynn, about a mile distant. Messengers were speedily despatched for physicians, and for the Rev. M. Badin. The latter arrived at 2 o'clock the same night, having rode about sixteen miles in little more than two hours. He found M. Sal-

---

* For the honor of human nature, we must observe that this was a man of no standing in the country; and that his brutality is almost single in the early history of Kentucky. The lad of whom mention is made above, is now one of our most respectable citizens.

mon insensible, reciting occasionally prayers in Latin, and acting as though he fancied himself at the holy altar. M. Badin administered to him the last sacraments, and remained with him till his death, which took place on the following night, the 10th of November. His remains were conveyed to the church of Holy Cross, where they were interred with all the ceremonies of the Roman Ritual.

M. Badin wept bitterly over the death of a friend and fellow-labourer, to whom he was so sincerely attached. He composed for him an Epitaph in Latin verse, of which the following is a translation:

"Here lies Anthony Salmon, a French Priest of eminent virtue, who preferred exile to schismatical wealth, leaving father, mother, and country. Let piety weep, and religion pour forth her prayers," for his repose.*

The worthy patriarch of the American Church, Bishop Carroll, seemed to take a special interest in the missions of Kentucky. In the same year of M. Salmon's death, he sent out another zealous missionary to labour in this distant field. The Rev. Mr. Thayer arrived in Kentucky in the year 1799. He was the first native of America who exercised the holy ministry in our State. He had been a Presbyterian or Congregationalist minister at Boston; and had been reared with all that bitter hostility to the holy Catholic church so common to his sect.

While yet a Protestant preacher, he determined to travel through Europe. He reached Paris, while Benjamin Franklin was residing there, in

* "Hic jacet Antonius Salmon virtute verendus,
Presbyter e Gallis; prœtulit exilium
Schismaticis opibus; fratres, matrem, arvaque linquens:
Det pietas fletus, Religioque preces."

quality of Minister of the United States to the French Court. He visited Franklin, and requested to be appointed his Chaplain. The philosopher-statesman made him the characteristic reply: that he could "say his own prayers, and save his country the expense of employing a Chaplain." Thus foiled in his object, Mr. Thayer proceeded to Rome, which he reached, probably, about the year 1781. He repaired thither with the full expectation of being able to collect facts to establish conclusively the idolatry of the Catholic church; but he left the "Eternal City" an ardent Catholic himself.

The immediate occasion of his conversion was his witnessing the wonderful miracles operated at the tomb of the venerable Labre. These he ridiculed, at first; but a long and rigid scrutiny convinced him that they were the work of God. His next inference was natural—that the religion in favour of which such prodigies had been operated, must be the religion of Christ; since God cannot stamp the broad seal of his approbation on falsehood and error. His conclusions were strengthened by a full examination of the evidences which demonstrate the truth of Catholicity. With a simple and docile heart, he committed himself wholly to the teaching of God, whose light and grace he fervently invoked in prayer. A new light broke upon his mind; and his previous prejudices vanished like the mists before the rising sun. He soon beheld himself in the clear and unclouded day of Catholic truth; and returned humble thanks to God for having thus vouchsafed to transfer him from the region of doubts and darkness, into the admirable light of His Blessed Son!

Ardently did he pant for an opportunity to impart to others, reared up with similar prejudices, the new light which had broken upon his own spirit. He determined to cast all human considerations to the winds, and to devote his whole subsequent life to the sublime occupation of endeavouring to enlighten others, especially his countrymen. The better to qualify himself for this undertaking, he resolved to enter into the Catholic ministry. Accordingly, after the necessary previous studies, he was ordained priest in Paris; after which he speedily returned to the United States.

He was stationed in Boston, the theatre of his former labours as Protestant minister. He held weekly conferences on the truths of the Catholic faith; and his discourses, delivered with much earnestness and eloquence, attracted great crowds of his Protestant fellow-citizens. He published a detailed and well-written account of his conversion, in which he clearly and forcibly stated all the motives which had led him to take this important step. He thus endeavoured to convey his own convictions to the minds of his countrymen, both from the pulpit and through the press. His zeal led him into various controversies with the Protestant preachers; and he always showed himself able to give an account of the "hope which was in him." Still he had the mortification to find, that the Americans, who are so easily misled by novelties of whatever species, are very slow to change their religious opinions, especially in favor of what is old and painful to human nature. He found that *conviction* and *conversion* were two different things; and that, though he could flatter himself with having brought about the former state of mind in many, he was cheered by but few evidences of his having secured the latter.

Feeling, probably, that "no prophet is received in his own country," he left Boston; and, after having visited Canada, offered his services to Bishop Carroll, for whatever mission in the Union he might think proper to assign him. As we have said, Bishop Carroll sent him to Kentucky. Here he remained for about four years, during two of which only he was engaged in the ministry.

He left Kentucky in 1803; and subsequently went to Ireland. He exercised the holy ministry for many years in Limerick, where he contributed greatly towards the revival of piety. The year of his death we have not been able to ascertain with precision; but it certainly occurred some time before the year 1822. When M. Badin was in Paris during this year, he received, from a respectable Irish gentleman of Limerick, a glowing account of his zealous labours and edifying death. Among other particulars, the gentleman alluded to mentioned the fact, that Mr. Thayer had induced obout two hundred of his penitents to make their meditation daily.*

* In the facts detailed in this chapter, we have followed the admirable report on the Kentucky missions, drawn up by M. Badin, in 1822, and published in the Annales. (*loco sup. cit.*) We have added several important facts, derived from the oral statements of the Very Rev. M. Badin, and from other aged persons, who were well acquainted with the individuals of whom we have spoken.

CHAPTER VI.

Early History of the Chief Protestant Sects in Kentucky—From 1784 *to* 1820.

Our authorities—Father Rice—His opinion of the first Protestant preachers in Kentucky—A "speck" of Religion—Wrangling and Sectarism—A frightful picture—Causes of religious decline—Avarice in preachers—The great hurricane of religion—Origin and doctrines of the Cumberland Presbyterians—Fierce and indomitable spirit of Presbyterianism—Origin of the "New-Lights"—Singular *manifesto*—Sentence of deposition—A curious document—Origin of the Campbellites—Presbyterian dissensions—A preacher twice convicted of slander—Another condemned—Disunion among Baptists—The "great revival" in Kentucky—Col. Stone's description of it—Farther particulars—*Jerking, jumping, falling* and *barking* exercises—The Shakers in Kentucky—Curious religious statistics—Reflections.

BEFORE we proceed farther in our rapid sketch of the early history of the Catholic missions in Kentucky, it may be well to pause a little, in order to survey the cotemporary history of the principal Protestant sects. These often came into collision, not only with each other, but with the Catholic church. Differing in almost all else, they united in the principle of hatred of the Catholic religion. And we cannot fully understand the early history of the latter, in our State, without examining the corresponding phases in the history of the former.

Our sketch, confined, as it necessarily must be, to one chapter, will be very brief and summary, embracing only some of the principal facts and features in the history of the most conspicuous among the early sects of Kentucky. We shall state nothing which is not undoubted, and little that cannot be satisfactorily proved from respectable Protestant authority. To show that we mean to be impartial, we will farther remark, that our chief authority will be a work of some antiquity, and of considerable weight among the sects themselves.*

One of the first preachers, if not the first, who emigrated to Kentucky was the Rev. David Rice, of the Presbyterian church. He was born in Virginia, in 1733; removed to Kentucky in October, 1783; and died in 1816, being 83 years of age. The author of his Memoirs gives us rather a singular account of the motives which induced him to emigrate to our State.† It seems that he had a large family to provide for; and his removal to Kentucky was prompted more by the desire of securing the good things of this world, than by that of spreading the Gospel. Speaking of his first visit to the country, the writer above referred to says:

"He accordingly was induced at a convenient time to ride out and see the country, not principally with a view to preach the Gospel, nor even with the view of moving there soon, if ever; but merely to become acquainted with the country, and if all circumstances were encouraging, to procure settlements for some of his numerous family."‡

* The title of the book is as follows: "An outline of the History of the Church in the State of Kentucky, during a period of forty years, containing the memoirs of Rev. David Rice, and sketches of the origin and present state of particular churches, and of the lives and labours of a number of men who were eminent and useful in their day. Corrected and arranged by Robert H. Bishop, Professor of History in Transylvania."—Lexington—1824, 1 vol. 12mo. pp. 420.
† Work just quoted, chap. viii. p. 65 seqq.   ‡ Ibid. p. 66.

And he finally consented to emigrate thither, only after he had obtained a *substantial* call, in the shape of an instrument of writing, signed by three hundred men.*

So much for married preachers—for Father Rice, as he is styled, was a fair specimen of all of them in this respect. Their conduct fully verifies the saying of St. Paul: "He that is with a wife is solicitous for the things of the world, how he may please his wife, and he is divided."† Should a minister of God be divided?

Father Rice describes the religious condition of the people, on his arrival in Kentucky, in the following words:

"After I had been here some weeks, and had preached the Gospel at several places, I found scarcely one man, and but few women who supported a credible profession of religion. Some were grossly ignorant of the first principles of religion. Some were given to quarrelling and fighting, some to profane swearing, some to intemperance, and perhaps most of them totally negligent of the forms of religion in their own homes."‡

He had not a much better opinion of his first fellow-labourers in the ministry of Kentucky, of whom he says:

"They were men of some information, and held sound principles, but did not appear to possess much of the spirit of the Gospel. Upon this my spirits sunk pretty low, verging on a deep melancholy." To which the writer of his Memoirs adds: "A melancholy prospect indeed to a pious mind. Like priest, like people—genuine piety scarcely discernible in either—the spirit of the

---

* Ibid. p. 67.
† I. Corinthians, chap. vii. 33.—Read the whole chapter.
‡ Work before referred to—p. 68.

world animating all."* Wonder if Father Rice himself "possessed much of the spirit of the Gospel?"

According to his testimony, the early Baptists and Methodists were not a whit better than their Presbyterian brethren. He says:

"The Baptists were at this time pretty numerous, and were engaged in some disputes among themselves, about some abstruse points, which I suspected neither party well understood. About the same time, two Methodist preachers came to the country, who, though they were rather passionate in their addresses, seemed to be men of tender Catholic (!) spirit, and advocates for good morals. For some time their coming encouraged and revived me, in some degree, but as soon as they had gained a little footing in the country, they began to preach what they called their principles, that is, those doctrines which distinguish them from other societies. This, so far as I could learn, produced its genuine effects—a party spirit and alienation of affections among the people. This sunk me into my former melancholy. To me it appeared that all our religious societies, Presbyterians, Baptists, Methodists, &c. &c., were in a fair way to destroy both the spirit and the practice of religion, and sink it into contempt."†

At length, Father Rice was cheered by "a little reviving in the midst of bondage:" yet this was but a trifling forerunner of another mighty revival that was to come—a mere speck of cloud on the horizon, which portended the coming of the awful hurricane of religion which was soon to sweep over Kentucky. Of this hurricane we will soon

* Ibid. p. 69–70. † Ibid. p. 70.

speak at some length; of the *speck*, the author above cited speaks as follows:

"On this commenced a small revival of religion in Mr. Rice's congregation, and in several other places adjoining. A number of professors appeared to be strengthened and comforted—a number of hypocrites undeceived—and a number of sinners were made to cry out, what shall we do to be saved? The awakening and seriousness continued for several months, adding a small number to the church on every sacramental occasion, and inducing a few to give themselves up to God in the work of the ministry."*

The spirit of wrangling and sectarism has ever been the plague-spot of Protestantism: never did this spirit manifest itself more fully than during the period of which we are speaking. We have already seen some instances of its early developement: we will here add a few more, to show that time, instead of remedying, rather served to aggravate the evil. After he had been many years in the country, Father Rice addressed "two epistles to the citizens of Kentucky," besides a tract against slavery. From the second of these epistles we present the following extracts, bearing on the subject:

"In the midst of all this error and confusion"— he had been speaking of the evils of sectarism— "many of our professors are mere lifeless, orthodox formalists, who are more inclined to expose error with violence, than to humble themselves and pray for a reformation. They boast of the soundness of their principles, and their strong attachment to them, but at the same time in practice deny the power of godliness," &c.†

* Ibid. p. 76-7.   † Ibid. p. 348.

And again: "A melancholy consequence of all this is, that many are filled and almost overwhelmed with perplexing skeptical doubts.

"Some are doubting of their own religion; not because it appears to them unscriptural, but because they see many, whom they esteemed better Christians than themselves, either turned back to a course of vice, or carried away with gross errors. Others doubt of the reality of the religion of almost all others, and think it nothing but a delusion and disorder of the passions. Others conclude, or at least have some apprehension, that there is nothing in experimental religion at all; that it is all a mere delusion, arising from the temperament of the body, or excited by passionate addresses, animal exertion, or the like. Others imagine that because ministers are disputing about the doctrines of religion, there is no truth in any of them; but that all are doubtful at least. Too many conclude that there is no reality in religion at all; but that it is all priest-craft, or king's-craft: that the only way is to make the most of this miserable world, having nothing better to expect. The youth, the poor unhappy youth, find themselves free from the restraints of religion, and rejoice in their liberty; are skeptical in their opinions, and hasting to a confirmed and inveterate infidelity; they neglect religious worship, or attend it without reverence or any serious thoughts of improvement."*

This is truly a fearful picture, as startling as it is graphic. Could Father Rice now arise from his grave, he might draw a similar portrait of our own times; or rather, he would find that not one light or shade of his original picture would now

---

* Ibid. p. 349-350.

need retouching. Such, then, are thy acknowledged fruits, oh Protestantism! Such are the dreadful evils which thou hast left as an heir-loom to mankind!

The author of the book from which we are quoting, timidly "ventures to suggest some of the reasons why the Gospel, faithfully and affectionately preached, has not produced the effect desired."* These reasons, he says, are chiefly: a too great worldly spirit, the want of piety, and the want of mutual love.

"There is too much of the policy of the world in every one of the churches—too much dependence on those who are avowedly men of the world; and too little dependence upon our common Master, and the energies of his Spirit. There is not a want of *personal* piety among us, but there is a great want of *family* piety....... Lastly and chiefly—there is a great want of the love of the brethren among us. We have not Christian confidence in one another."†

To these causes for the decline of religion, we should add another, which has, perhaps, done more extensive mischief to the Protestant sects, than any thing else: avarice among the preachers. This is freely admitted by the candid historian of the sects in Kentucky. Near the close of his summary sketch of the Baptist churches, which, he says, had been torn by "a great deal of unhallowed controversy," he adds the following general remarks:

"By looking back to the reflections of Father Rice, we will find him lamenting over the money making and speculating spirit among the Presbyterians. The facts which have been brought before us in the history of the Baptists render it ex-

* Ibid. p. 157.   † Ibib. p. 158.

tremely probable that genuine religion has suffered much among them from a similar spirit. A private difference between a preacher and a leading member of his church, about the exchange of two slaves, convulsed the whole Elkhorn Association, and ended in a permanent separation of brethren who had before walked together in unity. The first pastor of the church at Washington, one of the first and one of the largest churches in the State, lost his character and property by land speculation. And farther, Benedict* makes the remark: "the churches do but little for their preachers—very few receive to the amount of a hundred dollars a year for their services; but few of them, however, are very poor. They have from necessity found the means of supporting themselves. Many of those who settled early in the country have become wealthy."†

Certainly the preachers were never known to neglect their own interest for the salvation of souls. They are often remarked as the keenest traders of the country. And many of the unfortunate personal and doctrinal controversies which tore the bosom of most Protestant sects in the early period of their history in Kentucky, are fairly traceable to rival claims of preachers for good situations—or good *calls*, as they are styled—and to bitter animosity growing out of that rivalry. Sometimes, however, they were caused by fanaticism. According to our author, the Cumberland Presbyterians originated in this latter way. As the origin of this sect is both curious in itself, and fairly connected with our subject; and as it is moreover intimately associated with one of the most aston-

* In his "History of the Baptists," 2 vols. 8vo. 1813.
† Ibid. p. 301.

ishing displays of fanaticism furnished by the annals of mankind, we may be pardoned for dwelling at some length on this branch of the subject. We will, however, do little more than abridge the statement of the Protestant church historian of Kentucky, already often quoted. He says:

"The years 1800 and 1801 were distinguished by an uncommon religious excitement among the Presbyterians of Kentucky. This excitement began in Logan county, and soon extended all over the State, and into the *neighbouring States and territories.* Besides increased attention to the usual and ordinary seasons and modes of worship, there were during the summer of these years, large camp-meetings held, and four or five days and nights at a time were spent in almost incessant religious exercises. At these meetings hundreds, and in some cases, thousands of people might have been seen and heard *at one and the same time*, engaged in singing, and prayer, and exhortation, and preaching, and leaping, and shouting, and disputing, and conversing. It was in meetings and in exercises of this kind, that the Cumberland Presbyterians had their origin.

"Previous to the first meeting of the Kentucky Synod, (Presbyterian) which was in October, 1802, all the ministers and churches south of the Kentucky river were under the inspection of one Presbytery, and it was within the bounds of this Presbytery, and particularly in the settlements on the waters of Green river and Cumberland, that the religious excitement was greatest. It was supposed by many good men, that the Holy Ghost was poured out upon the churches in a degree nearly equal to what was seen and felt on the day of Pentecost,(!) and consequently, that ministerial gifts and ministerial graces were bestowed in greater abundance, and to a greater extent, than any of that generation had ever witnessed. Hence at the fall meeting of Presbytery, in 1801, it was proposed that the ordinary rules of the Presbyterian church respecting literary qualifications, and the length of time to be spent in the regular study of divinity, by all candidates for the holy ministry, should be dispensed with, and that four men, who were produced, should be taken immediately under trials for license; and a majority of members of Presbytery being in favour of the measure, it was adopted, though strenuously opposed by a respectable minority."[*]

Shortly afterwards the Presbyterian Synod of Kentucky divided this district into two Presbyteries, one of which—the Cumberland Presbytery, newly erected—was composed chiefly of those who were in favor of the new discipline in regard to ministers. This Presbytery licensed ministers by wholesale, and soon filled the south of Kentucky with preachers, as remarkable for their confident enthusiasm, as they were for their ignorance. These men were possessed of a rude species of eloquence, which gained favour with the common people. The number of these irregularly appointed preachers soon swelled to thirty; and they were increasing so rapidly as to bid fair, in a very short time, to outnumber the regularly appointed ministers of the Kentucky Synod.[†]

This body took the alarm; and, in the meeting held in October, 1805, a committee composed of ten among the leading ministers, and six ruling elders, was appointed to confer with the members of the Cumberland Presbytery on the subject. They were vested with "full synodical powers,"

[*] Ibid. p. 117—118.   [†] Ibid. p. 118—119.

and the conference was to be held at Jasper meeting house, in Logan county. They appeared at the appointed place on the 3rd of December, 1805; when they commenced their inquiry. But the advocates of the new system of extraordinary heavenly lights were not disposed to abide by the judgment of this ecclesiastical body.

"The Committee was stigmatized with the unhallowed name of an 'Inquisition,' sent down by the Synod to destroy the revival of religion, and to cut off all the young preachers, because they had not learned Latin and Greek."*

"The most of the members of the commission were *nick-named*, and given some appellation, either to affix stigma or confer an encomium, as the fruitful and ingenious inventors thought the individuals were favourable or unfavourable to their cause. Under such very unpleasant and forbidding circumstances did the commission meet and transact their business—only one man in the settlement, living some three or four miles from the meeting-house, opened his door and his heart for the reception and accommodation of the commission."†

The whole affair terminated, as might have been anticipated, in an open schism of the Presbyterian church in Kentucky. Both parties adhered tenaciously to their respective opinions, and no accommodation could be effected. The champions of the Spirit were not likely to be convinced by the reasoning of their less favoured brethren. We have room merely to give one passage in the long and bitter controversy which ensued; and we give it as an illustration of the Protestant rule of faith, in its theory and practice, which, in the in-

*Ibid. p. 121. † Ibid.

stance we are going to allege, were strangely at variance.

"The Commission then requested, in a friendly manner, the majority of the Cumberland Presbytery, 'to give the reasons why, in licensing and ordaining persons to preach the Gospel, they required them to adopt the Confession of Faith so far only, as they in reason think it corresponds with the Scriptures?' The answer was, 'that the Confession of Faith was human composition, and fallible, and that they could not in conscience feel themselves bound any farther than they believe it corresponds with Scripture.'"[*]

The answer, it must be confessed, was a poser, based, as it clearly was, upon the Protestant rule of faith—private judgment, or the Bible as expounded by each individual for himself. The Committee, instead of solving the difficulty, proceeded to suspend all the newly appointed preachers, and to cite the majority of the Cumberland Presbytery before the Presbyterian Synod of Kentucky. This body, as well as the General Assembly of the Presbyterian church in the United States, fully sanctioned the high-handed proceedings of the Committee: and thus was the schism consummated.[†]

The excluded ministers were not much troubled at the decision: they set up for themselves, and soon overspread the southern portion of Kentucky, the State of Tennessee, and part of Alabama. In 1823, they had nine Presbyteries, of which only two were in Kentucky.[‡] They differ from the Presbyterian church, not only in church discipline, but also in some doctrinal points, especially those connected with grace and predestination.

[*] Ibid. p. 122.   [†] Ibid. p. 124, seqq.   [‡] Ibid. p. 126.

On these points, they seem to approach the doctrines of the New School: they maintain that "God provides salvation for all mankind," and that He wills and decrees neither sin nor the damnation of any one.* On the original ground of quarrel, they seem to have relented somewhat; and they now encourage literary qualifications in their preachers.† Such was the origin, and such the principal features in the early history of the Cumberland Presbyterians.

The "general outpouring of the Spirit" in 1800, and in the summers of the two following years, not only originated the Cumberland Presbyterians, as we have just seen, but it also gave rise to other dissensions and sects. The Spirit of God is a Spirit "of peace and not of dissension;" but the spirit of which we are speaking had different characters altogether: it was as prolific of new sects, as it was superabundant in its communications! Our Blessed Saviour has said: "by their fruits ye shall know them"—a golden rule, by which error is immediately distinguished from truth. The former is manifold, inconsistent, and contradictory; the latter is one, uniform, and unchangeable.

Every where, and at every period of its history, the Presbyterian church has been marked by a spirit of dissension, not only in regard to other denominations, but also within its own bosom. The fierce and relentless spirit of John Calvin still lives in his disciples. Even the close ties of sympathy, rendered stronger by common necessities and dangers, in the newly settled wilderness of Kentucky, could not extinguish this *combative* spirit of Presbyterianism. Its hoarse notes of dis-

---

* See extracts from their "Confession of Faith", Ibid. p. 127.
† Ibid. p. 128.

cord were mingled with the roaring of the wild beasts, and the ferocious war-whoop of the Indians!

The Cumberland Presbyterians were one, and the "New-Lights" another off-shoot of early Presbyterianism in Kentucky. Of the manner in which the latter sect had its origin, the author to whose authority we have already often appealed, speaks as follows:

"The people of whom we propose to give a short sketch in the following article, had their origin at the second meeting of the Synod of Kentucky, which was in September, 1803. They have been known in the language of the day under various names. They have assumed to themselves the exclusive name of "the Christian Church." They have usually been called "New-Lights, or Stoneites," &c. &c.; and if they are known at all in the future history of the church, they will be denominated Pelagian or Socinian heretics."(!)*

At the above named Synod, two leading preachers, of whom the principal was Barton W. Stone, "were accused of disseminating doctrines contrary to the publicly received doctrines of the Presbyterian church."† The accused protested against the proceedings of the Synod, and proved hopelessly refractory. They determined not to have their Christian liberty (!) abridged, and to set up for themselves. Accordingly, in June, 1804, they issued the following singular circular:

"We hereby inform you, that we have made an appointment for a general meeting of Christians at Bethel, seven miles below Lexington, on Thursday before the second Sabbath of October next.

*Ibid. p. 130.   † Ibid.

The design of the meeting is, to celebrate *the feast of love,* and unite in prayer to God for *the outpouring of his Spirit.* The place of meeting was chosen as a centre for the States of Ohio, Kentucky, and Tennessee, that all who are engaged in the common cause of our Lord and Saviour Jesus Christ, may unite, and swell the solemn cry : *Thy Kingdom come! Even so, come Lord Jesus!* Brethren, the grace of our Lord Jesus Christ be with you all. Amen.

"P. S. We will meet prepared to encamp on the ground, and continue for several days."*

The call was responded to by "a meeting sufficiently numerous to alarm the heart of the Ecclesiastic."† All attempts at reconciliation proved abortive; and in the year 1808, the Synod passed the following singular decree against the authors of the new sect:

"Resolved, That the above mentioned R—— M—— Barton W. Stone, &c. &c. &c., be DEPOSED, in the name of Christ; and by the authority committed to us, they are hereby DEPOSED from all the functions of the Gospel ministry, and cut off from our communion."‡

But the leaders had anticipated this blow, and had already prepared themselves for it. In the fall of 1803 they had separated from the Synod, and had organized themselves into a new Presbytery, which, singularly enough, was dissolved, by their own free consent, in the following June, at a meeting held in Springfield. They were opposed to the doctrines of the Decrees and of Predestination, as well as to all creeds and confessions of faith.|| Their opposition to all church authority, was one of the main reasons which prompted the

* Ibid. p. 131-2. † Ibid. ‡ Ibid. p. 133. || Ibid. p. 134.

sudden dissolution of their Presbytery. On the occasion they published a document under the solemn title: "the last will and testament of the Presbytery of Springfield." The following is an extract from this curious paper:

"With deep concern they viewed the divisions and party spirit, which have long existed among professing Christians; principally owing to the adoption of human creeds and forms of government. While they were united in the name of a Presbytery, they endeavoured to cultivate a spirit of love and unity with all Christians; but found it exceedingly difficult to suppress the idea, that they themselves were a party separate from others. This difficulty increased in proportion to their success in the ministry," &c.* Hence they resolved on a dissolution, as "there was neither precept nor example in the New Testament for such confederacies as modern church Sessions, Presbyteries, Synods, General Assemblies, &c."†

These principles, which, it must be avowed, embody the essence of original Protestantism, gave rise, shortly afterwards, to the new sect of which Alexander Campbell is now the great champion and leader—the second in succession from Barton W. Stone, who, we belive is, however, still living. This new sect has become numerous, especially in the west; and it goes under the various names of "Reformers," "Christians," "Disciples" and "Campbellites," which latter is the more usual denomination among the uninitiated. This sect—which yet professes to be no sect!!—is not yet old enough to have obtained a fixed *Christian* name! And, yet, with the charm of novelty, it has swept off vast numbers from the other sects, especially from the Baptists.

* Ibid. p. 135. † Ibid. p. 135-6.

Dissensions and quarrels seem to be the heirloom of early Presbyterianism in Kentucky: and in this respect Calvinism in our State has been but consistent with its general spirit and character every where, and at every time. We have already given several instances of this spirit: we must yet furnish one or two more.

Among the first Presbyterian preachers who came to Kentucky was the Rev. Adam Rankin, who settled at Lexington in 1784 or 1785.*

"In Oct. 1789, Mr. Rankin was arraigned before the Presbytery of which he was a member, on a general charge of slandering his brethren in the ministry. After a delay of something better than two years, the charge was considered by Presbytery as substantiated, and Mr. Rankin was required to submit to what censure might be deemed necessary. Mr. Rankin, instead of submitting, declined all farther connection with Presbytery, and received on the spot what was called the right hand of fellowship, from a considerable number of the bystanders. He proceeded immediately to organize separate societies—for which cause, as well as for contumacy, the Presbytery, at a subsequent meeting, solemnly *deposed* him from the ministerial office."†

The author continues:

"Whatever was the truth in the case, the great majority of the people, who adhered to Mr. Rankin, sincerely believed that he was a slandered man, and that other men of the Presbytery were the slanderers—and that Mr. Rankin had suffered, and still was suffering, for his sincere, and ardent, and

---

* See Ibid. p. 140. This author, let it be remembered, seems to be a Presbyterian himself—a circumstance which greatly enhances the value of his testimony, whenever his brethren are concerned. † Ibid. p. 141.

consciencious attachment to the exclusive use of Rouse's version of the Psalms of David, in opposition to Watt's Imitation. Hence they considered him and themselves, as faithful testimony-bearing men, for what they called the Scriptural Psalmody, in opposition to psalms and hymns of human composition, and of human authority."*

In May, 1793, Mr. Rankin and his adherants attached themselves to the Associate Reformed Church, into which body they were received at a general Synod held in Philadelphia. With his new co-religionists he did not, however, fare better than he had with the old. The charge of slander was again branded on his brow, by a commission appointed by the General Synod of the Associate Reformed Church. The condemnation is couched in the following strong language:

"Their decision on the whole of the premises is—That the Rev. Adam Rankin, convicted before them of lying and slandering his brethren, is a scandalous person, and ought not to continue in the exercise of the Christian ministry; and they accordingly did, and hereby do, in the name, and by the authority of the Lord Jesus Christ, the only King and Head of the church, suspend him, the said A. Rankin, from the office of the Gospel ministry, forbidding him all and every one of the proper acts thereof, until he be lawfully restored thereto. Done at Léxington, State of Kentucky, this 17th day of September, 1818."†

Signed by the Commission—four in number.

Another Presbyterian preacher of high standing in the communion, the Rev. James McChord, of Lexington, became involved in difficulties with his own church. For having published a work

* Ibid. p. 141-2. † Ibid. p. 142-3.

which was supposed to contain unsound doctrine; he was arraigned before his own Presbytery, in October, 1815, and suspended from the exercise of the ministry. He appealed to the General Synod, which confirmed the decision of the inferior tribunal, in May, 1817. Upon this, "he put in a declinature of their authority, and appealed to churches who might be disposed to do him justice;" alleging that the proceedings of the tribunals which had condemned him had been "illegal and unrighteous."*

This chapter would extend to too great a length, did we propose to exhibit all the facts in the early history of the Presbyterian church in Kentucky, setting forth its fierce and wrangling spirit. The instances already given will suffice for our purpose; and we must hasten on to other matters.

The Baptists of Kentucky were scarcely more united than the Presbyterians. Disunion, in fact, has ever been the heritage of error, as union has been always the distinctive mark of truth. The Baptists of Kentucky emigrated to the State chiefly from Virginia. They brought with them across the mountains the divisions by which the society was rent in the "Old Dominion." The chief sects were the Regular and the Separate Baptists: the former strongly Calvinistic, while the latter were much more numerous.† These divisions having, in Virginia, coalesced into one body, styled the "United Baptists," in the year 1787, the Baptists of Kentucky, were strongly stimulated to follow the example. But many attempts at reconciliation proved unsuccessful, until at length, if we are to believe our author, the pacification was brought about by means of the great revival of 1800–1–2.

* Ibid. p. 174–5. † Ibid. p. 290.

But, as the sequel proved, this was a mere truce, not a permanent union. Some years afterwards, the Baptists of Kentucky were divided into various warring sects, among which the most prominent were those of the Open and Close Communion, and the Ironsides, so called; and now the denomination is dreadfully rent by its controversies with the Reformers or Campbellites.

Our historian discourses after this wise of the influence of the great Revival on the controversies among the Baptists of Kentucky.

"But in the time of the great revival, the outpourings of the Divine Spirit, and its softening influence on the minds of the saints, prepared the way for that reconciliation and union, which all their weighty arguments and assiduous endeavours had not been able to accomplish. This astonishing work, in the year 1800 and following, prevailed most powerfully among the Separate, as well as the Regulars. The churches and members were now much intermixed. All were visited and refreshed by the copious and abundant rain of righteousness which was poured upon the land; and regardless of names, they unitedly engaged in enjoying and forwarding the precious and powerful work."*

This same great revival was truly an "astonishing and precious work"—the most astonishing perhaps, if not the most precious, that ever was witnessed in the world! It marked an era in the Protestant church history of Kentucky. It was on the whole so very singular, that we will be pardoned for dwelling on it in some detail. And first, we will give a pretty accurate account of the revival, furnished by a distinguished living Pro-

* Ibid. p. 292-3

testant writer; and then we will add some additional particulars gleaned from other authentic sources.

In a late work,* Col. Wm. Stone, of New York, thus speaks of this "great revival:"

"About thirty or thirty-five years ago, there was an extensive revival of religion (so called) in Kentucky, characterized by the greatest fanaticism, accompanied by a great variety of bodily affections, and running into many painful excesses. These fanatics were reducible to various classes, some of which were affected by the '*falling* exercise;' and others, by what was called 'the *jerking* exercise;' others were moved by the Spirit to propose 'the *running* exercise;' and others again, 'the *climbing* exercise'—all of which exercises are sufficiently indicated by their names. It was a frequent occurrence for a number of people to gather round a tree, some praying, and others imitating the barking of dogs, which operation was called, in familiar parlance among them, 'treeing the devil.'(!) It was stated also concerning the same people that in their religious assemblies, or other places of worship, religious professors of zeal and standing, would get out into the broad aisle, and go down upon their knees together, playing marbles, and other childish games, under the notion of obeying the saying of the Saviour—'Except ye be converted, and become as *little children*, ye cannot enter into the kingdom of heaven;' others would ride up and down the aisle of the church, on sticks, &c.

"It was farther said, that the religious leaders, or at least one of them, by the name of McNamara, would affect to personate Satan: that on a certain

---

* "Mathias and his Impostures." N. York 1835, 1 vol. 12mo. p. 312–13.

occasion during Camp-meeting he was creeping about among the peoples' feet, exclaiming, 'I am the old serpent that tempted Eve:' when approaching, in this manner, to a Scotchman, who was on the ground as a spectator, the man lifted up his heel, and stamping on the face of the minister, replied: 'The seed of the woman shall bruise the serpent's head.' This man, McNamara, was regarded among them with superstitious reverence, insomuch, that it was common for them to sing, in worship, a hymn having for its chorus—'glory to God and McNamara!' A pious friend of the writer, who was at the time a student of theology under the late Dr. Mason, states that these facts were reported by his fellow-students from Kentucky, one of whom actually heard the blasphemous chorus sung! And yet all these affections, these 'fantastic tricks,' which might well 'make angels weep,' were fully believed to be the work of the Holy Spirit—the fruits and evidence of conversion—and it would have been bold impiety and blasphemy to doubt it."

The writer adds to this statement—for the substantial accuracy of which all the older inhabitants of Kentucky will willingly vouch—the following judicious reflections:

"What sober Christian does not shrink with pain, sorrow, and disgust, from proceedings like those just related, carried on under the name of religion, and with an impious confidence referred to the direct agency of the Holy Spirit? And yet they are scarcely more extravagant or revolting than have been witnessed in our own day, and in some of the most enlightened regions of our own State. Look at the present condition of the churches of western New York, which have become in truth, 'a people scattered and peeled.'"*

To understand more fully how very "precious and astonishing" this great revival was, we must farther reflect: 1st. That it produced, not a mere momentary excitement, but one that lasted for several successive years : 2ndly. That it was not confined to one particular denomination, but, to a greater or less extent, pervaded all; 3rdly. That men of sense and of good judgment in other matters, were often carried away by the same fanaticism which swayed the mob; 4thly. That this fanaticism was as wide-spread, as it was permanent—not being confined to Kentucky, but pervading most of the adjoining States and territories; and 5thly. That though some were found who had good sense enough to detect the imposture, yet they were comparatively few in number, and wholly unable to stay the rushing torrent of fanaticism, even if they had had the moral courage to attempt it.

Such are some of the leading features of a movement in religion, (!) which is perhaps one of the most extraordinary recorded in history, and to which we know of but few parallels, except in some of the fanatical doings of the Anabaptists in Germany, during the first years of their history. The whole matter furnishes one more conclusive evidence of the weakness of the human mind, when left to itself; and one more sad commentary on the Protestant rule of faith. Here we see whole masses of population, spread over a vast territory, boasting too of their enlightenment and Bible-learning, swayed for years by a fanaticism, as absurd as it was blasphemous; and yet believing all this to be the work of the Holy Spirit!! Let Protestants after this talk about Catholic igno-

* Ibid. p. 313-14.

rance and superstition! Had Catholics ever played the "fantastic tricks," which were played off by Protestants during these years, we would perhaps never hear the end of it.

The picture drawn above by Col. Stone is not only not exaggerated, but it even falls short of the original, in many of its features. Besides the "exercises" which he mentions, there was also the *jumping* exercise. Spasmodic convulsions, which lasted sometimes for hours, were the usual sequel to the *falling* exercise. Then there were the "exercises" of *screaming*, and *shouting*, and *crying*. A Camp-meeting during that day exhibited the strangest bodily feats, accompanied with the most Babel-like sounds. An eye-witness of undoubted veracity, stated to us, that in passing one of the camp-grounds, he noticed a man in the "*barking* exercise," clasping a tree with his arms, and dashing his head against it until it was all besmeared with blood, shouting all the time that he had "treed his Saviour"!! Another eye-witness stated, that in casually passing by a camp in the night, while the exercises were at the highest, he witnessed scenes of too revolting a character even to be alluded to here.

One of the most remarkable features, perhaps, of these "exercises" is, the apparently well authenticated fact, that many fell into them, by a kind of sympathy, almost in spite of themselves, and some even positively against their own will! Some who visited the meetings to laugh at the proceedings, sometimes caught the contagion themselves. There seems to have then existed in Kentucky a kind of mental and moral epidemic—a sort of contagious frenzy—which spread rapidly from one to another.

Yet the charm was not so strong that it could not be broken, as the following incident, related to us by a highly intelligent Protestant gentleman, clearly proves. Some young ladies of his acquaintance came from one of those meetings to pass the night at his father's house. They were labouring under great nervous excitement, and, in the course of the evening, began to *jerk* most violently. The father, one of the most intelligent men in Kentucky, severely rebuked them, and told them bluntly, that he would "have no such behavior as this in his house." The reproof was effectual, and the *jerking* spirit was exorcised!

Among the early sects of Kentucky, the Shakers are not the least remarkable. In the spring of 1805, three members of this fraternity visited Kentucky.* They soon made proselytes; and they now have two flourishing establishments: one in Mercer, and the other in Logan county. They are disciples of Ann Lee, and date back their origin to the respectable antiquity of the year 1750. They condemn marriage as unlawful, and profess to believe that the milennium, or second resurrection, has already come. On the Trinity, they teach a curious medley of blasphemies, among which the principal is, that the Word was communicated to the *man* Jesus, and that the Holy Ghost, whom they hold to be a female, was personally imparted to the *woman* Ann Lee; and her they view as having been necessary to complete the work of the Redemption.† Their worship con-

* "An outline of the History of the Church," etc. before cited. p. 138.
† See one of their standard works, printed in 1808, at Lebanon, Ohio. See also an able article on the subject in the "Annales de la Propagation de la Foy," vol. 3. p. 216, seqq.

sists in dancing till they are covered with perspiration, and are on the point of dropping with exhaustion. They own nothing individually, but live in common, under their superiors, who feast their disciples occasionally with particular revelations from Mother Ann!*

We will conclude this hasty sketch of the early Protestant sects in Kentucky, by the following curious statistical table, exhibiting the religious complexion of the population of our State, in the year 1820. We are indebted for it to the work which we have already so often quoted.

"According to the census of 1820, the population of Kentucky stood thus:

Whites,	434,644
Slaves,	126,732
Free people of colour,	2,759
Other persons,	182
Total,	564,317

According to the documents to which we have

---

* For more information on the doctrines of the Shakers, see a very curious, rhapsodical, and blasphemous book, lately published by the sect in the east, entitled: "A Holy, Sacred, and Divine Roll and Book, sent forth by the Lord God of Heaven to the inhabitants of Earth.—Read and understand, all ye in mortal clay.—Pp. 222; Canterbury, New Hampshire, 1843." This book purports to be a new revelation from heaven—a sort of new bible; a second Joe Smith and Mormonite concern. Seldom have we read so much incoherent blasphemy within the same compass. Though the book purports to be wholly divine, yet it is curious to notice that a committee of the Shakers found it necessary to append to it some corrections and explanations! Verily, this *is* the age of humbuggery, imposture, and *enlightenment!*

had access at this time, the Christian population stands thus:

Baptists,	21,680
Methodists,	20,850
Presbyterians,	2,700
Cumberland Presbyterians,	1,000
Others,	500
Total,	40,730

The number of whites, male and female, under 10 years, about	166,100
The number of blacks, do. do.	24,350
Total,	190,450

From the whole population,	564,317
Take the number under 10,	190,450
And there remain,	373,867
From this number, take the number of Church members,	46,730
And there remain,	327,137

To be brought under the influences of a Christian profession."*

This table exhibits a truly frightful religious condition of the Protestant sects in Kentucky, in the year 1820. The author does not take into the account either the Roman Catholics—did he think them Christians?—or the Episcopalians: and his statement may have other defects, for ought we known. Still, as far as it goes, it cannot have been far out of the way. Making every due al-

* Ibid. p. 306-7.

lowance, it still appears, then, that, up to the year 1820, the Protestant sects of Kentucky, with all their parade about religion, the Sabbath, and the Bible, did not succeed in making Christians of more than *one-eighth* of the whole population over ten years of age!! And that, up to that time, *seven-eighths* of the adult population had not been "brought under the influence of a Christian profession."!! What became of all the converts made in the "great revival?"

The Protestant historian estimates the whole number of preachers employed in Kentucky, in the year 1820, at two hundred. Taking this as the basis of his remarks, he makes the following commentary on the statistical table given above— a commentary which strongly confirms its substantial accuracy:

"Suppose there are two hundred preachers actually employed every Sabbath, and that each has an audience of 200, there will be only 40,000 worshippers in all: a number somewhat less than the number of church members. Yet, taking all the circumstances connected with the arrangements of the different churches throughout the year, into view, we are persuaded that the average number of regular Sabbath day worshippers does not exceed this number. Now take this forty thousand from five hundred thousand, the population of the State, and you have four hundred and sixty thousand, every Sabbath, who are not attending public worship any where."*

This is truly a startling and appalling statement! It exhibits the frightful condition in which Protestantism left Kentucky, after nearly forty years' exertion for the conversion and enlightenment of

* Ibid. p. 308.

its people! The religious statistics of no Catholic country in the world present any thing one hundredth part so sad and afflicting. And yet Protestant preachers are in the habit of sneering at the ignorance and superstition of Catholic countries!! And even in Kentucky, they have lately gone so far as to get up "holy leagues" for evangelizing "the ignorant and priest-ridden Italians!" Better, by far, extend their superfluous zeal on their own people. Those who, by their own showing, have beams in their own eyes, should not be so *very* solicitous about extracting the motes from the eyes of their neighbours.

CHAPTER VII.

M. Badin again alone.*—From 1803 *to* 1805.

Death of missionaries—M. Rivet and General Harrison—But three Catholic missionaries in the whole West—Labours of M. Badin increase—No rest in this life—Anecdote of Bishop David—M. Badin *not* dead—Fruits of his labours—Piety of early Catholics—Zeal to attend church—"Uncle Harry," a pious negro—Hospitable Catholics of the olden time—Distinguished men of Kentucky, friends of M. Badin—Joe Daviess—Converts—Judge Twyman—Mrs. Onan—Singular charge against Catholics—Is the Pope antichrist?—Zealous Catholic laymen—Anecdotes—Celibacy—Having two wives—The "Water-witch"—Asking a sign—Divorces—Praying by Proclamation—How many Commandments?—"Principles of Catholics"—Discussion with preacher McHenry—Famous sermon on Baptism.

DIVINE Providence, as we have seen, had already sent several missionaries to our State, to labour in conjunction with the Very Rev. Vicar General, M. Badin. But death and the hardships of the mission had gradually deprived him of all these fellow-labourers; and he was again left alone. M. Salmon had died in 1799; and M. Fournier in February, 1803: and Rev. Mr. Thayer had left Kentucky early in the spring following.

To add to the afflictions of M. Badin, and to increase still more his solitude, death had also de-

* The facts contained in this chapter rest chiefly on the detailed oral statements of M. Badin; of which statements accurate notes were taken at the time.

prived him of the dear and intimate friend, whose letters had so often poured the balm of consolation into his afflicted heart. M. Rivet, the zealous pastor of Vincennes, had died during the previous winter of 1802–3. He had won the respect and secured the warm friendship of the late lamented President Harrison, who at that time resided at Vincennes, as Governor of the Northwestern Territory. Governor Harrison visited him in his last sickness, did all that kindness and friendship could do to procure him every species of comfort, both bodily and mental, and received his last breath.

The melancholy intelligence of the death of his friend, greatly afflicted the heart of M. Badin, which had been already deeply touched by similar scenes nearer home. Forlorn and desolate in heart, he remained alone in Kentucky for more than seventeen months, during which time he had no opportunity to pour his griefs into the ear of a brother clergyman. Besides himself, there were at that time but two other Catholic missionaries in the whole northwest: the Rev. Donatien Olivier, at *Prairie du Rocher*, in Illinois; and the Rev. Gabriel Richard, at Detroit, in Michigan.

The former was a native of Nantes, in France, and was one of the oldest Catholic Missionaries in the Valley of the Mississippi. His residence was at *Prairie du Rocher*, but he visited St. Louis, St. Genevieve, Cahokias, Kaskaskias, and sometimes Vincennes.* The latter was also a native of

---

* He died at the Seminary of the Barrens, in Missouri, on the 29th of January, 1841, at the advanced age of 95 years. This venerable missionary was admirable for his child-like simplicity and unaffected piety, which he exhibited to his last breath. Truly he was a model for missionaries—a mirror for the clergy! See his obituary in the Catholic Advocate, vol. vi. p. 23.

France. He was a zealous and pious Sulpician, as remarkable for his talents, as he was for the polish and sweetness of his manners. He was elected a Delegate to Congress, by his fellow-citizens of the Michigan Territory. He died of the cholera, in the summer of 1832, a few weeks before Bishop Fenwick. He did much for the Catholic religion in Michigan: in fact, he may be viewed as the founder of the Catholic missions in that district.*

When M. Badin was thus left alone, his missionary duties greatly increased. He had to supply the place of his two deceased brethren, as well as that of Mr. Thayer. The Catholic population of Kentucky was also daily on the increase, chiefly by emigration from Maryland. On his first arrival in the State, the number of Catholic families did not, perhaps, exceed three hundred: ten years had elapsed; and the number was now swelled to nearly a thousand. These were scattered over the whole State; and to visit them all, even occasionally, required almost supernatural exertion in one solitary missionary.

M. Badin continued to reside at St. Stephen's, as the most central point of his vast mission. But he lived almost entirely on horseback. He had no rest, day nor night. His natural activity of mind and body, was stimulated by a lively sense of duty, and a feeling of the awful responsibility of his charge. When worn down by labour, his friends often advised him to take some rest; but he was wont to answer them, that he expected no

---

* The town and church of Detroit were burned by accident, in the year 1805. The church was subsequently rebuilt by the exertions of M. Richard. In the northwest and southwest there are now thirteen Bishops, and more than two hundred and fifty priests!

repose in this life.* He was always cheerful, in the midst of all his labours, and God preserved his health unimpaired for the benefit of his people.

His labours and hardships were so great, in fact, and he had to pass through so many dangers, that his death was reported more than once. The following humorous instance of the kind may not be here wholly out of place. While he was walking the streets of Louisville, on Easter Tuesday, 1806, he met Mr. Pennington, the editor of a newspaper, then published in that place. The editor seized his hand and shook it warmly, congratulating him that he was not yet dead! He then conducted him into his office, and showed him a very laudatory obituary notice, some impressions of which had been already struck off! M. Badin, of course, contradicted the account.

In the midst of his multiplied duties, M. Badin was cheered by the abundant fruits with which God had blessed his labours. Disorders had, in a great measure, disappeared, and piety had revived. He was much consoled by the increased devotion of his people, the lives of many of whom were truly edifying. They listened attentively to the instructions of their pastor, which were often as lengthy as they were zealous; and, what was better still, they reduced them to practice. Especially were they assiduous in attending church on Sundays, whenever they had an opportunity to do so. They did not seek to exempt themselves from this duty, by light pretexts of the weather or of indisposition.

---

* On this subject, we may be pardoned for giving the following anecdote. When the late lamented Bishop David saw the portrait of M. Badin, for the first time, he raised his hands and eyes in admiration, and said, smiling: "It is the first time he was ever at rest in his whole life!" The remark had as much truth as wit.

AGAIN ALONE. 115

They seem to have complied faithfully with the sufficiently rigid regulation made by M. Badin: that those who had horses should ride ten miles, and those who had none, should travel on foot five miles, to church. They were also faithful in attending to the advice of their pastor, who exhorted such as were unable to hear Mass on Sundays, to say the whole Rosary, or to recite the Mass prayers at home, in the presence of their families.

Besides these exercises of piety, the zealous missionary had recommended public prayer in families, morning and evening, followed by spiritual reading and catechism for the children and servants; and he had the satisfaction to learn that his advice in this respect was generally followed by the Catholics under his charge. Especially, was he gratified by the regular and numerous attendance at the Holy Sacrifice on Sundays.* Large multitudes flocked to the church, at an early hour, often from a distance of eight and ten miles. So great was the eagerness to hear Mass, and to have an opportunity of approaching the Sacraments, that many repaired to the church several hours before the dawn. Sometimes, even, they would remain in the church during the whole night; often, too, in the dead of winter! At that early period, there were few articles of foreign manufacture in the country; and both men and women often came to church clad in buckskin and covered with blankets, with moccasins on their feet, and handkerchiefs about their heads, instead of hats and bonnets.†

---

* See the condensed statement of M. Badin, published in the "Annales"—p. 30-31—*sup. cit.*

† See *Supra* chapter ii.

Among the models of piety, which abounded during the time of which we are treating, we cannot omit to say a few words concerning one who was as eminent for his virtue, as he was lowly in condition. The name of the truly pious and exemplary negro servant, commonly called "Uncle Harry," is familiar to most of the older Catholic settlers of Kentucky. He was truly a model of every Christian virtue. On the death of his master, he became the property of infant heirs. An old and faithful family servant, he was left by the executor to his own choice in the selection of his employment. He determined to go to the salt-licks, thinking that there he could earn most by his labour, for the benefit of the young heirs. Before departing, however, he determined to consult M. Badin on the step he was about to take. His pastor endeavoured at first to dissuade him from his purpose, representing the hardships he would there have to undergo, the distance from church, and the danger to which his salvation would be exposed.

"Uncle Harry" replied to this last reason, with the utmost simplicity of faith: "that God would protect him from danger, and that the Blessed Virgin would take care of him." M. Badin yielded. At the licks, "Uncle Harry" was a model of piety for all. When any one of his fellow-servants was sick, he was always called for; and on these occasions, he did every thing in his power to console and instruct the sick person, by the bedside of whom he was wont to recite his beads, and to say all the prayers he knew. Sometime afterwards he was publicly sold, and purchased by a man who was not a Catholic. He obtained permission to see M. Badin, whom he induced to purchase him, promising that his labour should more than indemnify him for whatever expense he might incur. A year or two later, M. Badin visited him while he was labouring in the field: he appeared sad and dejected, and on being asked the reason, he replied, that he was fearful that he might die before he could repay his kind master what he had expended. M. Badin comforted him, and the good negro again put on a cheerful countenance.

He said prayers morning and night, with the other servants, who had great respect for his virtue. He gave them the most comfortable beds, and often spent the night in prayer, taking but a brief repose, on the hard floor. In the church, he always knelt as immoveable as a statue; and was often there for hours before the rest of the congregation. His whole life, in fact, seemed to be one continual prayer: and he died, as he had lived, praying. He expired without a struggle. One morning he was found dead, sitting upright on a stool, his hands clasped in prayer, holding his beads, and his countenance irradiated with a sweet smile. His death occurred in 1806.*

Among the Catholics of these times, who were most distinguished for their piety and liberality to the church, we may mention Anthony Sanders, Thomas Gwynn, Teresa Gough, and Henrietta Boone. The last named laboured indefatigably during fifteen years, for the benefit of the church, and her servants cleared the farm adjoining St. Stephen's—the present site of Loretto. Messrs. Sanders and Gwynn were conspicuous for their generous hospitality to the first Catholic missionaries of Kentucky. Their houses were ever the home of the Catholic clergy.

---

* Those who were acquainted with "Uncle Harry" will know that the picture above drawn of him is not too highly coloured. Virtue is admirable, wherever found, and God often chooses the humblest individuals as His most special favourites.

M. Badin was acquainted with the most celebrated men in Kentucky. He numbered among his friends, Judge Rowan, Gen'l. Todd, Judge Nicholas, Richard M. Johnson, Robert Alexander, and Joe Daviess. A finished scholar, a man of great vivacity and wit, and the countryman of La Fayette, he was every where welcomed by the first families of the country. His first acquaintance with the famous Joe Daviess began by the latter's calling accidentally at his house, to inquire his way, which he had missed; and the acquaintance thus began, soon ripened into a warm mutual friendship. Joe Daviess had never before seen a Catholic priest, and he was astonished to find in the first one he saw, a man so thoroughly intelligent and polite. He borrowed some Catholic works, and promised to make himself better acquainted with the Catholic doctrine.

M. Badin won and secured the esteem of all these men without flattering them : on the contrary, he often told them his mind very plainly; while he not only did not conceal any doctrine or practice of his church, but openly avowed and defended them all,—"in season," and sometimes, perhaps, "out of season." His frankness pleased the open and chivalrous Kentuckians of his day, and won him many friends.

He also made many converts during his missionary career in Kentucky. We will say a few words concerning two of these. Judge James Twyman had fought in the battle of the Blue Licks, from which he narrowly escaped with his life. He afterwards became a distinguished lawyer. By hearing Catholic instructions and reading Catholic books, his intelligent mind soon discovered that the Catholic was the true church, and that without her pale there was nothing but wavering and uncertainty. Manning's "Shortest way to end Disputes," was the work which chiefly struck him as conclusive in its arguments. Knowing how dangerous it was to tamper with divine grace, he did not delay to enter into the Catholic church: conversion in him immediately followed conviction.

Nor was he slow to avow or defend the faith which he had embraced from conviction, as the following incident will show. While he was attending the court at Washington, in Mason county, the people sitting at dinner, in the public tavern, began to abuse and laugh at the Catholics, for their stupidity in adoring images and worshipping the Virgin Mary, &c. Judge Twyman listened in silence, and when they had done, he arose, and, after a pause of a moment, to rivet attention, he said, slowly and deliberately: "look at me: do you think I am a fool? I am a Roman Catholic! I was raised a Protestant, but embraced the Catholic religion after a long and careful examination." The announcement created quite a sensation; and not another word was said against Catholics in his presence.

The other convert alluded to, was Mrs. Onan. She was very intelligent, and was well versed in the Bible, though she could not read. She was often attacked by the preachers, who made every effort to gain her over to their sects: but she was able to quote Scripture, as well as they, and often much better. M. Badin used to say Mass at her house. While visiting her, in the year 1808, she informed him that a neighbouring Baptist preacher had, on the Sunday previous, attempted to prove that the Catholics—vulgarly called *Romans*—had actually crucified Christ, by showing, from the Bible, what part Pilate and his Roman soldiers had taken in the crucifixion! She asked M. Badin's advice on the subject, and also, whether it would not be better, that she should go to refute his absurdity? M. Badin told her that she would do much better to stay at home, and say her prayers, and let the preacher alone. Mrs. Onan repressed her zeal, and continued faithful and exemplary until death.

This reminds us of another incident, in which a Catholic lady of no great learning, effectually refuted and silenced a preacher, who had assailed her with the expectation of persuading her to abandon Catholicity. He began his tirade, by expressing his surprise, "that a lady of her well known sense, should be a follower of the Pope, who was certainly the beast of the Revelations, and the antichrist," &c. The lady, Mrs. S——n, quietly continued her knitting, until the preacher, G—— W——, had fairly wound up his invective; then raising her eyes, she quietly asked him: "do you know grammar, sir?" Somewhat taken aback, on being thus catechized, he answered in the affirmative. "Well," resumed Mrs. S——n, "is Antichrist *singular* or *plural?*" He answered, "*singular.*" "Are two hundred and fifty-six Popes *singular* or *plural?*!!" He answered: "they are *plural.*" "Therefore," concluded Mrs. S——n, "the Pope is *not* antichrist." And she quietly resumed her knitting; while the preacher left her, complaining, that she was incorrigible, and kept in woful ignorance by her priest!

In the remote stations there were several zealous and exemplary laymen, who contributed greatly towards keeping up the true Catholic spirit in their respective neighbourhoods. In the long intervals between the visits of the pastor, they nistructed the children in the catechism, and had meetings in their houses, on Sundays, where they said the Mass-prayers, and read good books in common. Among the most zealous of these laymen, we may mention a Mr. Durbin, of Madison county, who was often known to ride to St. Stephen's—eighty miles distant—with young couples, whom he thus prevented from marrying out of the church.

We may as well here relate, several anecdotes connected with M. Badin's many rencounters with the preachers or leading men among the Protestant sects in Kentucky. Some of these incidents belong to a later period; but we will give them now, as we may not have occasion to refer to them in the sequel. A volume might be filled with these anecdotes, in which M. Badin often showed the readiness of his wit, as well the depth of his learning. We will select a few of the more striking; premising, that M. Badin made it a rule not to seek controversy, nor to decline it, when it was thrust on him. He was always ready "to give an account of the hope that was in him;" and circumstances gave him many opportunities to do so. He had, too, something pointed and *piquant* in his manner and style, to which it is impossible to do full justice, in a rapid written description.

On one occasion, while he was travelling on horseback, in Scott county, he was overtaken by a man named Shannon, a shrewd and intelligent Protestant gentleman of the neighbourhood. The conversation soon turned on the subject of religion. Mr. Shannon objected particularly to the celibacy of the clergy, which he represented as unscriptural, dangerous, and impracticable. He concluded his argument, by asking emphatically: "When you vowed celibacy, did you know that it would always suit you to live unmarried?" M.

Badin instantly answered, by asking another question: "When you vowed at the altar to be always faithful to your wife, did you *know* that she would *always* suit you?" The man was non-plussed.

On another occasion, when he was riding, at the distance of about four miles from Bardstown, a preacher attacked him on the same point—a usual hobby with Protestants. "M. Badin," said he, "there are some things in your church which I like; but there are others which I never could understand." "Very probably;" dryly answered M. Badin. After an awkward pause, the preacher continued: "for instance, M. Badin, I never could understand why it is that you priests do not marry." "I *am* married," replied M. Badin. "What, *you* married," quoth the preacher; "you really astonish me!" "I *am* married, I tell you," persisted M. Badin. "And please tell me," resumed the preacher, "where is your wife?" M. Badin answered: "I am married to the Holy Catholic Church of God!" "Oh!" said the preacher, "*I* am married to the church, too, but I have another wife." M. Badin.—"Then you have *two* wives— one of them must be an adulteress—now take your choice between your *church* wife, and your *woman* wife! The Scripture says: 'No man can serve two masters'—and *surely*, no man can serve two *mistresses!*" The preacher, who had expected to make his companions laugh at the priest's expense, now found the laugh turned against himself!

A preacher once asked him pompously, profanely using the words of our Blessed Lord: "What do men say that I am?" M. Badin answered instantly: "they say you are a preacher and a *water-witch!*" The answer was a palpable hit: the preacher was then at the house of Gen'l. Walton, who had sent for him to ascertain the site of salt water on his farm, by means of the divining rod!

A Dr. Brown once asked him to work a miracle, in order to establish the truth of his doctrine. M. Badin immediately answered, in the words of our Blessed Saviour: "a wicked and adulterous generation asketh for a sign: and no sign shall be given it."*

Once, M. Badin was at Frankfort, during the session of the Legislature. Many applications for divorce were made, even at that early day. A very intelligent member of the Senate, one day asked him, in presence of several others—"Why it was that Catholics never applied for a divorce, though all other denominations were in the habit of doing so?" M. Badin answered, smiling: "Do you not know the reason? We priests know *how* to marry people—your preachers are mere bunglers at the business: they do not understand what Christ said—'what God hath joined together, let not man put asunder.'"†

M. Badin had a notorious servant, named Jared, who was a shrewd fellow, and seemed to have caught a little of his master's wit. We must relate one instance of this. About the year 1812, President Madison issued a proclamation, appointing a certain day for fasting and prayer. On this day, a Protestant gentleman was riding by St. Stephen's; and observing Jared in the field, he shouted out to him, and asked him "to whom do you belong?" "To priest Badin," answered Jared. Stranger. "Well, why is not your master at church, praying for the government? Does he not know that this is the day named in the proclamation?" Jared. "Massa prays for the government

---

* St. Math. xvi. 4.   † St. Math. xix. 6.

every Sunday, and even every day: we Catholics do not pray by proclamation only. But, massa, why are not *you* at church, praying for the government?" The man rode on.

We must yet relate one more anecdote concerning a passage between a preacher named Rogers, and an ignorant and not very exemplary Catholic, named Wimpsatt. This man, a quiet, silent sort of a person, happened on one Sunday, at the house of a Mr. McAdams, on Pottinger's Creek, when Rev. Mr. Rogers preached. After the sermon, the man of the house strongly pressed his Rev. guest to attempt the conversion of the "ignorant Roman." The preacher set about the work with great zeal, abusing the Pope, the priests, &c., most unmercifully; Wimpsatt all the while observing a dogged silence. This circumstance emboldened the preacher, who began to catechize him in a tone of triumph, winking all the time at his host, who was present. Among other things, he asked W. "How many Commandments are there?" Wimpsatt hesitatingly answered—"*nine*." "Oh," quoth the preacher, "and that's all your priests have taught you! Only *nine* Commandments?" "There *used* to be ten," quietly answered W., "but the other day your brother preacher Skaggs ran away with one of them, the *ninth!*" This man Skaggs was married, and had just run away with a neighbour's wife! The laugh was now against preacher Rogers; and the conversation dropped.

Great and truly lamentable was the prejudice with which Protestants of that day viewed every thing Catholic. It was founded, in general, on the grossest ignorance of Catholic principles—an ignorance which was studiously kept up by the preachers, who, nevertheless, were constantly declaiming against the priests, for keeping their people in ignorance! To dispel this ignorance, and to soften down Protestant prejudice, M. Badin published his "Principles of Catholics." It was printed in Bardstown, in 1805; and was the first Catholic work ever published in the west. Like every thing else he wrote, it was solid, clear, condensed, pointed, and well written.* Owing to his overwhelming occupations, and to the scarcity of candles, M. Badin was compelled to write a portion of it by moonlight. The tract was read with avidity, and no doubt did much good.

The increase of Catholics in Kentucky, and the growing prospects of the church, stimulated the zeal of the preachers, who often declaimed till they were hoarse, against "the errors and abominations of popery." M. Badin was more than once compelled to come in collision with them. In 1798, the Rev. Barnabas McHenry, a Methodist preacher of great power of lungs and volubility of tongue, publicly challenged him to an oral discussion. The challenge was accepted, and the parties met at the house of Philip Davis, on Hardin's Creek, in presence of a large concourse of people. After the preliminaries had been arranged, the discussion commenced, and lasted for several hours, the two disputants speaking alternately.

M. Badin had brought with him four Bibles, in English, French, Latin and Greek; and he opened the discussion by protesting his firm belief, and that of his church, in every thing contained in this inspired volume. He proved that it was a calumny to say, that the Catholic church is an en-

---

* A volume of considerable size might be made up of the various writings of M. Badin, which are well worth preserving in this form. We have reason to hope that something of the kind will be hereafter published.

emy of the Bible, which she carefully preserved for fifteen hundred years, before any of the modern Protestant sects had ever been heard of. Mr. McHenry rejoined with great volubility, declaiming in the usual strain against the "abominations of popery," but studiously avoiding a direct answer to M. Badin's pointed question—"Where did you get your Bible?" After repeated efforts, M. Badin was not able to hold him to the question; and the discussion terminated, preacher McHenry affecting great indignation at the manner in which he had been handled by the priest.

Mr. McHenry refused to meet M. Badin a second time, but sent a challenge to M. Fournier, who he thought was not so well versed in the English language. M. Fournier answered, "that when he would have done with M. Badin, he would then hold himself in readiness; but that for the present he declined to interfere." After waiting some time, Mr. McHenry was at length induced by his own people to send a second challenge to M. Badin; and the parties again met at the same place. To abridge the discussion, and to make it have some useful result, M. Badin proposed that each of the disputants should speak alternately for ten minutes only; and that each should adhere strictly to the matter in hand. These terms were, with great reluctance, at length acceded to by the other party.

M. Badin opened the discussion, by proving from the Bible the necessity of a regular mission, in order lawfully to preach the Gospel. He then asked Mr. McHenry for his credentials and mission to preach, and begged him not to decline the question, but to give a direct and explicit answer. The preacher replied, that he derived his orders and mission from Dr. Coke, who had been ordained by John Wesley; that he, in his turn, had been ordained by the Church of England, which latter church had derived its orders from the Church of Rome. After giving this genealogy of his sect, he triumphantly concluded, that he had the same authority to preach as M. Badin himself, having derived his mission from the same source! M. Badin rejoined by asking the following questions:

"1st. How could an idolatrous church, such as you say the church of Rome was, constitute a lawful Christian ministry? 2nd. What authority had the church of England to separate from that of Rome; and how could she still have a lawful mission, after the separation, when the Roman Catholic Church had withdrawn from her all the jurisdiction which she had originally bestowed? 3rd. How could John Wesley lawfully separate from the Church of England, from which he had avowedly derived his orders? 4th. How could he, being a mere priest—if that—validly consecrate Dr. Coke a bishop, when all antiquity proclaims, that only a bishop can validly consecrate a bishop?"

The preacher was non-plussed; he did not answer directly one of these searching questions, though M. Badin repeated them over and again, and refused to pass to other matters, till they had been satisfactorily answered. Mr. McHenry at length became vexed, and refused to dine at Mr. Davis' house with M. Badin, alleging that his business called him home immediately! As he was mounting his horse, M. Badin invited him to pay him a visit occasionally at St. Stephen's: the preacher declined, and rode off, M. Badin calling after him, and saying, with a smile: "Well, since

J

you will not visit me, I am determined to visit you." He was not again challenged to discussion by preacher McHenry, or by any other.

We will conclude this chapter, and with it our account of M. Badin's early missionary career, by briefly relating another scene of a somewhat different character, which occurred some years later. In the year 1812,* a great controversy was carried on in the vicinity of Bardstown, between the Baptists and the Presbyterians, on the subject of Baptism. The two principal champions were, the Rev. Mr. Lapsley, a Presbyterian, and the Rev. Mr. Vardaman, a Baptist minister. The latter was a man of stentorian lungs, and of considerable popular eloquence. He produced quite a sensation, and made many converts from the ranks of the Methodists and Presbyterians. Great excitement prevailed in consequence. While the controversy was at its highest point, the Rev. Mr. Lapsley happened to meet with M. Badin, whom he immediately invited to preach on the subject in Bardstown. M. Badin said: "he was always ready to preach; but that he must tell the truth, and preach the doctrine of the Holy Catholic Church."

An appointment was accordingly made, for a day in June of that year, and the sermon was to be delivered in the Court-house of Bardstown. M. Badin attended, on the appointed day, with a large supply of Bibles and ponderous folio volumes, containing the writings of the Fathers, and the decrees of the Councils. The concourse was so great, that it was deemed expedient to adjourn to a neighbouring wood, where there had been erect-

---

* For the truth of this account we confidently appeal, not only to M. Badin's statement, but to the testimony of all the eye and ear witnesses of the discussion, some of whom are still living. The affair created great sensation at the time, and is still well remembered.

ed a stand for preaching, which had been used by the Methodists at a recent camp-meeting. The Rev. Mr. Lapsley was present, but not the Rev. Mr. Vardaman.

M. Badin, entrenching himself behind his formidable battery of books, held the vast multitude enchained for three hours, two of which he devoted to the special benefit of the Baptists, and the third, to that of the Presbyterians. His discourse was very pointed and learned. When he was in the midst of it, the rain set in, and he proposed to adjourn the meeting; but so great was the anxiety of the people, to hear him, that they shouted out to him, to "continue on, for that they did not regard the rain."

M. Badin first proved infant Baptism, and the validity of other modes besides immersion, chiefly from the ancient Fathers and Councils; and then he proceeded to exhibit and refute the errors current among the Presbyterians and Methodists, concerning the nature and effects of the Sacrament. He showed that these sects could not satisfactorily prove infant Baptism, and that by other modes than immersion, from the Scriptures alone— their only rule of faith—and that their only hope to succeed in the controversy was, to adopt the Catholic rule of Scripture interpreted by tradition and church authority. The last hour of his powerful sermon tended, in no small degree, to throw a damper on the triumphant enthusiasm which the Methodists and Presbyterians had manifested during the first two hours. Still, all admired his learning and acute reasoning; and his famous sermon on Baptism was long remembered in this vicinity.

CHAPTER VIII.

The Rev. Charles Nerinckx—His Early Life and Labours.—From 1805 *to* 1811.

M. Nerinckx—His childhood and early history—Curate at Malines—And at Everbery Meerbeke—His care of children—Revival of piety—His austerity—Is persecuted and compelled to fly—His retreat at Terremonde—Escapes to the United States—A "floating hell"—Reaches Baltimore—Sent to Kentucky—His arrival and early labours—His spirit of prayer and mortification—His courage and zeal—His cheerfulness and kindness to the poor—His narrow escapes in crossing rivers—His wolf adventure—His adventure with Hardin—His bodily strength and toils—The churches he built—His labours in the confessional—A touching devotion—The fruits of his zeal—The secret of his success—A touching incident.

For more than two years M. Badin had been left alone, in charge of the extensive and laborious missions of Kentucky. To his persevering zeal and indomitable energy of character, these missions were, in a great measure, indebted under Providence for their establishment and progress. And he has been justly styled by a venerable personage, "the founder of this Diocess, and of the several congregations of this immense region."*

Divine Providence at length took compassion on the forlorn condition of M. Badin, and sent him a zealous and indefatigable auxiliary, who was to

* Letter from Bishop Flaget to Bishop England, dated December, 1824—published in the Catholic Miscellany—No. 23.

relieve him of a great portion of the heavy burden, which had been long weighing him down, and exhausting his energies. In the annals of missionary life in the west, few names are brighter than that of the Rev. Charles Nerinckx. A native of Belgium, and, like most of the other early Catholic missionaries in the west, a victim of the French Revolution, he arrived in Kentucky in the summer of 1805; and he laboured with unremitting zeal in this missionary field, for nearly twenty years. Some particulars of the early life of this illustrious priest cannot but prove interesting; especially to those in whose memories his virtues are yet freshly embalmed.*

Charles Nerinckx was born on the 2nd of October, 1761, at Herffelingen in Haynault. His parents were distinguished for their virtues and their strong attachment to religion. His father was a physician of some eminence in the profession; and his mother seems to have been a woman of great piety. The tender mind of Charles was imbued with a deep and abiding religious feeling. At an early age, he was placed in the elementary school of Ninove, where he commenced his studies. At the age of thirteen, he was removed to the College of Geel, in the province of Kempen; whence he was afterwards sent to the University of Louvain, where he entered on the study of philosophy. His parents determined to spare no expense which might be necessary to give him a thorough education; and they were highly grati-

* The biographical notice of M. Nerinckx, published in the London "Catholic Miscellany and Repository of Information" for April 1825, is the basis for the following sketch, which is a recast of that notice, with many additional details, drawn from the recollections of some among the oldest Catholic settlers in Kentucky, as well as from the statements of M. Badin.

fied to find that Charles corresponded so well with their parental solicitude, and that he more than fulfilled their highest expectations.

Having completed his academic course, and duly consulted God in prayer, the young Charles resolved to study for the church. Accordingly, in the year 1781, he was sent by his parents to the Seminary of Malines, where he entered on the study of Theology. Here he was still more remarkable for tender and solid piety, than he was for the rapid advancement he made in his studies. Though he far outstripped his companions, yet he did not permit himself to be elated with his success. He referred all his actions to God, to whom he was united by a habitual spirit of prayer. He concealed his success, even from his own eyes, under the garb of a deep internal humility; and from those of his companions, under the veil of an unaffected modesty. He feared the praises of men more than others usually seek them.

His studies completed, he was ordained priest in 1785: and in the following year was appointed *cure*, or pastor of Malines, the Archiepiscopal city. He filled this important post for eight years, and gathered there the abundant first-fruits of his ministry. The good people of Malines yet remember his piety and laborious zeal, the effects of which they still feel. The rectory of Everbery Meerbeke, half way between Malines and Brussels, having become vacant by the death of the aged incumbent, M. Nerinckx was appointed to fill it by the general suffrage of a board of examiners, who, after the searching examination, or *concursus*, recommended by the Holy Council of Trent, for such cases, unanimously awarded him the palm over all other candidates. Though loath to leave Malines, where the people were much attached to him, yet he hesitated not to enter upon the new field of labour thus opened to him by Providence.

The extensive parish of Everbery Meerbeke was in a neglected and deplorable condition. The parish church was in a dilapidated state, and the people had been much neglected, in consequence of the age and infirmities of his predecessor in the pastoral office. M. Nerinckx immediately set about remedying all these evils; he repaired the church, and was assiduous in his efforts to revive piety among his new parishioners. Believing that the hearts of the parents could be most effectually reached through their children, he spared no pains to instruct the latter, and to rear them up in the most tender sentiments of piety. He gave them catechetical instructions on every Sunday evening after Vespers. To do this the more successfully, he divided the parish into sections, and distributed the children into regular classes; which he taught himself, or through pious catechists whom he had selected; and he had the names of all the children of his parish carefully registered. He soon won the hearts of the children, and was able easily to obtain their regular attendance at catechism. He frequently inculcated on them a tender devotion to the Holy Virgin, and taught them to sing canticles, which he had composed in her honour.

The effects of this discipline were soon discernable. The children were prepared for their first communion, and soon became models of piety for the whole parish. The hearts of the parents were touched; and the most neglectful or obdurate among them, were gradually brought to a sense of duty. Piety was seen to flourish in a parish, before distinguished only for its coldness and negligence. Numerous pious confraternities in honour of the Blessed Virgin were established, as well as associations for visiting the sick, and for other charitable objects. Thus, by the zeal of one man, aided by the Divine blessing, a total reformation was effected in a short time; and the parish of Everbery Meerbeke became a model for all others.

M. Nerinckx, though kind and polite to all, was rather austere in his manners, as well as rigid in his discipline. He was, however, always much more rigid with himself than with others. He never lost a moment, nor allowed himself any recreation. He paid no idle visits for mere pastime: he visited the different families of his parish only on duty, and generally on Sunday evenings. He knew well that a priest who does his duty has little time to spare for idle conversation. Wherever good was to be done, or a soul to be saved, there was he found, by day or by night, in rain or in sunshine, in winter or in summer. When not actually engaged in the ministry, he was always found at home, employed in prayer or in study. He was an enemy of promiscuous dances, and he succeeded in abolishing them throughout his parish.

It was natural that a man of so much zeal, and one who had done so much good, should be viewed with an evil eye by the infidel leaders of the French revolutionary movement, who had recently taken possession of Belgium. An order for his apprehension was accordingly issued; and M. Nerinckx was compelled to fly from his dear parish, which he left a prey to the devouring wolves. In 1797 he secreted himself in the hospital at Terremonde, which was under the charge of twelve or fifteen hospitalier nuns, of whom his aunt was superioress. Here he remained for seven years, during all of which time he carried his life in his hands. He acted as chaplain to the hospital, the former incumbent having been banished to the Isle of Rhe. He bore his persecutions with entire resignation to the holy will of God, and edified all by the practice of every virtue. He encouraged the good nuns to persevere in their heavenly calling of mercy. He said Mass for them every morning at 2 o'clock, and then retired to his hiding place before the dawn.

In this retreat he had full leisure to apply to study, and he lost not a moment of his precious time. He wrote Treatises on Theology, on Church History, and on Canon Law; and his manuscripts would have filled eight or ten printed octavo volumes. These he was often afterwards solicited to publish; but his modesty took the alarm, and he was inflexible in his refusal. In the hospital were shut up many of the prisoners who had been made in the revolutionary battles fought in Belgium. Some of these were horribly maimed. M. Nerinckx did all he could, in his dangerous situation, to assuage their sufferings and to impart to them spiritual succour. At the dead hour of night, he often stole to their cells, at imminent hazard of his life, and administered to them the holy Sacraments: and when they were hurried to execution, he viewed them from his hiding place and imparted to them the last absolution.* Often, too, he visited by stealth his dear parish of Everbery Meerbeke, administering the Sacraments to his people, consoling them in their sufferings, and strengthening them in the hour of danger.

---

* One of these poor prisoners, while going to execution, was observed to hold in one hand—the maimed stump of the other, which had been cut off by the Jacobins!

Beset with dangers, and uncertain as to the duration of the dreadful storm which was then sweeping over Europe, M. Nerinckx at length determined to bid adieu to his unhappy country, and to emigrate to the United States. Here "the harvest was great, and the labourers few;" and no impediment was placed in the way of a free exercise of religion, according to each one's conscientious convictions. He accordingly made his escape, in a vessel which sailed from Amsterdam to the United States, on the 14th of August, 1804.

He had a long and dangerous passage of ninety days. The old and ricketty vessel was often in imminent danger of foundering at sea; and to add to the distress, a contagious disorder carried off many of the passengers and crew. Still they were not chastened under the rod of affliction; the heart of M. Nerinckx often bled over their wickedness, which he was wholly unable to check; and he afterwards was in the habit of styling this ill-fated ship, "a floating hell." The Captain, in particular, was a very profane and wicked man. M. Nerinckx was wont to ascribe his preservation from shipwreck, to a special interposition of Divine Providence.

He reached Baltimore about the middle of November, and immediately offered his services to the Patriarch of the American church—Bishop Carroll,—for whatever mission in the United States he might think proper to assign him. Bishop Carroll received the good exile with open arms, and immediately sent him to Georgetown to prepare himself for the American mission, by learning English, with which, as yet, he was wholly unacquainted. M. Nerinckx was then in his 45th year; and yet he applied himself with so much ardour to the study of the English language, as to be able in a few months to speak and write it with considerable facility.

Bishop Carroll was well aware of the forlorn condition of M. Badin, who was alone in Kentucky; and he determined to send the new missionary to his assistance. And had he sent us no other, Kentucky would still have ample reason to be forever grateful to him for the invaluable treasure he sent in M. Nerinckx.

The good missionary hesitated not a moment to comply with the wish of his new superior. What cared he for the dangers, privations, and labours which he foresaw he would have to endure on the arduous mission to which he was hastening? Had he not been already trained to this severe discipline of the cross; and had he come to America to rest on a bed of down, and to dally with luxuries? From an early period of his life, labours and sufferings had been his daily bread; and now he was too much accustomed to them any longer to feel any apprehension on their account. He was, on the contrary, rejoiced to enter on a mission which no one else wished, or was indeed willing to accept.*

He left Baltimore in the spring of 1805; and, after a long and painful journey, reached Kentucky on the 5th of July following. He immediately applied himself zealously to the labours of the mission, which he cheerfully shared with M. Badin, the Vicar General. For the first seven years he resided with M. Badin, at St. Stephen's; afterwards, he took up his residence chiefly near

---

* This additional circumstance we learned from M. Badin, to whom we are also indebted for some other details in the sequel, superadded to what is stated in the notice above referred to. See also brief statement of the missions of Kentucky in the "Annales"—*sup. cit.*

the church of St. Charles, which he had erected on Hardin's Creek, and named after his patron Saint. But he was seldom at home: he lived on his scattered missions, and passed much of his time on horseback.

His labours in the arduous field upon which he had now entered were as great as their fruit was abundant. With his whole soul, he devoted himself to the work of the ministry. He even seemed to court labours and sufferings for their own sake. Of a powerful frame, and of herculean constitution, he never spared himself. His rest was brief, and his food was generally of the coarsest kind. He generally arose several hours before day, which hours he devoted to prayer and study. In fact, he seemed to be always engaged in mental prayer, no matter how numerous or distracting were his employments.

He appeared to live solely for God, and for his neighbour. Performing his duty was his daily bread. And though old age was fast creeping over him, yet he relaxed in nothing his exhausting labours. His soul was still fresh and vigorous; and God so preserved his health, that, even at the age of sixty, he seemed gifted with all the strength and vigour of youth.

He seldom missed offering up the Holy Sacrifice daily, no matter what had been his previous fatigues or indisposition. Often was he known to ride twenty-five or thirty miles fasting, in order to be able to say Mass. His missionary labours would be almost incredible, were they not still so well remembered by almost all the older Catholics of Kentucky.

His courage was unequalled: he feared no difficulties, and was appalled by no dangers. Through rain and storms; through snows and ice; over roads rendered almost impassable by the mud; over streams swollen by the rains, or frozen by the cold; by day and by night, in winter and in summer; he might be seen traversing all parts of Kentucky in the discharge of his laborious duties. Far from shunning, he seemed even to seek after hardships and dangers.

He crossed wilderness districts, swam rivers, slept in the woods among the wild beasts;* and while undergoing all this, he was in the habit of fasting, and of voluntarily mortifying himself in many other ways. His courage and vigour seemed to increase with the labours and privations he had to endure. As his courage, so neither did his cheerfulness, ever abandon him. He seldom laughed, or even smiled; but there was withal an air of contentment and cheerfulness about him which greatly qualified the natural austerity of his countenance and manners. He could, like the great Apostle, make himself "all to all, to gain all to Christ." He appeared even more at home in the cabin of the humblest citizen, or in the hut of the poor negro, than in the more pretending mansions of the wealthy.

He was averse to giving trouble to others, especially to the poor. Often, when he arrived at a house in the night, he attended to his own horse, and took a brief repose in the stable, or in some out-house; and when the inmates of the house arose next morning, they frequently perceived him already up, and saying his office, or making his

---

* Sometimes when he was asked by those at whose house he had arrived in the morning—"where he had slept on the previous night?"—he would answer cheerfully: "with Captain Dogwood"—the name of a tree abounding in the woods of Kentucky.

meditation.* He made it an invariable rule never to miss an appointment whenever it was at all possible to keep it. He often arrived at a distant station early in the morning, after having rode during all of the previous night. On these occasions, he heard confessions, taught catechism, gave instructions, and said Mass for the people generally after noon; and he seldom broke his fast until three or four o'clock in the evening.

In swimming rivers, he was often exposed to great danger. Once, in going to visit a sick person, he came to a stream which his companion knew to be impassable. M. Nerinckx took the saddle of his friend—who refused to venture—placed it on his own, and then remounting the horse, placed himself on his knees on the top of the two saddles, and thus crossed the flood which flowed over his horse's back. On another occasion, he made a still more narrow escape. He was swept from his horse, which lost its footing and was carried away by the current; and the rider barely saved himself, and reached the other shore, by clinging firmly to the horse's tail.

On one of his missionary tours, he narrowly escaped being devoured by the wolves, which then greatly infested those portions of Kentucky which were not densely settled. While travelling to visit a distant station, in what is now Grayson county, but what was then almost an unreclaimed wilderness,† he lost his way in the night. It was the dead of winter, and the darkness was so great, that he could not hope to extricate himself from his painful situation. Meantime, while he was seeking a sheltered place, where he could take

---

* This often occurred, especially at the station on Clear creek, Hardin county.

† And what is now little better.

some repose, the famished wolves scented him, and came in hundreds, fiercely howling around him. With great presence of mind, he immediately remounted his horse, knowing that they would scarcely attack him while on horseback. He hallooed at the top of his voice, and temporarily frightened them off; but soon they returned to the charge, and kept him at bay during the whole night. Once or twice they seemed on the point of seizing his horse, and M. Nerinckx made the sign of the cross and prepared himself for death : but a mysterious Providence watched over him ; and he escaped after sitting his horse the whole night.* With the dawn, the wolves disappeared.

As we have said, he was a man of powerful frame and herculean strength. A proof of this will be presented in the following singular adventure, which is well known to all the older Catholics of Kentucky.

He was in the habit of rigidly enforcing order in the church, during the celebration of the divine mysteries. Protestants, and persons of no religion, often attended church, led thither chiefly by curiosity. These sometimes did not conform to the rules of propriety : and M. Nerinckx, who was little swayed by human respect, was not slow to admonish them of their faults in this particular. As he was not very well versed in the English language, and was by nature rather plain and frank, his admonitions were not always well understood, or well received. Once, especially, a man by the name of Hardin—a youth of powerful frame and strength, and somewhat of a bully—

* This adventure we learned from an aged citizen of Grayson county.

took great offence at something which M. Nerinckx had said, and which it seems he had entirely misunderstood. He openly declared that he would be avenged on the priest, the first time that he would meet him alone.

An opportunity soon occurred. M. Nerinckx was going to the church of St. Charles, from St. Stephen's, when Hardin waylaid him on the road. Springing from his hiding place, he seized the bridle reins of M. Nerinckx's horse, and bid him stop, "for that he intended to give him a sound drubbing." At the same time, he cut one of the stirrup leathers, and ordered the rider to dismount; an order which was promptly complied with. M. Nerinckx remonstrated with him; told him that he had meant in nowise to offend or injure him; and that his profession wholly forbade him to wrangle or fight. Hardin, however, persisted, and was in the act of striking the priest, when the latter took hold of him, and quietly laid him on the ground, as though he had been the merest child; observing to him, meantime, with a smile, "that he would neither strike or injure him, but that he felt authorized to see that himself received no injury at his hands." In this position he held him motionless on his back, until he had obtained from him a promise, that no farther attempt should be made on his person.

After this rencounter, M. Nerinckx quietly remounted his horse, and proceeded on his journey; Hardin as quietly moving off in the other direction. On arriving at the church, one of his friends asked M. Nerinckx, "how it had happened that his stirrup leather had been cut?" He replied, by simply stating the adventure in few words; and observing, with a smile, "that these young buckskins could not handle a Dutchman!" After this he never was heard to speak of the affair; but Hardin was wont to say to his friends, "he had often thought before, that he had handled men; but that he really never had hold of one, before he met priest Nerinckx, who, he verily believed, had something supernatural about him."[*]

M. Nerinckx often manifested his great bodily strength in the course of his laborious life. He erected no less than ten churches in Kentucky; two of which—those of Holy Cross and of Lebanon—were of brick; and the rest of hewed logs. He was not content with directing the labours of others: he was seen intermixing with the workmen, aiding them in cutting timber, in clearing out the undergrowth, and in every other species of hard labour. He generally worked bareheaded under the broiling sun: and, in removing heavy timber, or as it is commonly called, *rolling logs*, he usually lifted against two or three men of ordinary strength! He built his own house, chiefly with his own hands; and was wont to say cheerfully, "that his palace had cost him just $6 50 in money!"

He had charge of six large congregations, besides a much greater number of stations, scattered over the whole extent of Kentucky. Wherever he could learn that there were a few Catholic settlers, there he established a station, or erected a church. The labour which he thus voluntarily took on himself, is almost incredible. To visit all his churches and stations generally required the space of at least six weeks.

---

[*] We have followed the version of the adventure given by the late Vincent Gates, the pious attendant and almost indivisible companion of M. Nerinckx; and for it we are indebted to a nephew of Mr. Gates. We mention this, because the occurrence has been related in different ways.

He never took any rest or recreation. He seemed always most happy, when most busily engaged. He seldom talked, except on business, or on God, on virtue, or on his missionary duties. On reaching a church or station, his confessional was usually thronged by penitents, from the early dawn until mid-day. Before beginning to hear confessions, he usually said some prayers with the people, and then gave them a solid and familiar instruction on the manner of approaching the holy tribunal. If he seemed austere out of the confessional, he was in it a most kind, patient, and tender father. He spared no time nor pains to instruct his penitents, all of whom, without one exception, were deeply attached to him. To his instructions chiefly in the confessional, are we to ascribe the piety and regularity of many among the living Catholics in Kentucky.

But it was on the children and servants that he lavished his labour with the greatest relish. Thoroughly to instruct them, and prepare them for their first communion, was his darling employment. He thought no time nor labour, that was devoted to this favourite object of his heart, too long or ill-spent. For this purpose, he usually remained a week at each of the churches and stations. During this time, he had the children and servants daily assembled, and devoted his whole time to them. He thus renewed in Kentucky the edifying scenes which had been witnessed in his former parish of Everbery Meerbeke, in Belgium. The children were much attached to him; and he possessed a peculiar tact in winning their hearts, and stimulating them to learn their catechism, and to be virtuous. He distributed them in regular classes, and awarded premiums to the most deserving. Thus he laid, broad and deep, the foundations of Catholic piety in Kentucky.

In Kentucky, also, as in Belgium, he sought to inculcate a tender devotion to the Blessed Virgin. The first church which he erected he dedicated to God under her invocation, and called it Holy Mary's, after her. His churches were generally built in the form of a cross: the two arms of which, with one half of the body, were occupied respectively by the men and women, who were always kept separate.

After Mass, he was in the habit of practising a devotion, as beautiful as it was touching and impressive. He went to the centre of the church, where, surrounded by the little children, who so dearly loved him, he knelt down, and, with his arms extended in the form of a cross,—the children raising also their little arms in the same manner—he recited prayers in honour of the five blessed wounds of our Divine Saviour. The parents often joined the children in this moving devotion. After this, he led his little congregation, composed chiefly of children, into the adjoining graveyard, where he caused them to visit and pray over the graves of their deceased relatives and friends.

God blessed his labours with fruits so abundant and permanent, as to console him for all his toils and privations. He witnessed a flourishing church growing up around him, in what had recently been a wilderness, inhabited only by fierce wild beasts and untameable savages. He saw, in the virtues of his scattered flock, a revival of those which had rendered so illustrious the Christians of the first ages of the church. M. Badin had laid the foundation; and, like a skillful architect, he reared the superstructure, in that portion of the

K

flock entrusted to his charge. The results of his labours prove how much one good man, with the blessing of God, can achieve by his single efforts, prompted by the lofty motive of the Divine glory, and directed with simplicity of heart to one noble end.

Yet, though learned and of solid judgment, he was not remarkable for brilliancy of talent, for engaging address, or for pulpit eloquence. His discourses were plain, matter of fact, instructions, delivered in broken English, and with little rhetorical ornament. He was, on the whole, rather a tiresome and disagreeable speaker; yet was he listened to with great attention, and his words sunk deeply into the hearts of his hearers.

The whole experience of the church has proved, that however valuable mere human eloquence may be, and however efficient for the conversion of men, it is still utterly powerless, when unattended with a special grace in the preacher, which enables him to reach the *hearts* of his hearers. The history of the church in all ages has proved the truth of the Psalmist's declaration: "Unless God build the house, in vain doth he labour who buildeth it." "Paul may plant; Apollo may water: but God giveth the increase." Men of the least reputation for popular eloquence, have often effected the greatest amount of good. Jealous of his glory's being shared with men, God often does the most by the feeblest instruments. And it is on this principle, that twelve unlettered fishermen converted the world—confounding the philosophers, confuting the rhetoricians, and silencing the oracles of paganism.

We would not be understood as intending, by this digression, to disparage mere human learning or eloquence. Both are highly useful, and even, to some extent, necessary, especially in our *enlightened* (!) day. But we have meant to imply, that mere human gifts, however great or useful, are only subordinate to gifts of a higher kind. Men are not to be converted merely "by the persuasive words of human wisdom;" but by invoking the divine blessing through constant prayer, and by preaching, with simplicity, and in union with God, "Christ, and Him crucified." This did the good M. Nerinckx; and this is the true secret of his great and astonishing success in the holy ministry.

We shall have occasion in the sequel to recur to the subject of M. Nerinckx's missionary career in Kentucky. Then will we more appropriately speak of his establishments, which were founded after the arrival of the Bishop in Kentucky. We will close the present chapter, already long enough, by relating one more incident in the life of this good missionary.

The Catholics were so much dispersed, that he was often called to a distance of fifty and even a hundred miles, to visit the sick. On one occasion, he was called to see a Mr. Keith, who lived in Bourbon county, eighty miles off. The messenger arrived at the residence of M. Nerinckx early in the morning; and stated that he had left the sick man in a dying condition. M. Nerinckx lost not a moment. At five o'clock in the morning, he mounted his famous horse, "*Printer;*" and after riding during the whole ensuing night, reached the house of Mr. Keith, at six o'clock the next morning.

The poor man was already dead. He had just breathed his last. Ardently had he desired the succours of religion in his last struggle; repeatedly had he asked, "whether the priest was coming?"

In his anxiety, he had dragged himself to the door of his cabin, to direct his straining eyes, now almost set in death, in the direction in which he expected the minister of God to approach!

M. Nerinckx remained for some time with the afflicted family of the deceased, comforting them with the assurance that God had no doubt mercifully accepted the will for the deed in the deceased. He prayed with them over his remains, which he followed to their last resting place. He took occasion from the manner of his death to make a deep impression on the minds and hearts of the living, whom he exhorted "to be always ready, for they knew not the day nor the hour," when death might surprise them. After thus doing all the good he could accomplish, he returned, deeply affected by the scene he had witnessed.

CHAPTER IX.

*The Dominicans in Kentucky.**—*From* 1805 *to* 1824.

Early missionary labours of the Dominican Order—The English Dominicans—College at Bornheim—Departure for America—Arrival in Kentucky—Founding of St. Rose—The new noviciate—Bishop Concannon—Father Wilson's learning, virtues, labours and death—Father Edward Fenwick—His zeal and labours—"Stray Sheep"—Humorous adventure with an old lady—His missionary labours in Ohio—Founding of St. Joseph's, Somerset—Nominated first Bishop of Cincinnati—His success and death—The missionary labours of the Dominicans in Kentucky—Father Willet—College of St. Thomas Aquinas—Monastery of St. Magdalen's.

THE white mantle of St. Dominic had appeared in the midst of many a dreary wilderness, which it had been the means of converting into a blooming garden of Christian civilization. Clad in this emblem of purity, the sons of St. Dominic had tamed the fierceness of the savage, had enlightened his understanding, and had moved his heart to embrance the religion of Christ.

* We regret that we are not able to give a fuller history of this distinguished Order in the west. The Dominicans in Kentucky did much and wrote little: and we have been able to find no documents wherewith to compose a full history of their labours in our Diocess. The facts, however, which we will give may be relied on: they are based on notes kindly furnished us by one of the oldest and most distinguished living members of the order.

From the thirteenth to the sixteenth century, they were among the chief pioneers of Christian civilization. Wherever nations or tribes were to be converted to Christianity, there were they to be found, ready to make every sacrifice, to endure every privation, and to peril life itself to insure triumph to the Cross. Their blood has been poured out like water, in every quarter of the globe, and among almost all the tribes of the earth. In the heart of Asia, and amid the burning sands of Africa—on the banks of the Euxine and the Caspian Seas—along the waters of the Nile, the Euphrates, and the Ganges, might they be found, far away from their brethren, toiling, and labouring, and dying for the propagation of the faith.*

On the first discovery of America, we find them accompanying every expedition of exploration and conquest, mitigating the horrors of invasion, and erecting the Cross by the side of the banner of earthly conquest. The names of Olmedo, and of Las Casas—not to mention a hundred others almost equally illustrious—shine conspicuous in the annals of Spanish conquest in America: amidst the gloomy horrors of war, they brightly gleam, like stars in a dark night!†

It was in the plan of Divine Providence, that our infant missions should be blessed with a branch of this illustrious Order. For their establishment in Kentucky, as well as for most of our other early missionaries, we are indebted to the horrors of the French Revolution—Providence thus drawing good out of evil, as the bee extracts honey from the bitterest flowers. In every age of

---

* For facts under this head, see Becchetti's Church History—a continuation of that by Cardinal Orsi—*passim*.

† See Prescott, Robertson, and other historians of the Spanish Conquest.

the church, persecution has been thus instrumental in disseminating the Gospel, even as the storm scatters the seeds of the plants over the surface of the earth.

In consequence of the bitter and long continued persecution of the Catholics in England, the English Dominicans, like their other clerical brethren, in England, were compelled to expatriate, and to locate themselves on the Continent. They accordingly established an English Dominican Province in Belgium, and had a flourishing College at Bornheim. Early in the year 1805, this beautiful institution was seized on and broken up by the French revolutionary troops. At this disastrous period, Father Thomas Wilson was President, and F. Edward Fenwick was procurator of the college. The latter was thrown into prison, whence he was, however, shortly afterwards delivered, chiefly in consequence of his being an American citizen. The President and the other members of the Order escaped to England.

On entering the college, the rapacious French troops seized upon every thing of value upon which they could lay their hands. On this occasion, F. Wilson showed his presence of mind, by casting a valuable watch into a back garden, adjoining the college, whence he recovered it on the departure of the French troops.

Shortly after their arrival in England, the members of the province petitioned their General to be sent to America, the native country of F. Fenwick. The request was granted, and F. Fenwick, in consequence of his many virtues, and of his being an American, was named Superior. The colony immediately set sail, and soon landed safely in America.

Twenty-one years had elapsed since F. Fenwick had set foot on the soil of his native country. Born in 1768, in St. Mary's county, Maryland, of respectable and wealthy parents, descended from the Fenwicks of Fenwick Tower in Northumberland, England, he had been sent abroad by his parents, at the age of sixteen. At this age he had entered the Dominican college of Bornheim, where, after having completed his education, he had taken the habit of St. Dominic, and made his religious profession. Promoted to holy orders, he had been for many years professor or procurator of the institution, edifying his brethren by his exemplary conduct, and his unaffected piety. And now he returned to his native country, invested with the sacred order of the priesthood, and prepared to enter upon a new and more extensive field of usefulness.

The members of the Order who accompanied F. Fenwick to the United States were three in number: FF. Thomas Wilson, William Raymond Tuite, and R. Anger; all natives of England. They presented themselves to Bishop Carroll, who welcomed them warmly to his extensive Diocess, which then embraced the whole territory of the United States. When F. Fenwick applied for advice as to the most suitable location for the new Dominican province, Bishop Carroll recommended the distant and destitute missions of Kentucky. To his tender solicitude for the prosperity of our infant missions, we had, early in the same year, been indebted for the invaluable services of M. Nerinckx; and now we were to be indebted to the same goodness, for a whole band of zealous and efficient missionaries.

In the fall of the year, 1805, F. Fenwick paid a visit to Kentucky, to examine the country, and to decide on the most fitting situation for the new establishment. Having satisfied his mind on the subject, he returned to Maryland, late in the same, or early in the following year. In the spring of 1806, he and his brethren removed to Kentucky, where they established themselves in the present Washington county, on a farm which had been purchased with the rich patrimony of F Fenwick. The new establishment was called St. Rose's, after the Virgin of Lima—the pro to-saint of the Dominican Order in America. Thus F. Fenwick was the founder of the Dominican Order in the United States; and he was afterwards destined to be the father and founder of the missions of Ohio, and its first Bishop.

Having thus founded St. Rose's, F. Fenwick determined to commit the destinies of the new establishment to another, whom, in his humility, he sincerely believed better qualified than himself to conduct it with success. He accordingly obtained from the General of the Order permission to resign his office of superior, in favour of F. Thomas Wilson, who, by an extraordinary privilege, was named Provincial for an indefinite period.* F. Fenwick then became a private member of the Order; preferring rather to live under obedience, than to incur the responsibility of commanding.

Under the vigorous administration of F. Wilson, the establishment of St. Rose, was soon in a flourishing condition. To him, under God, were its prosperity and permanency mainly ascribable. In 1808, a noviciate was opened, which was soon filled with candidates for admission into the Order. These young men combined the exercises of the active, with those of the contemplative life. They spent some hours of each day in manual labour, aiding the workmen in making

* *Usque ad revocationem.*

brick, and in building the present church and the other edifices adjoining.*

The infant institution was greatly aided by a bequest left it about this time by a distinguished member of the Order. The first Bishop of New York, the Rt. Rev. Dr. Luke Concannon, was a Dominican, and a warm personal friend of his brethren who had recently settled in Kentucky. He died at Naples, in 1808, on the eve of his embarkation for America. He bequeathed his valuable library, besides $2,000 in money, to the convent of St. Rose. He had also intended to establish a branch of his Order in the new Diocess over which he had been called to preside, but death prevented his design.

On his arrival in Kentucky, F. Wilson was about forty-five years of age. Of refined and highly polished manners, as well as amiable, modest and learned, he was universally admired and beloved. He was of retiring habits, and much devoted to prayer and study. He was one of the most learned divines who ever emigrated to America. For many years he had been professor of Theology at the College of Bornheim, in Belgium; and he still continued to discharge the same duty at the newly established convent of St. Rose. He had written much—probably an entire course of theology, adapted to the wants of England and America—but shortly before his death, his large collection of manuscripts suddenly disappeared. It was believed that, through a motive of exaggerated humility, he had himself committed them to the flames, on the eve of his death. It will be remembered, that in this respect, he had the same

---

* See M. Badin's "Statement of the Missions of Kentucky," in the first volume of the "Annales," &c., page 40, *note—sup. cit.*

feelings of modesty as the Rev. M. Nerinckx. Much as we admire humility, we cannot but regret the loss which its excess thus occasioned the American church.

After F. Fenwick had been consecrated first Bishop of Cincinnati, in 1822, F. Wilson accompanied him to his new Diocess, in quality of Theologian. After remaining in Ohio for six months, during which time he greatly aided the new Bishop with his wise counsels, he returned to St. Rose. Here he died, in the same odour of sanctity in which he had lived, in the summer of 1824. Long and reverently will the Catholics of Kentucky remember his virtues, which are still freshly embalmed in the recollection of his brethren. He was a bright ornament of an illustrious Order, and its early history in the United States is identified with his biography.

Another ornament of the Order in North America, less brilliant, but, perhaps, more useful still, was the illustrious F. Edward Fenwick. After he had resigned the office of superior, he became a general missionary. He was seldom at home, and lived almost constantly on horseback. His zeal for the salvation of souls was as boundless as it was untiring and persevering. He traversed Kentucky in every direction, in quest of scattered Catholic families, whom he was wont to designate as "stray sheep." Often was he known to ride thirty or forty miles out of his way, to visit a lonely Catholic family, of whose existence he had been informed. Though not gifted with great natural talents, he possessed a peculiar tact for winning souls to Christ. His manners were of the most familiar, affable, and winning kind. He could adapt himself to every emergency, and to every description of character and temperament.

Frank, open, and sincere by nature, and an American himself, he possessed an instinctive talent for dealing with Americans, whether Catholics or Protestants. Multitudes of the latter were converted to Catholicity through his agency.

Often, after a long and painful ride, he reached, at night-fall, the house of a distant Catholic family, which he had determined to visit. Before dismounting from his horse, he frequently, on these occasions, entered into familiar conversation with his new acquaintances, by telling them, "that he had travelled out of his way in quest of 'stray sheep;' and asking them whether they had heard of any such in that vicinity?" Having thus established a sort of intimacy, he explained to them in the course of the evening, the symbolical meaning of "stray sheep," and he seldom failed of his object. On one occasion, however, he was not so successful, as the following amusing incident will show.

He was sent for by an old lady, not a Catholic, who lived at a distance of four miles. Having no horse at the time, he was compelled to perform the journey on foot, in a dark night, and over bad roads. On reaching the house, he found the old lady sitting by the fire, surrounded by her friends. She stated to him very gravely, that knowing him to be a very kind-hearted man, she had sent for him in order to procure twenty-five cents' worth of tobacco, of which she then stood greatly in need! F. Fenwick, though excessively wearied, could not suppress a laugh at the old lady's vexatious conceit: he handed her the money, stating that he was not in the habit of carrying tobacco in his pockets; and on leaving the house, simply requested her, with a smile, to send to him for the money the next time she needed tobacco, and not to put him to the trouble of travelling four miles on foot.

But it was on the new missions of Ohio, that F. Fenwick was destined most to signalize his missionary zeal. Of this mission he was the first pioneer and founder. He penetrated into the State, for the first time, in the year 1810. He then found, in the vicinity of Somerset, only three Catholic families, of German extraction, numbering in all about twenty members. He traversed the State in all directions, and was gratified to be able subsequently to discover there many other scattered families of Catholics. These he visited occasionally, saying Mass for them, instructing the children, and administering the Sacraments. The first churches of this new mission were founded by him.

In the year 1818, or 1819, a gentleman living near Somerset, Ohio, made a present to the Order of a fine farm, on condition that F. Fenwick would erect on it an institution similar to that of St. Rose, in Kentucky. The generous offer was accepted; and with the approbation and advice of Bishop Flaget, whose Diocess then embraced Ohio, F. Fenwick, accompanied by his nephew, F. N. D. Young, proceeded to Ohio, to found the new establishment. It was called St. Joseph's, and is now one of the most flourishing convents of the Order in the United States.

In 1822, F. Fenwick was nominated by the Holy See first Bishop of Cincinnati. Thinking himself wholly unfit for the responsible office, he fled and buried himself in his distant missions in the forest. He soon, however, found that it was as impossible for him, as it had been for Jonas of old, "to fly from the face of the Lord." He reluctantly accepted the appointment, and was consecrated at St. Rose, by Bishop Flaget.

Our scope and limits will not permit us to enter into the details of his subsequent career, in the episcopacy. Suffice it to say, that he laboured for ten years, with indefatigable zeal, in this new and wider sphere of usefulness; and that he had the satisfaction to find, that God abundantly blessed his labours. When he first visited Ohio, he was able to find but twenty Catholics; at his death, he left about forty thousand, whose spiritual wants were attended to by thirty missionaries. Great numbers of those had been added to his ever increasing flock, by conversion.

He died, as he had lived, in the midst of his labours. He was on a visitation of his extensive Diocess, which embraced Ohio and Michigan. He had fallen sick at *Saulte Sainte Marie*, on Lake Superior; and when he reached Michillimackinac, his life was despaired of. Still he continued his visitation. On the 25th of September, 1832, he calmly breathed his last, thirty miles from Canton. He had said Mass, and written two letters on the previous day. Thus died Bishop Fenwick, a faithful missionary to the last, and a martyr to his zeal.[*]

The Order of St. Dominic in Kentucky had thus laid the foundations of the Ohio missions, and given to the newly established Diocess of Cincinnati its first Bishop. It had established in Ohio a branch of the Order which was soon to rival the mother institution itself. Still, though few in number, the Dominicans determined to extend yet more the sphere of their usefulness.

[*] See an obituary notice of him in the Catholic Telegraph, vol. 2. No. 11. p. 85.

They entered with relish and indefatigable zeal on the missions of Kentucky. They had charge of several flourishing congregations in this Diocess. They attended the old congregation of St. Anne's on Cartwright's Creek, until the year 1819, when the tottering log church was taken down, and the congregation attached to it was merged in that of St. Rose. This had already become one of the most numerous in the whole Diocess.

They also had charge of the large congregation attached to the church of St. Pius, in Scott county; as well as of that at Lexington. The former was attended to successively by FF. R. Anger and S. H. Montgomery; the latter, for several years, by F. Wm. T. Willet. The last named was a native of Kentucky, and had been one among the first novices who had entered the Order at St. Rose, where he had been ordained in 1816, together with FF. Richard P. Miles, Samuel H. Montgomery, and N. D. Young. He was a man as remarkable for his talents, as he was for his zeal and virtues. In Lexington, he won the hearts of all who knew him. Humble, affable, charitable, of easy and polished manners, and an excellent preacher, he was an efficient and devoted missionary. But his health was bad; his constitution was a prey to that insidious and fatal malady—consumption; and he fell a victim to this disease on the 9th of May, 1824. He was interred at Lexington, in presence of a vast concourse of people, of all denominations; and his virtues are still vividly remembered.*

* A neat and plain sepulchral monument was erected over his remains; and our only source of information as to his life and the date of his death, was a brief obituary notice which appeared at the time in a Lexington paper, and the inscription on his tomb.

About the year 1809, F. Wilson had established, adjoining the convent of St. Rose, the College of St. Thomas Aquinas. This institution continued to flourish for about ten years. The novices and younger members of the Order acted in the capacity of professors and officers in this college, the subsequent decline of which is mainly ascribable to the increasing demand for their services on the missions, of which the Dominicans had taken charge in Kentucky and Ohio. So great, in fact, was this demand, that it was found impossible to keep up the institution, the exercises of which were accordingly closed in 1819 or 1820. It had, however, already educated many of the youth of Kentucky, both Catholic and Protestant, and had done great good to religion.

About this time, a new institution—that of the Sisters of the Third Order of St. Dominic—grew up under the auspices of the Dominicans in Kentucky. The new establishment, called St. Magdalen's, was situated about a mile from St. Rose. F. Wilson may be viewed as its original founder; but its subsequent prosperity and permanancy are mainly ascribable to one of the chief ornaments of the Dominican Order in Kentucky—the present Bishop of Nashville.*

---

* The following statement, kindly furnished us by the same Rev. gentleman to whom we are indebted for most of the facts contained in the preceding chapter, will show the present flourishing condition of the Sisterhood of the Third Order of St. Dominic.

It has now two houses: one, St. Magdalen's, near St. Rose's, in Kentucky; and the other, St. Mary's, in Somerset, Ohio. The convent of St. Magdalen, in Kentucky, has at present about eighteen professed members, and six novices. These religious ladies conduct a female boarding school, in which they usually educate from eighty to a hundred pupils. They have also recently opened a day-school in Springfield, which bids fair to flourish. They teach all the branches usually taught in such

The Order of Dominicans in the west, was subsequently, for a short time, divided into two distinct provinces, one of which embraced Ohio, and the other Kentucky: but, on the petition of the members to the General, the two provinces were reunited into one. It has given two distinguished Bishops, and many zealous missionaries to the American church. Among the latter, we cannot omit to mention FF. Polin and McGrady. They were both ordained together by Bishop Fenwick, in the year 1822; and, after having laboured with indefatigable zeal for many years, the former, on the missions of Kentucky, and the latter, on those of Ohio, they both met again at St. Rose, where they died within three days of each other.* F. Polin was a Mathematician, and a man of considerable talent; yet as humble as a child, and as mild as a lamb. He was universally beloved, and deeply regretted.

institutions. They recite daily in choir the office of the Blessed Virgin; and also, the office of the dead weekly; and they make vows for life.

About the year 1828, the Rt. Rev. Dr. Fenwick, Bishop of Cincinnati, being then Superior of the Dominican Order in America, desirous of extending the sphere of their usefulness, called four members of the sisterhood to Ohio, and established them at Somerset. They began their labours in a small house which had been purchased for their establishment by Dr. Fenwick. In a very short time they became so popular, that the Catholics of the vicinity united to aid them in enlarging their house, so as to enable them to receive boarders. They named their convent St. Mary's; and put it under the protection of the great Queen of Virgins. So rapidly has this establishment increased, that it numbers now more than twenty professed Sisters, besides novices; and educates about a hundred young ladies annually.

* See their obituary notices in the Catholic Advocate, vol. 3, p. 390. F. Polin died on the 24th, and F. McGrady, on the 27th of Dec., 1839; and each was in his 40th year. F. Raymond Tuite died in 1836 or 1837.

CHAPTER X.

The Trappists in Kentucky—*From* 1805 *to* 1809.

Goodness of Providence toward the Missions of Kentucky—The Cistercian and Carthusian Monks—The Abbe De Rance—His early life, disorders, and conversion—His exemplary penance—Attempts a reform of the Order—The Trappists—Their rules and austerities—Dispersed by the French Revolution—Some of them escape to America—Father Urban Guillet—The Trappists at the Pigeon Hills, in Pennsylvania—Their arrival in Kentucky—Their edifying life and austerities—The number who died in Kentucky—Cross in the moon—Departure for Missouri—Delay at the mouth of the Ohio—Sublime spectacle—Ascent of the Mississippi—Curious accident—The Trappists at Flourissant—And at Monk's Mound—The Indians—Curious fact in acoustics—Deaths at Monk's Mound—Return to Europe—Incidents of travel—Remarks on a passage in the "American Notes" of Charles Dickens.

It would seem that Divine Providence had cast an eye of particular benevolence on the early missions of Kentucky, and watched over them with a special care. The first that was established in the west, the church of Kentucky was destined to

---

* We have derived the facts contained in this chapter from an aged and respectable individual, who came out to America with the Trappists, and remained with them until their final return to Europe, in 1813. Though not himself a regular member of the Order, yet he lived in the same community with the Trappists, and was thoroughly acquainted with their history and institute.

become the mother and foundress, as well as the model, of many others. She was to be the fruitful mother of many spiritual children, who "would rise up and call her blessed." From the original Diocess of Bardstown, no less than *nine* others[*] have already sprung into existence; many of them, under the fostering care of the present venerable Patriarch of the western church.

And, as if to prepare the church of Kentucky for this wide extension, and to increase her fecundity, God seemed lavish of his favours in her regard. He had already sent zealous missionaries to labour in her ample field—to water it with their tears, and to gather from it fruits ripe for heaven: and now He sent out to the same portion of His vineyard, a band of pious contemplatives, who were to fertilize it with their prayers, and to diffuse the sweet odour of sanctity throughout the whole western wilderness.

The Trappists were a branch of the Order of Cistercian Monks, originally founded by the great Saints Stephen and Bernard, in the twelfth century. This was one of the most austere religious Orders ever established in the church. It was intended to revive, in the western portion of the Christian church, the bright examples of primitive sanctity furnished in the lives of the eastern solitaries, of the third and fourth centuries. St. Bruno,[†] St. Bernard, and St. Stephen were to the western, what St. Anthony, St. Pachomius, and St. Basil, had been to the eastern church: and the Cistercians and Carthusians of the west, were the

---

[*] Including that of Little Rock, Arkansas, about one-half of which lay within the original limits of the Diocess of Bardstown.

[†] St. Bruno was the founder of the Carthusians, an Order still more austere than that of the Cistercians.

counterpart of the monks of Syria and of the Thebais, in the east. Both were devoted, in a life of entire seclusion from the world, to the constant practice of prayer, of mortification, and of all the evangelical counsels.

Like most of the religious Orders, the Cistercians had, in course of time, relaxed somewhat of their primitive fervour. They had become less devoted to austerity and to prayer, and had imbibed no little of the spirit of the world, which they had renounced. Fervent members of the Order had, at different times, laboured, with greater or less success, both by word and by example, to stem the downward current, and to restore the society to its original condition. Among these zealous men, whom Divine Providence raised up from time to time, none were perhaps more conspicuous, or succeeded in effecting more good, than the famous Abbe de Rance.

A native of France, of a wealthy and ancient family, the nephew of Bouthillier de Clavigni, the French Secretary of State, the young de Rance was yet more distinguished for the vivacity of his intellect, and the brightness of his genius. So precocious, in fact, was his understanding, that he had already completed his Latin and Greek studies, and, with the aid of his preceptor, had published a new edition of the Greek poems of Anacreon, in his thirteenth year! Young, gay, wealthy, full of wit and of talent, he soon became the idol of the court, and soon too, alas! was contaminated by its vices. With all the enthusiasm of his nature, he gave himself up a willing victim to the gay pleasures and gilded vanities of the world.

But Divine Providence had a higher destiny in reserve for him, and mercifully withdrew him from the delusions in which his young spirit had been temporarily involved. Disgusted with the world, which, however it smiled on him, could not satisfy his longing aspirations after happiness, young de Rance determined to bid farewell to it for ever, and to seek in solitude that happiness, which his heart could not find amid the giddy dissipations of Paris. He wished also to atone for his past disorders, by a life wholly devoted to prayer and penitential austerity. He accordingly left Paris, sold his ample patrimony of Veret, gave the proceeds to the charity hospital of the Hotel Dieu, at Paris; and, of all his immense property, he reserved for his support only the priory of Boulogne, and the Abbey of La Trappe.

After having taken the advice of three learned and pious French Bishops, he resolved to enter the Order of Cistercians, of which his Abbey of La Trappe was an establishment. He was accordingly admitted a novice of the Order, in 1663, and made his profession in the following year, at the age of thirty-eight.

The young religious soon shone forth a bright example to his brethren. He deplored the sad falling off of the Order from its primitive fervour, and resolved to exert himself to the utmost to restore it to the condition in which it had been left by St. Bernard. He had all the qualities for a reformer—zeal, humility, piety, and unshaken firmness of purpose; and the Holy See, viewing him as the very man for the emergency, gave him ample powers to effect a thorough reformation of the Order in France.

Stimulated by his example, and moved by his burning eloquence, the monks of La Trappe soon embraced the proposed reform. La Trappe became, under de Rance, what Clairvaux had been under St. Bernard. But the reformer was not so successful with the other houses of the Order, which declined being brought under the rigid discipline which he had re-established at La Trappe. Those who embraced the reform were called Trappists, from the mother establishment. In course of time, several other houses of Trappists were established in France, Germany, Switzerland, and Italy.

The different establishments of the new reform continued to flourish for about a hundred years. Every where they exhibited the brightest examples of every virtue. Throughout the solitudes which they inhabited, there reigned a perpetual silence, interrupted only by anthems of praise to the Almighty. Their rule also enjoined manual labour, rigid mortifications, and perpetual abstinence from flesh, and even from fish and eggs. Those who were wearied or disgusted with the world, and wished to do penance for their sins, found a secure and charming retreat at La Trappe. Attracted by the sanctity of the monks, and stimulated by the illustrious example of de Rance, many persons of wealthy and noble families renounced the world, and sought in this rigid Order to atone for past faults, and to aspire to perfection.*

At length, the furious storm of the French Revolution scattered the humble glories of La Trappe. After having blighted the most fertile and lovely provinces of France, its ravages extended to the wilderness itself, which it rendered still more desolate, by banishing from it the voice of prayer. The Trappists were compelled to fly;

* The famous Baron de Geramb, a German nobleman of distinction, is an example of this. Many of our readers are familiar with his recent beautiful and edifying works.

and a branch of the Order sought shelter in the United States.

The Trappists sailed for America in 1804—the same year that the Rev. Mr. Nerinckx embarked for our shores. On the 15th of August of that year—the Feast of the Assumption of the Blessed Virgin Mary—they established themselves at the Pigeon Hills, near Conawago, in Pennsylvania. Father Urban Guillet, a native of France, was their Superior during the whole time of their sojourn in America. He was a man of great piety, of indefatigable zeal and activity, and of singular meekness and suavity of manners. He won the hearts of all who became acquainted with him.

The original number of Trappists who emigrated to America was twenty-five, of whom eight were priests, and seventeen lay-brothers. These were subsequently farther augmented by two other smaller colonies, consisting of three priests and several lay-brothers. They were from various parts of France, Switzerland, and Italy. Besides the regular members of the Order, there were also many boys attached to the establishment. These were not, however, subject to its severe discipline. Under the eye of the monks, they were trained to piety and learning, and were taught various trades. When they attained the proper age, they were received into the Order, if their inclinations prompted them to ask admission, and if it was thought that they had a true vocation.

The Trappists remained at the Pigeon Hills for only one year. Desirous of breathing a purer atmosphere of solitude, they determined to penetrate farther into the wilderness. Father Urban had already visited Kentucky, and selected a situation for the new establishment, on Pottinger's Creek, near Rohan's *knob*, about a mile from the church of Holy Cross. To this place the Trappists removed in the fall of 1805; and here they remained for about three years and a half—until the spring of 1809.

On their arrival in Kentucky they opened a gratuitous school for boys, whom they endeavoured to train up in virtue and learning. This was the first Catholic school of any note that was established in our State. It continued to flourish for nearly three years, and contributed greatly to the spiritual improvement of the rising generation. Under the care of the monks, many youths, besides being imbued with the elements of learning, were reared to the practice of virtue, and were prepared for their first Communion.

The Catholics of Kentucky were greatly edified by the piety of the good monks. Their example diffused through the new settlements the sweet odour of piety. Though their institute did not permit them to engage actively in the labours of the missionary life, yet Father Urban often visited the sick, and discharged other duties of the ministry, in case of necessity. But the hands of the good solitaries were ever stretched forth in prayer on the mountain of God, while their missionary brethren were labouring in the plain. And there is no doubt, that their fervent prayers and penitential austerities drew down an abundant blessing on the infant missions of Kentucky. Sinners are converted and souls are saved more by prayer than by preaching; at least, the latter is wholly powerless unless united with the former.

While in Kentucky, the Trappists relaxed in nothing the rigor of their institute. They observed a perpetual silence. They slept on boards, with nothing but a blanket for their covering, and a coarse canvass bag stuffed with straw for their pillow. They gave but four hours in the twenty-four to repose—from eight o'clock, P. M., until twelve. At midnight they arose to sing the Divine Office in common, after which they never retired to rest. They took but one meal in the day, at three o'clock, P. M.; with a slight collation at night, from Easter until Ascension day. They never ate meat, butter, eggs, nor fish: their food consisted of the coarsest bread, and of vegetables plainly dressed. On Good Friday, they took nothing but bread and water. Their life was thus a continual penance and prayer.

But, in the climate of Kentucky, these rigid austerities were not compatible with health. The constitutions of many among the monks were greatly impaired; and five priests and three lay-brothers fell victims to disease, and were buried in the cemetery adjoining the church of Holy Cross. These afflictions, and the ardent desire which Father Urban had conceived of labouring for the conversion and civilization of the Indian tribes, together with the aspiration after still greater solitude, determined him to emigrate with his Order still farther westward.

But before we follow this remarkable band of monks in their onward pilgrimage to the far-west, we will briefly relate a singular natural phenomenon which they witnessed while in Kentucky, and for which we are indebted to the same eye-witness to whom we owe the other details of this chapter.

In the year 1808, the moon, being then about two-thirds full, presented a most remarkable appearance. A bright and luminous cross, clearly defined, was seen in the heavens, with its arms intersecting the centre of the moon. On each side, two smaller crosses were also distinctly visible, though the portions of them most distant from the moon were more faintly marked. This strange phenomenon continued for several hours, and was witnessed by the Trappists on their arising, as usual, at midnight, to sing the divine praises. The largest cross was about sixteen diameters of the moon in length, and four in width: the smaller ones were of about one-third this magnitude. The breadth of each arm of the largest cross was just that of the moon's diameter. Our readers may have learned through the public newspapers, that a phenomenon somewhat similar, though not altogether so remarkable, was lately witnessed in various parts of the United States.

Having resolved to remove farther west, the Trappists built a flat-boat, near the house of Capt. J. Rapier, on the Beech Fork, about three miles from Bardstown; and having launched it, and placed their effects on board, they patiently awaited the coming of a freshet to bear them to the Ohio river. They were enabled to depart from Kentucky early in the spring of 1809; and they proceeded without accident to the mouth of the Ohio. Here they were delayed for three weeks, awaiting the arrival of a body of boatmen, whom Father Urban, who had travelled by land to St. Louis, had promised to send to meet them at this point, in order to aid them in the difficult ascent of the Mississippi.

During their stay at the mouth of the Ohio, the monks landed on the Illinois side of the river, near the site of the present town of Cairo. Here they felled and sawed timber, and fitted up a temporary altar, at the foot of a large, widely-branching tree, and there they daily sang the divine praises, and offered up the Holy Sacrifice of the New Law. It was, perhaps, the first time that the voice of prayer had been heard amidst those dense and unreclaimed forests: the first time that the Holy victim had been there offered up! There is something truly grand and sublime in the spectacle presented by this first solemn act of worship at the confluence of the two great rivers which water the Mississippi Valley! It was a solemn dedication of the whole Valley to the service of the Living God.

At length, almost despairing of the expected aid from St. Louis, the Trappists set to work to prepare their boat for the ascent of the Mississippi. They sawed timber, covered the boat with planks, erected a large mast, and fitted to it a temporary sail. When they had completed these preparations, they were cheered by the arrival of sixteen sturdy Canadian boatmen, or *voyageurs*, sent to their assistance by Father Urban. On examining the boat, the Canadians declared that the mast and sail were useless, and a mere encumbrance; and that the only means of conveying the boat to St. Louis would be, to tow it along the banks by means of ropes. This was a laborious and tedious operation, which consumed a whole month: whereas, in one of our modern steamboats, the ascent is now accomplished with ease in thirty-six hours.

On the arrival of the boat at St. Louis, the Trappists learned that Father Urban had determined to fix the new monastic establishment at Flourissant, where there is at present a flourishing institution of the Jesuits. The boat was accordingly towed up the Mississippi and Missouri rivers, to the point on the latter nearest to Flourissant. An accident occurred at the mouth of the Missouri, which greatly endangered the safety of the boat, and may serve to show the peculiar dangers attending this species of navigation.

In attempting to draw the boat into the rapid current of the Missouri, the tow-line broke, and the boat shot rapidly down the stream. All the able bodied men were on the shore, and only the infirm and disabled were on board. The boat continued to descend the Mississippi during almost an entire day, before the boatmen on the shore were able to check it; and several days' hard labour were required to regain their former position, and many more to reach their destination.

At Flourissant the Trappists remained for one year, during which time they continued to practice all the religious austerities of their Order. In 1810, M. Jarot, a French Catholic of Kahokias, made them a present of a farm in Illinois, lying on the banks of the Mississippi river, about six miles above St. Louis. To this place they immediately removed, and here they continued for nearly three years. This was their fourth and last resting place in the United States.

They soon set to work and built up a little village on the bosom of the prairie, in the immediate vicinity, and around the foot of a cluster of Indian mounds, one of which, larger than the rest, is still called Monk's Mound. These mounds were, probably, the great burial places of the Indian tribes; and the cluster formed a sort of "city of the dead." In excavating for the foundation of their houses, the monks discovered bones, idols, beads, implements of war, and various other Indian antiquities.

During their stay at Monk's Mound, the Trappists were often in great danger from marauding bands of Indians. Many person were killed and scalped in the immediate vicinity of the place;

and the youths belonging to the establishment were often compelled to join parties of the white people who were organized for the pursuit and chastisement of the savages. Still, the monks themselves were never molested in their own establishment. The savages seemed even to be awed into reverence for their sanctity; and often did they pause in the vicinity of the rude Trappist chapel, to listen to the praises of God chanted amidst the bones of their own fathers.

Father Urban had conceived an ardent desire to open a school for the instruction and civilization of the Indian tribes: he intended to teach their children the various trades of civilized life, while their minds would be gradually imbued with the elements of Christianity.* But untoward events, and the speedy recall of the Order to Europe, prevented him from carrying this benevolent design into execution.

At the time that the Trappists established themselves in Illinois, the Indian war of the northwest was beginning to rage. It terminated in the full discomfiture of the savages, at the famous battle of Tippecanoe, on the 7th of November, 1811. It is a remarkable fact in the history of acoustics, that the Trappists distinctly heard the report of the cannon fired at Tippecanoe, though they were about two hundred miles distant from the scene of action. A peculiar state of the atmosphere, and the circumstance that the sound passed uninterrupted over immense level prairies, may enable us to account for this curious fact, which is stated on respectable authority.

* See the Statement of M. Badin, on the Missions of Kentucky, published in the "Annales de la Propagation de la Foy" —vol. 1, No. 11, 1823, p. 32-3.

In Illinois, the monks were scarcely more fortunate, in regard to health, than they had been in Kentucky. They there lost by death two priests and five lay-brothers of the Order, all of whom were buried at Monk's Mound. Thus, during their whole stay of nearly nine years in the United States—from 1804 to 1813—they lost seven priests and eight lay-brothers, making a total of fifteen; besides a few others who may have died in Pennsylvania and Missouri. It was apparent that the climate was not congenial to their health, while practising the rigid austerities enjoined by their Order.

This and other reasons soon caused their return to Europe. The fury of the French Revolution had subsided; and Napoleon Buonaparte had set up again the altars which it had thrown down or desecrated. When religious freedom had been thus restored, the General of the Order recalled the Trappists from America, to reoccupy the establishments from which they had been banished in Europe.

Father Urban immediately prepared to obey the call of his Superior. In the month of March, 1813, the establishment at Monk's Mound was broken up. The property was disposed of, and the monks embarked with their more valuable moveables, at St. Louis, in a keel boat bound for Pittsburgh. Their trip was long, painful, and attended with many dangers. To exhibit the difficulties of travelling on our western waters at that time, we will here mention a few of the incidents attending this voyage on the Mississippi and Ohio rivers.

The boat pursued its course during the day, and usually landed at night, when the crew bivouacked in the woods. On reaching the mouth of the

Ohio river, the whole country was found to be inundated, as far as the eye could reach, and it became impossible to effect a landing. A day or two afterwards, the boatmen discovered a house on the Illinois side, on the site of the present town of America, about 15 miles above the mouth of the river. They were overjoyed at the sight; and, having landed, they endeavoured to enter the building. But they found the doors barricadoed, and the whole house pierced with port-holes, for protection against the savages. It was a kind of solitary block-house erected in the wilderness. After waiting in suspense, for several hours, they at length observed a white man, in the garb of a hunter, slowly and cautiously approaching the house, with his musket levelled. They showed themselves, and shouted out at the top of their voice, that they were friends. The hunter ran hastily towards them, gave them a cordial welcome, and having bid his wife to unbar the doors of his castle, introduced the strangers, and made them sharers in his best cheer. He told them that he had been living alone for several years in this place, and that the precautions they had noticed, had often secured him and his family from the horrors of Indian massacre.

On reaching Fort Massac, the boat was brought to by the garrison stationed there; and in attempting to land, the steersman ran it on a rock, which accident well-nigh caused it to founder. On landing, a few miles below Shawneetown, they were near being robbed, and perhaps murdered, by a band of eight suspicious looking men, who successively arrived at the landing shortly afterwards, in two large pirogues. It was believed, that these men had perhaps followed the boat from St. Louis, with a view to possess themselves of the money and valuable cargo which they knew it contained. The monks were alarmed at an early hour of the night, and immediately repaired with Father Urban, to the boat, which was pushed off from the shore, and tied to a tree in the middle of the river. The probable robbers finding that their plot was discovered, and anticipating, perhaps, a warm reception, made no attempt upon the boat; and, in the morning, they had disappeared.

The rest of the journey was performed without any farther adventure worthy of notice. The Trappists embarked for France, and bade a final farewell to the United States. While all the members of the Order, both priests and lay-brothers, thus returned to Europe, many of the young men who were attached to it remained in America; generally devoting themselves to the trades which they had learned among the Trappists.*

We will close this rapid and very imperfect sketch of the Trappists in America, by an expression of deep regret, that a man of Mr. Dickens' good sense and general good feelings, should have so far forgotten himself, as to have penned that libellous passage in his "American Notes," in which he speaks of the Trappists as gloomy, and self-destroying fanatics, and seems even to rejoice over the death of many of their number in America. In an ignorant and bigoted Protestant, we might have excused this atrocious sentiment: but we are wholly at a loss to account for it in the accomplished and refined Boz—a name which has done so much to elicit sympathy for the oppressed and the suffering.

---

* Three of them settled in Bardstown, where one of them is still living.

Carnal-minded Protestantism never could understand nor relish a life of retirement, of self-denial, of penance, and of mortification. To it, the spirit and utility of these practices are wholly unintelligible. The example of Christ himself, and that of St. John the Baptist, and of all His Saints, fail to correct the erroneous feelings on this subject. "The sensual man perceiveth not the things which are of the Spirit of God." And the man who would speak, as Mr. Dickens has spoken, of the retirement and austerities of the Trappists, would, if not restrained by human respect from carrying out his principle, also sneer at similar observances in the life of Christ himself!

We grant that austerity and bodily inflictions may be carried too far. But the numerous deaths which occurred among the Trappists in America, were, perhaps owing to their not being occustomed to the climate, at least as much as to any indiscretion they may have been guilty of in practising the hard penances enjoined by their rule. We do not find that a similar mortality attends the Order in France and in other countries of Europe, where it has been long established. On the contrary, the European Trappists, like the ancient solitaries of the Thebais, are famous for their longevity. The experience of mankind has clearly established the fact, that, where one man dies prematurely from voluntary abstinence, ten thousand die by eating too much. And the longevity of ancient and modern cenobites has proved the entire truth of the old adage: "if you would eat *long*, you must eat *little*."

CHAPTER XI.

The Arrival of the Bishop in Kentucky.

Efforts of M. Badin to have a Bishop nominated for Kentucky—His journey to Baltimore—Edifying incident at Brownsville, Pennsylvania—The Rev. M. Flaget—His early life—Arrival in America—Labours at Vincennes—In Havana—And at Baltimore—His qualities—Appointed first Bishop of Bardstown—Firmly declines accepting—Compelled to yield—Consecrated—The Rev. M. David—Difficulties and delay at Baltimore—Extracts from the Bishop's correspondence—Incidents of the journey to Kentucky—The Arrival—The ceremonies of taking possession of his See—Apostolical poverty—Religious statistics of Kentucky on his arrival—And of the Northwest—The Bishop removes to St. Thomas', and to Bardstown—The first priest ordained in Kentucky—His zeal and labours—Eulogy of Bishop Flaget.

HITHERTO we have treated of the early missions of Kentucky. We must now speak, though necessarily with great brevity, of Kentucky as a Diocess; of the life and apostolical labours of its first Bishop, and of the many institutions for piety and education, which, with the divine blessing, he was enabled to rear.

Long and ardently had the Rev. M. Badin desired and prayed, that God would vouchsafe to send a Bishop to take charge of the extensive missions under his direction. After the arrival in Kentucky of the Rev. M. Nerinckx, of the Dominicans, and of the Trappists, he had enjoyed more leisure, and had some time to breathe. Still, he had employment enough to exercise his zeal to the full. He continued, in the capacity of Vicar General, to have the charge of the whole missonary district. The yearly increase of the Catholics, the building of new churches, the organization of additional congregations, and the general solicitude for the welfare of the entire mission, were sufficient to engage his whole thoughts, and allowed but little rest, even to one of his active mind and body.

For nearly fourteen years he had been labouring in the missions of Kentucky; during a considerable portion of the time, alone and unaided. Often had he wished to confer with the venerable Bishop of Baltimore on the condition and wants of this distant portion of his vast Diocess. The communication with his superior by letter was then very difficult and uncertain; and the number and weight of his employments had hitherto prevented him from visiting Baltimore. Now, however, he felt that he could undertake the journey without detriment to his missionary duties. Accordingly, in the spring of 1807, he set out for Baltimore. One great object of his visit to Bishop Carroll, was, to represent to him, in the strongest light, the importance of having a Bishop appointed for Kentucky.

We must briefly relate a little incident which occurred on this journey. He seldom omitted any opportunity of preaching, or of doing good. When he had reached Brownsville, Pennsylvania, he was invited to preach; and the Methodist meeting-house was politely tendered to him for this purpose. A large concourse of people were in attendance, anxiously desiring to see the priest, and to hear what he had to say. M. Badin ascended the pulpit, and having made the sign of the cross, and said some preliminary prayers, he began his discourse, with a good humoured smile, somewhat in this characteristic way: "My dear brethren: you have been in the habit of hearing the Gospel incorrectly preached, and of hearing the doctrines of the Holy Catholic Church misrepresented from this place: I mean to tell you the truth, and the whole truth." He then clearly stated the Catholic doctrine, furnishing scriptural proofs as he advanced, and answering the most common objections. He proved that Catholics, far from rejecting the Bible, were really its best friends and truest expounders; and that, but for the Catholic church, Protestants would not even have the Bible.

His discourse made a deep and lasting impression. Among his hearers was a Major Noble, a man of considerable talent and standing in that vicinity. After the sermon, he invited M. Badin to his house; and after having conversed with him at length on the doctrines and practices of Catholicity, he determined to become himself a member of the church. M. Badin had the consolation to baptize him and to offer up the Holy Sacrifice in his house.

Mrs. Noble was still deeply prejudiced against the Catholic church; but she became uneasy in mind, and after having prayed, and read attentively some Catholic works which M. Badin left with the family, she too resolved to become a Catholic. On his return from Baltimore, M. Badin had the great happiness to baptize her, and all the other members of the family.

On his arrival in Baltimore, M. Badin was kindly received and warmly welcomed by the venerable Bishop Carroll. He lost no time in representing to the Bishop the condition and necessities of the missions of Kentucky; and in strongly urging the appointment of a Bishop to take charge of them. He recommended for this situation the Rev. M. Flaget, a distinguished Sulpician, whose ardent zeal, tender piety, and long experience in the missions of America, fitted him in a peculiar manner for the office of the episcopacy. Providence seemed to point to him as the very man for the emergency.

As we have elsewhere seen, this virtuous and eminent clergyman had come to America in 1792, in company with the Rev. MM. David and Badin; and he had therefore been in the country for nearly sixteen years. He had already performed the arduous noviciate of the western missions, and had become schooled to the difficulties and dangers attending them. Bishop Carroll had sent him to Vincennes in the year 1792;—one year before M. Badin was sent to Kentucky. In Vincennes, M. Flaget had laboured with indefatigable zeal, for more than two years. In that and the other French Catholic stations in the northwest, he had effected much good, and done much to revive piety among those entrusted to his charge. He had undergone much toil, suffered many hardships, and escaped many dangers from the hostility of the Indian tribes.

Especially had he signalized his zeal and devotedness during the prevalence of the small-pox, which raged with great fury among the French population during his brief stay at Vincennes. Wherever the fearful disease made its appearance, there was he to be found, attending to the spiritual and temporal wants of the sufferers, and exerting himself to the utmost to assuage their ills, and to pour the balm of consolation into their afflicted spirits. In short, he had been one of the very first and most efficient pioneers of Catholicity in the west.

Late in the year 1794, he returned to Baltimore, by the way of New Orleans; and was succeeded at Vincennes by M. Rivet, of whom we have already spoken. He was afterwards sent, with some brother Sulpicians, to the Island of Havana, where he spent some time in the attempt to build up a Catholic College. While there, he became acquainted with the present King of the French, Louis Philippe, who was then a fugitive from his country, and in great distress. The people of Havana made up a considerable sum of money for his benefit, and appointed M. Flaget to hand over the amount to the illustrious exile.

Various circumstances having caused the failure of the attempt to establish a college of the Sulpicians at Havana, M. Flaget and his associates returned to Baltimore. Here M. Flaget spent his time in teaching, and in the various duties of a college life; edifying all by his humility, his tender piety, his charity, and all the qualities which mark the gentleman and the Christian priest. He was, moreover, blessed with a strong frame, and an iron constitution. In fine, he possessed all the qualities requisite for the first Bishop appointed in the west.

Such was, at least, the opinion of Bishop Carroll, who was an excellent judge of character, and intimately acquainted with M. Flaget. Old age and infirmity were now beginning perceptibly to steal over the venerable Patriarch of the American Church; he found that the whole Union, of which he was Bishop, and the See of New Orleans, of which he was administrator, formed too heavy a burden for the shoulders of one man, now worn down with years and fatigue, both of body and mind. He accordingly recommended to the Sovereign Pontiff, the sainted Pius VII., the erection of four new Episcopal Sees, and the appointment of four new Bishops, for Boston, New York, Philadelphia, and Bardstown. The Pontiff acceded to the request: the four new Sees were erected in 1808; and Bishop Carroll was promoted to the rank of Archbishop.

M. Flaget was nominated first Bishop of Bardstown. His See embraced the whole northwestern territory of the United States, or that which lay north of the 35th degree of north latitude, including the present States of Michigan, Ohio, Indiana, Illinois, Missouri, Kentucky, Tennessee, and about one half of Arkansas, besides the two territories of Wisconsin and Iowa—seven and a half States, and two territories. From this great mother Diocess of the west, ten have now sprung up— including that of Little Rock. The See of Bardstown bears to the west, nearly the same relation, as that of Baltimore does to the whole United States: each is a mother church, to which many spiritual daughters look up with gratitude and reverence.

On receiving the news of his appointment, the humility of Bishop Flaget immediately took the alarm. He could not discover in himself those exalted qualities which all others perceived. He persisted in a refusal of the nomination for two whole years; and, the more effectually to get rid of the burden with which he was threatened, he determined to leave the United States, and to visit his native country. But he had scarcely reached Paris, when M. Emery, the venerable Superior of the Sulpicians, put into his hands a letter from

Pope Pius VII., in which he was commanded to accept the appointment without farther delay. Longer resistance would have been in manifest opposition to the will of heaven, and Bishop Flaget submitted to his fate with resignation.

His friends in France urgently pressed him to receive the episcopal consecration in his native country; but Bishop Flaget resolutely declined, alleging that a sense of propriety prompted him to be consecrated in Baltimore, by Archbishop Carroll. He accordingly made little delay in France. He returned to Baltimore, where he was consecrated by the Archbishop, on the 4th day of November, 1810, the Feast of St. Charles Borromeo, towards whom he had always cherished a particular devotion.

In the new career which Divine Providence now opened to Bishop Flaget, he had the consolation to be aided by the advice and assistance of one among his oldest and best friends. The Rev. J. B. M. David, had been the sharer in his exile from France, and the companion of his voyage to the United States, in 1792. He now cheerfully offered his services for the new Diocess, to the charge of which God had called his distinguished friend.

The Rev. Dr. Emery, the Superior of the Sulpicians, to which congregation both belonged, had already appointed M. David Superior of the Seminary which Bishop Flaget intended to form, in order to rear up clergymen for his new Diocess. The Bishop rightly judged, that he could not hope to be blessed with general or permanent success, without the resource of a Theological Seminary; and the event proved, that he could not have selected a more valuable or efficient instrument for carrying this design into execution, than the one whom obedience and Christian friendship thus assigned him.

Besides M. David, Bishop Flaget had, associated with him for the Diocess of Bardstown, a Canadian priest, a subdeacon,* and two young laics. The three last named were to form the *nucleus* of his Theological Seminary. But unforeseen difficulties now presented themselves. The new Bishop had not the means to defray the necessary expenses of himself and companions on the long and painful journey to Kentucky. In this emergency, the charity of his numerous friends in Baltimore came to his assistance. A subscription was set on foot, and the necessary amount was promptly collected.

Still it was not until the spring of the following year, 1811, that the Bishop was enabled to commence his journey westward. Two letters which, during this interval, he addressed to the Very Rev. M. Badin, now his Vicar General in Kentucky, unfold the embarrassment which he felt, as well as the state of his feelings in entering upon his new charge. We will be pardoned for here furnishing extracts from this portion of his correspondence.†

"God is my witness," writes the good Bishop to M. Badin, "that I seek not for riches ; I would rather die a thousand times than be subject to this disorder. The less of the goods of this world we possess, the less will our minds be made uneasy.

---

* The present Rt. Rev. Coadjutor Bishop, Dr. Chabrat.

† Copious portions of these letters are given by M. Badin, in his Statement "of the Missions of Kentucky," P. 37, seqq., often quoted already. He prefaces the extracts with the appropriate remark: "l'homme se peint dans ses ecrits"—"the man paints himself in his writings." They are also published, in an English translation, in the U. S. Catholic Miscellany, for Dec. 1, 1824.

But there are some expenses which it is absolutely necessary to meet, and it is your business to devise the means. I must calculate on your friendship for me. It will then be your business, my dear Badin, henceforth to provide for me the means of living. And, after all, you have brought it on yourself; for, were it not your seeking, they would never have thought of making me Bishop. We have eight or nine trunks of books and other necessaries, and the distance is very great, and the carriage very dear; the expense of our journey, and the carriage of our packages, must exceed $500, and we have nothing. Here, then, we must stay, till Providence relieve us. However, to make my expenses as light as possible, I shall leave at Baltimore a servant who has offered himself to me gratis. I shall even leave my books too, as I do not reckon them essential; and I will only take M. David with me. He and I are fully satisfied to live just as you do, be your table ever so poor, and be your accommodations ever so moderate.

"If the episcopacy presented to me only difficulties of this kind, I should not have made so great a stir about accepting it. Providence hurries me on, in spite of myself: I was well on my way, travelling by sea and by land, to shake off a yoke which it was sought to fasten on me; and I have only my pains for my reward. God seems to require of me to bow my head, and to suffer this burden to be placed on it, though it is likely to crush me. Alas! if I stop long to consider my weakness, I shall become so far depressed in spirits, as not to be able to take one step on the long path which lies open before me, and which I must now traverse. To sustain my courage, I am frequently constrained to recollect, that I have not intruded myself into this august ministry; but that all the superiors whom I have on earth have, in one way or another, forced me to accept of it."

To assist the good Bishop in defraying the expenses of his journey westward, M. Badin had opened a subscription in Kentucky. But the poverty of the Catholics, and other circumstances, caused him subsequently to suspend it. Bishop Flaget alludes to the circumstance in the following passage, from another letter addressed to his Vicar General, which breathes a spirit similar to that already given.

"Be pleased to take notice, that we are seven or eight persons, and have but one horse among us. I intend to let M. David, as being the slowest of foot, have the use of him: I and my other companions will perform the journey on foot, with the greatest pleasure, and without the least difficulty. This manner of pilgrimage will be more to my taste, and, unless I am greatly in error, will derogate nothing from my dignity. I, however, leave every thing to your own prudence. For myself, I shall feel quite happy, if my money hold out to supply our wants as far as Louisville, where I expect to meet you. The rest of the journey will be at your cost.

"May the will of God be done! I would prefer a thousand times to walk, rather than create the slightest murmur: on this account, I approve of your having suspended the collection which had been commenced for us: it would only have alienated the affections of the people from me; still it is clear, that those good people, who were so anxious to have a Bishop amongst them, should pay the amount of his expenses in coming to them. There is nothing, I trust, which I would not do for the sanctification of my flock. My time, my labours, my life itself, are all consecrated to this object. And when I shall have done all this, I must still say, that I am an useless servant: I have done only that which I was bound to do."

In another letter, addressed, some years later, to the directors of the French Association for the Propagation of the Faith, Bishop Flaget thus graphically describes the difficulties of his situation, on being nominated first Bishop of Bardstown.*

"To give you a clear idea of the bishoprics of the United States, I propose to lay before you a brief statement of the condition in which I found myself, after the Court of Rome, on the representation of Bishop Carroll, had nominated me to the bishopric of Bardstown. I was compelled to accept the appointment, whether I would or not; I had not a cent at my disposal; the Pope and the Cardinals, who were all dispersed by the Revolution, were not able to make me the slightest present; and Archbishop Carroll, though he had been Bishop for more than sixteen (twenty) years, was still more poor than myself; for he had debts, and I owed nothing. Nevertheless, my consecration took place on the 4th of November, 1810; but for want of money to defray the expenses of the journey, I could not undertake it. It was only six months afterwards, that, through a subscription made by my friends in Baltimore, I was enabled to reach Bardstown, my episcopal See.

"It was on the 9th of June, 1811, that I made my entry into this little village, accompanied by two priests, and three young students for the ecclesiastical state. Not only I had not a cent in my purse, but I was even compelled to borrow nearly

---

* "Annales de la Propagation de la Foy"—vol. 3. p. 189.

two thousand francs, (about $380) in order to be able to reach my destination. Thus, without money, without a house, without property, almost without any acquaintances, I found myself in the midst of a Diocess, two or three times larger than all France, containing five large States and two immense territories, and myself speaking the language, too, very imperfectly. Add to all this, that almost all the Catholics were emigrants, but newly settled, and poorly furnished."

The good Bishop, with his companions, left Baltimore early in May, 1811; and they travelled over the mountains to Pittsburgh, where they embarked on a flat-boat, on the 22d day of the same month. The health of the good M. David was then "in as bad a condition as was that of the Bishop's funds:"* he had been exhausted by his previous missionary labours in Maryland. A letter of his, written to a friend in France, on the 20th of November, 1817,† furnishes some interesting particulars of the passage down the Ohio river.

"A Canadian priest had joined us, and the boat on which we descended the Ohio, became the cradle of our seminary, and of the church of Kentucky. Our cabin was, at the same time, chapel, dormitory, study-room, and refectory. An altar was erected on the boxes *(caisses)*, and ornamented as far as was possible. The Bishop prescribed a regulation which fixed all the exercises, and in

* From his letter cited below.
† This interesting document gives a clear and concise statement of the apostolic labours and establishments of Bishop Flaget, from 1810 to the date at which it was written. We shall have occasion often to quote it in the sequel. It was published in a French Journal—"Le Journal de Marseilles, et des bouches de Rhone, administratif, politique, commercial, et literaire." Oct. 17, 1818: No. 188.

which each had its proper time. On Sunday, after prayer, every one went to confession: then the priests said Mass, and the others went to communion. After an agreeable navigation of thirteen days, we arrived at Louisville, next at Bardstown, and finally at the residence of the Vicar General."

The party reached Louisville on the 4th of June. Here they were met by the good M. Nerinckx, who escorted them to Bardstown and to St. Stephen's, the residence of M. Badin. They reached Bardstown on the 9th, and St. Stephen's in the evening of the 11th, of the same month. Here they were welcomed by a large concourse of people, assembled to see their new Bishop for the first time; as well as by nearly all of the Catholic clergymen then in Kentucky. Among the latter, there were present, the Rev. Messrs. Badin, Fenwick, Wilson, Tuite, Nerinckx, O'Flynn, besides M. David, and the Canadian priest who accompanied the Bishop; making in all eight priests—more than had ever before been seen together in Kentucky.

The enthusiastic joy of the good people on seeing their Bishop among them, and the ceremonies which took place on the occasion, are so well described by M. Badin, in the Statement of the missions of Kentucky, already often quoted,* that we cannot perhaps do better than simply to translate from that document.

"The Bishop there (at St. Stephen's) found the faithful kneeling on the grass, and singing canticles in English: the country women were nearly all dressed in white, and many of them were still fasting, though it was then four o'clock in the

---

* P. 39. *note*, Annales, &c. vol. 1. *sup. cit.*

evening; they having indulged the hope to be able on that day to assist at his Mass, and to receive the holy Communion from his hands. An altar had been prepared at the entrance of the first court, under a bower composed of four small trees which overshadowed it with their foliage. Here the Bishop put on his pontifical robes. After the aspersion of the holy water, he was conducted to the chapel in procession, with the singing of the Litany of the Blessed Virgin; and the whole function closed with the prayers and ceremonies prescribed for the occasion in the Roman Pontifical."

From the same source, we borrow the following account of the Bishop's manner of life during the first year of his residence in Kentucky, during which time he remained at St. Stephen's with M. Badin.

"M. Badin had for his own lodging but one poor log house; and, in consequence of the expenses he had lately incurred in building a house for a monastery, which was burnt down ere it had been completed, it was with great difficulty that he was enabled to build and prepare, for the residence of his illustrious friend, and the ecclesiastics who accompanied him, two miserable log cabins, sixteen feet square: and one of the missionaries was even compelled to sleep on a matress in the garret of this strange episcopal palace, which was white-washed with lime, and contained no other furniture than a bed, six chairs, two tables, and a few planks for a library. Here the Bishop resided for a year, esteeming himself happy to live thus in the midst of apostolical poverty."

On the arrival of the Bishop in Kentucky, the condition and statistics of his Diocess were about as follows. There were more than a thousand Catholic families, including many who had been received into the church by the earlier Catholic missionaries. The Catholic population did not probably exceed, even if it reached, 6000. There were six priests, besides the Vicar General,* who administered the Sacraments to more than thirty different congregations or stations, about ten of which only had churches or chapels erected. The names of the churches then in Kentucky, are as follows: Holy Cross, St. Stephen's, Holy Mary's St. Charles, St. Ann, St. Rose, St. Patrick, St. Francis, St. Christopher, and St. Joseph. Besides these, the following were in progress of erection: St. Louis', St. Michael's, St. Clare's, St. Benedict's, St. Peter's, and St. John's. There was also one convent of Dominicans, and several residences for the clergy. Finally, there were six plantations belonging to the church, besides several bodies of uncultivated lands.†

Such were the resources of that portion of his vast Diocess which was embraced by Kentucky. The other parts of his charge in the northwestern States and territories, were not so well provided for. From a letter of Bishop Flaget, dated November 17th, 1817, it appears, that there were at that time, "on the river St. Laurence, near Lake Huron, about five thousand French Catholics, scattered over a space of eighty or ninety miles, with but one priest to administer to them the succours of religion. At Post Vincennes, on the Wabash, there were about a thousand Catholics,

---

* Seven Catholic priests had already died in Kentucky, including five Trappists.

† We have derived these statistics from a manuscript note of M. Badin, written many years ago, and appended to the printed letter of Bishop David, above quoted.

without any resident clergyman. Finally, in the State of Ohio, there were about two hundred German families of Catholics."*

After residing a year at St. Stephen's, Bishop Flaget removed, with M. David and the seminarians, to St. Thomas', where he fixed his abode for nearly eight years. About a year previous to the dedication of the new Cathedral of St. Joseph's at Bardstown, he took up his residence in this latter place.

The first priest whom he had the happiness to ordain, was M. Chabrat, his present Rt. Rev. Coadjutor. He had accompanied him from France to the United States, in the year 1810; and was already subdeacon, when he arrived in Kentucky. He was ordained priest at St. Rose, on the Feast of Christmas, 1811. He immediately afterwards commenced his missionary career in Kentucky; and continued for many years to labour with great zeal and success. He was one of our oldest, most laborious, and most efficient missionaries.

We cannot even attempt to give any adequate account of the apostolic labours of our venerable Bishop, during the long series of years that he has remained among us. Language would be indeed feeble, to pourtray the difficulties he had to encounter; the fatigue and toil he underwent, the privations he endured, the poverty with which he struggled, and the hardships he suffered, during his long missionary career in Kentucky. Nor is it necessary to dwell on these things at any great length. They are fresh in the memory of all our readers. His virtues are embalmed, and

* The letter was addressed to a friend at Aix, in France, and was published in an old French paper, from which we have translated the above extract.

his eulogy written in the hearts of his clergy and flock; and, in fact, in the minds of all the citizens of Kentucky, without distinction of creed. The noble institutions, literary, religious, and charitable, which have sprung up around him, constitute the best monument to his memory. He needs no other. These are the seals of his apostleship—these form the blooming crown of his labours and unquenchable zeal.

He always put himself at the head of his little band of zealous missionaries, sharing in their labours, and stimulating their zeal, both by word and by example. He visited regularly the various congregations of his Diocess, forming them to piety, and every where appearing as the father of his people. His words were full of unction and of divine sweetness, and moved all hearts. A man of God, and filled with the spirit of prayer, he transfused his own feelings into the minds and hearts of those whom he addressed. All respected and reverenced, and his clergy and people loved him as a father. He rejoiced with those who rejoiced, and wept with those who wept. Full of dignity and sweetness, he won all hearts.

To his clergy, especially, he was a model of every virtue, of unremitting zeal in the labours of the ministry, and of that spirit and practice of continual prayer, without which all the toil and efforts of the missionary were without profit. He never failed to make his meditation, and to offer up the Holy Sacrifice daily. Often was he known to ride on horseback twenty-five or thirty miles, fasting, in order to be able on that day to celebrate the Holy Mysteries.

What a consolation for him, in the evening of his life, to behold all his labours crowned with so astonishing a success! To behold himself surrounded by so many spiritual children, who rise up and call him blessed! To see so many flourishing institutions in his Diocess. To behold the west, which he entered as pioneer and first Bishop, now blessed with so many flourishing Diocesses, the chief pastors of which hail him as their venerable Patriarch!

CHAPTER XII.

***Rev. M. Nerinckx again—His Establishments and
Death.—From* 1811 *to* 1824.**

Rev. M. Nerinckx—Faithful unto death—A good soldier of the Cross—His Merits testified by Bishop Flaget—His success in making converts—Appointed administrator of New Orleans—Declines the honor—Affection of his old parishioners—His spirit and character—Founds the Society of Loretto—The objects of the Sisterhood—The Mother House—And branch Establishments—Bishop Flaget's testimony—Utility of the Society—Christian perfection—Reliance on Providence—Love of poverty—Continual Prayer—Mortification—Rules modified—Journey of M. Nerinckx to Missouri—His edifying death—Translation of his remains—His monument and epitaph.

WE have already endeavoured to give some account of the early life and apostolic labours of the Rev. M. Nerinckx. We cannot say too much of this excellent missionary, who, for nearly twenty years, laboured on our infant missions, with a zeal as commendable, as was the success of his exertions admirable. We do little, when we devote another chapter to the life, establishments, and holy death of this good man. The church of Kentucky will long cherish his memory, as that of one among her earliest and greatest benefactors.

To the very close of his life, he continued the same arduous missionary labours of which we treated in a previous chapter. Instead of moderating, he rather daily increased the number and weight of his employments. New opportunities of doing good and of saving souls, constantly presented themselves; and he seldom let one of them pass by unimproved. His zeal seemed even to grow with his years; and old age, instead of cooling, served rather to inflame its fervour. Finally, he died in the midst of his apostolic labours, toiling to his last breath, for the salvation of souls; and, like a good soldier, he fell on the field of battle, bravely fighting the battles of the cross.

His missionary labours, especially during the last years of his life, almost stagger belief. On this subject, we will give the testimony of a very competent witness—of one who knew him thoroughly, and fully appreciated his worth—of the venerable Bishop Flaget,[*] his ecclesiastical superior.

"During a considerable time, he had to serve alone with the Rev. M. Badin, who well deserves the title of founder of this Diocess—of the several congregations of this immense region. The continual travelling which M. Nerinckx was obliged to undergo, at all seasons of the year, and exposed to every inconvenience, would have terrified the most enterprising pioneer. As, at the time of his arrival, there were but one or two churches built, and the Catholics were scattered through the country, he went about from settlement to settlement, celebrating the holy mysteries from house to house—hearing confessions every morning, and obliged to fast almost every day in

[*] In a letter addressed to Bishop England, and published in the U. S. Catholic Miscellany, for Dec. 8th, 1824—a few months after the death of M. Nerinckx. We shall often have occasion to quote this document in the course of the present chapter.

the year. His instructions were extremely simple, and quite to the point. God alone can estimate the great fruit which they produced in all descriptions of persons.

"Feeling greatly the inconvenience which arose from celebrating the divine mysteries in rooms devoted to every worldly purpose, he did his best to inspire all Catholics whom he used to visit, with a zeal for constructing churches, and endowing them with lands for the support of pastors. His exertions, in this respect, were crowned with perfect success. The Catholic church of Kentucky has acquired much land, which is worth very little at present, but which will one day have considerable value. We count ten churches built solely by his exertions; also six convents of nuns, and as many oratories. He made two journeys to Europe, in order to procure the means necessary for those great works; and the valuables which he procured exceeded the amount of $15,000. This aid was principally drawn from religious Flanders.

"The attempt of death to snatch M. Nerinckx from us has been ineffectual; for he still lives among us in his works, and the monuments of the zeal of my virtuous friend are so multiplied in my Diocess, and his generous self devotion so well appreciated, that his name and that of his beneficent country are embalmed in the memory of my flock."

The labours of M. Nerinckx increased so much during the last years of his life, as almost entirely to exhaust his strength, and probably to hasten his death. Though blessed with an iron constitution and a herculean frame, yet incessant missionary toils and hardships, both in Europe and in America, had greatly impaired his health. He was seldom heard to murmur or to complain, yet he sometimes observed, towards the close of life, "that the care of three thousand souls in six different congregations, and in several stations besides, many miles apart, weighed heavily on a man of more than sixty years of age."*

Though he had something austere in his manner; and though he was a foreigner and spoke English very imperfectly, yet is it remarkable that he made, perhaps, more converts among Protestants, than any other missionary who ever laboured in Kentucky, if we except M. Badin. So true is it, that conversion is not ordinarily effected by human eloquence alone, or by any other mere human means, but by the grace and blessing of God, crowning with success the labours of the missionary. M. Nerinckx seldom made a missionary tour without receiving some one into the bosom of the Holy Catholic Church. In one of these excursions, he made no fewer than thirteen converts.† And those whom he received into the church were well grounded in the faith, and generally proved steadfast.

The transcendent merit of M. Nerinckx did not escape the eye of Bishop Carroll. Besides having charge of the whole territory of the United States, this venerable patriarch of the American church was also administrator of the Diocess of New Orleans, which had been for many years without a Bishop. On the division of his vast charge into five different Diocesses, and the erection of his own See into an archbishopric, he recommended to the Holy See the Rev. M. Nerinckx, as a

* From the sketch of his life published in the London Catholic Miscellany, quoted in a previous chapter.
† For this fact, we are indebted to the Very Rev. M. Badin.

suitable person to take charge of the vacant Diocess of New Orleans, in the character of administrator. The Sovereign Pontiff acceded to his request, and despatched a brief to that effect. The appointment of M. Nerinckx to this situation was intended as the forerunner of his consecration as Bishop of New Orleans.

The good missionary was with M. Badin when he learned the news of his appointment. He meekly bowed his head, and observed to his friend, beginning with the words of the Psalmist: "Bonitatem et disciplinam et scientiam docendus, docere non valeo"—"Having myself to be taught goodness, and discipline, and knowledge, I am not able to teach these things to others." He mildly, but firmly refused the proffered honor. Desirous of retaining him in Kentucky, where his labours were so fruitful, M. Badin, in conjunction with the Dominican Fathers of St. Rose, petitioned the Holy See, that he might not be compelled to accept an office, which would tear him from a field of labour in which he had already proved so eminently useful. They also represented, that the great delicacy of conscience characteristic of M. Nerinckx, would render him exceedingly unhappy in so arduous a situation, if it would not wholly unfit him for its responsible duties.

The Pontiff yielded to the entreaties of M. Nerinckx, thus supported by the suffrage of his brethren in the ministry; and he did not insist on his accepting the appointment. When, however, the news of his nomination reached his old parishioners of Everbery Meerbeke, in Flanders, the ladies of the parish immediately set about preparing and making up a complete suit of episcopal ornaments, which they had almost ready to send to him, when they received the intelligence that he had firmly refused the proffered dignity.

We will now furnish our readers with a farther portrait of the character of M. Nerinckx, drawn by the hand of his Bishop, in the letter to Bishop England above quoted. It will be perceived that the picture is perfect, and needs no retouching.

"Nothing could exceed the devotion of M. Nerinckx to the Holy Sacrament of our altars; in this respect, he was a model for every clergyman. In his churches, you saw only plainness except about the altar; but his devotion led him to aim at magnificence in this place, especially as regarded the tabernacle, which was to contain the Holy of Holies. Every thing connected with the Holy Mysteries called forth the exercise of this devotion. Never did he permit a day to pass without celebrating Mass, unless grievously ill, or engaged in a long journey; and a rule of his monasteries is, to keep up, even during the night, the perpetual adoration, by a succession of two sisters to two sisters, before the Holy Sacrament, to pay their homage to the God who loved us so dearly, as, after having suffered death for us, to give us, under the sacramental veils, His flesh to eat: and to repair, in some degree, the disrespect, with which this Sacrament is treated by the ingratitude of the human race."

The Bishop continues: "This good man had also great filial piety to Mary, the Mother of Jesus, and he desired to excite this affection for the Mother of our Saviour in all those with whom he had any intercourse. He admired her spirit of patient love and resignation in sufferings, especially when she beheld her dearly beloved—her Creator and her Son—upon that Cross, at the foot of which she was weeping. Often did the pious ejaculation, which he was in the habit of teaching to others, escape from his own lips: "Oh! suffering Jesus! Oh! sorrowful Mary!" In all the churches which he attended, he established the Society of the Holy Rosary, and the Confraternity and Sisterhood of the Scapular; and almost all the Catholics of his congregations, are still enrolled in one or more of those pious societies.

"Nothing could be more edifying than his piety towards the dead. It is quite impossible to pass by any of the numerous cemeteries which he has laid out, without feeling deep sentiments of religion, and having a sweet sensation of deep melancholy blended with the hope of the Christian. In the midst of each abode of the dead is reared the glorious emblem of the Christian's faith, a large cross, surrounded by a balustrade, for the convenience of the pious friends who come to pray for their departed brethren. At the head of each grave, you also find the emblematic cross, inscribed with the dates of the birth, death, and the name of the brother or sister, whose bones are there laid up in the hope of the resurrection. . . . He never permitted a week to pass without offering up the Mass for the repose of the departed. . .

"His love for retirement was such, that he never paid a visit of mere ceremony. Indeed, he never visited, except when the good of his neighbour or the duty of his ministry made it obligatory on him to do so. His watchings, even during his longest and most painful journeys, were very long, and were always spent either in study or in prayer. Prayer appeared to be his greatest, and only solace, in the midst of his continual labours."

Among the establishments made by M. Nerinckx, that of the Sisters of Loretto, or of "the Friends of Mary at the foot of the Cross," is the principal; and has proved of the greatest benefit to the Diocess of Kentucky. His objects in founding this invaluable Sisterhood were: to enable pious females to aspire to the lofty perfection of the religious state, and to promote, through their means, the Christian education of youth of their own sex, especially of those whose parents were needy and too destitute to defray the expenses attending the education of their offspring.

In the course of his long missionary career, M. Nerinckx discovered many young females who sought to practice a more perfect virtue than was campatible with the distractions of the world. They had caught no little of his own spirit of prayer, of disengagement from the world, and of lofty enthusiasm in the path of Christian perfection. He observed, too, many young girls who were raised in ignorance, and greatly exposed to temptation. He devised an admirable means of promoting the spiritual welfare of both these classes of females, in the establishment of the new Sisterhood of Loretto—which name he gave them out of reverence for the famous shrine of the Virgin, at Loretto in Italy.*

The foundation of the new society was laid on the 25th of April, 1812;—nearly a year after the arrival of Bishop Flaget in Kentucky. The mother establishment was called Loretto, and was erected on Hardin's Creek, near the church of St. Charles. The houses were built of wood, and were very poorly furnished. They were erected on one side of an oblong inclosure, in the centre

* In this city, the faithful pay reverence to the house in which the Holy Virgin lived at Nazareth. The identity of the two houses is established by the strongest evidence. See the learned work of the present Bishop of St. Louis, "On the Holy House of Loretto."

of which was reared a large wooden cross. The chapel of the Sisters occupied a central position in the buildings which stood on either side.*

The number of those who attached themselves to the new institute increased every year. Soon the buildings were too small for the number of applicants; and the pious founder was under the necessity of erecting new houses, and of creating branch establishments of the society. In twelve years from its commencement, the number of Sisters exceeded a hundred; and they had already under their charge six different schools for girls. In the letter above quoted, Bishop Flaget, after having denominated the Sisterhood the most valuable legacy which the good M. Nerinckx had left to his Diocess, speaks as follows of the condition of the society, in 1824, immediately after the death of the founder.

"Their number is over one hundred; they have charge of six schools. They give education to upwards of two hundred and fifty girls yearly in their houses, and take in some orphans *gratis*. The missionaries generally send the children whom they wish to prepare for their first communion to these monasteries, whenever they can, and they, as well as the boarders, are admirably well instructed in all that may be useful, both for this world, and for eternity."

This assiduous attention to the religious instruction of girls constituted, in fact, the principal utility of the pious society. It is difficult to estimate how much it has, by this means, contributed towards fostering and sustaining piety in this Diocess. Within the first ten years of its existence,

---

* While on a visit to his native country, M. Nerinckx had a print of the new establishment struck off, which he brought with him to America.

HIS ESTABLISHMENTS AND DEATH. 205

the Sisterhood had already prepared for their first communion eight hundred young ladies. These afterwards became mothers of families, and were able to instruct others; and thus the good was perpetuated from generation to generation.

M. Nerinckx watched over the new institution with the tender solicitude of a parent. He devoted to the spiritual instruction of the Sisters and of their scholars, all the time he could spare from the heavier duties of his missionary life. He endeavoured to infuse into them his own spirit of prayer and mortification. He laboured assiduously, both by word and example, to disengage them entirely from the world, and to train them to the practice of a sublime Christian perfection. He ardently sought to keep alive in their hearts the true spirit of the religious vocation; to make them despise the world, trample on its vanities, and devote themselves wholly to the service of God and of the neighbour, by a faithful compliance with the duties growing out of the three simple vows, of poverty, chastity, and obedience, they had taken.

Especially did he endeavour to impress upon them the obligation of placing implicit reliance on the good providence of God, not only in their spiritual, but also in all their temporal concerns. A favorite maxim which he had always in his heart, and frequently on his lips, was embodied in this golden saying: "do not abandon Providence; and He will never abandon you." How would that good heavenly Father, who "clothes the lilies of the field, and feeds the birds of the air," abandon those who had put all their trust in Him, and had devoted themselves entirely, both in body and soul, to His service?

In fact, this unbounded confidence in the providence of God, was almost the only legacy he was able to bequeath to the Lorettines. They had, in the commencement of their society, but little of this world's goods to depend upon. It was not difficult for them to practice the poverty which they had vowed: they were already extremely poor and destitute; and in fulfilling their vow, they had but to love and submit cheerfully to that which was a stern necessity of their condition. Their houses were poor and badly furnished; their clothing was of the plainest kind; and their food was of the coarsest.

M. Nerinckx himself set them the example of the poverty and mortification which their institute required them to love, as well as to practice. According to the testimony of his Bishop, "he himself led an extremely austere and mortified life; his dress, his lodging, his food, was poor; and he had filled his monasteries with this holy spirit. Those women sought for poverty in every thing; in their monasteries, in the plain simplicity of their chapels. The neatness, the cleanliness, the simplicity of their dwellings, and of their chapels, excited the wonder of their visiters."*

To keep up the constant practice and spirit of prayer in their houses, M. Nerinckx inculcated, besides regular and devout attendance at all the pious exercises of the community, distributed throughout the day, the utility of raising their hearts to God by a pious aspiration or ejaculation, whenever they would hear the clock strike, or would pass from one occupation to another.

Especially did he enjoin upon them a tender devotion to the Blessed Virgin, weeping at the foot of the cross, and a frequent repetition of the pious ejaculation: "Oh! suffering Jesus! Oh!

* In the letter to Bishop England, above quoted.

sorrowful Mary!" To feed and keep alive the spirit of piety, he recommended to them frequent visits to the Holy Sacrament of the altar; and we have already seen the provision which he made to keep up the perpetual adoration of Jesus Christ in this, the greatest mystery of His undying love for mankind.

To foster the spirit of humility and mortification, he recommended manual labour, and the love of being employed in the most menial offices of the house. To encourage them to practice these employments with cheerfulness and love, he pointed to the lowly life, and the voluntary hardships and privations of the Blessed Saviour; and to the great utility of such mortifications, for the atonement of sin, and the laying up of abundant merits in heaven.

This austerity was apparent in the body of rules which he drew up for the guidance of the society. They breathed the purest spirit of Christian perfection; but experience subsequently demonstrated, that some of them were too rigid for health, and ill-suited to the nature of the climate. Of this character were, the great exposure of the Sisters to every inconvenience of weather, while labouring hard in the fields, or forests, and the practice of going barefoot during a great portion of the year. As we have said, the poverty of the society at its commencement compelled hard labour; the other practice was adopted, with many others of a similar nature, to cherish a constant spirit of mortification. But these more rigid regulations were retrenched from the rule on its subsequent revision while its substance and spirit were fully retained.

The heart of the good founder was consoled by the early piety and fervor of the Sisterhood.

These appeared to enter into the entire spirit of their state, and to correspond, to the full, with his instructions. According to the testimony of the good Bishop Flaget,* "they were the edification of all who knew them: and their singular piety, and their penitential lives reminded one of all that we have read of the ancient monasteries of Palestine and of Thebais."

Thus did the good M. Nerinckx, alone and unaided, except by Divine Providence, found a society of pious ladies, which has already done, and will no doubt continue to do, incalculable good to religion in this Diocess. M. Nerinckx succeeded in doing, what M. Badin had been unable to accomplish. The latter, with intentions and views very similar to those afterwards entertained by the former, had constructed an edifice for a monastery at St. Stephen's : but before it could be completed, it was burned down by accident, and thus the whole design was frustrated. It was in the order of Providence, that the exertions of M. Nerinckx should be crowned with better success. His success, in fact, surpassed his own most sanguine expectations. The branches of his institution yearly multiplied, and soon Kentucky was too narrow a field for the exercise of its charity and zeal.

The good founder had been induced to send a colony of the Lorettines to Missouri; and he had already received gratifying accounts of the success which had there crowned their labours. Though almost exhausted with his missionary toils, and worn down by old age, he yet determined to pay a visit to this distant branch of the society, in order to encourage the Sisters in the path of usefulness on which they had entered.

* Letter before quoted.

Another principal motive of his journey to Missouri, was an ardent desire for the conversion and civilization of the Indians, who were there very numerous at that time. He had formed a plan to induce the heads of families and the chiefs of the savage tribes to send their children to the schools of the society, where they might be taught the English language, the elements of learning, and especially the catechism. This he conceived to be the best means of reclaiming the Indian tribes; and, in fact, it was but a carrying out of a favorite system which he had found so eminently successful, both in Europe and in America—that of reaching the parents through the piety of their children.

This was the last journey that the good missionary ever performed. He died in the midst of it, on the 12th of August, 1824, at the house of the Rev. M. Dahman, parish priest of St. Genevieve. He breathed his last, while closely engaged in the labours of the mission, and while panting for new means of promoting the glory of God and the salvation of souls. His death was worthy of his life. Calm, patient, collected, and resigned to the will of heaven; praying to the last, and longing to be freed from the prison of the body, and to be with Christ, the good priest bade farewell to this world, with a confident assurance of a blessed immortality in the next.

The fever of which he died he had contracted in the discharge of his missionary duties. The chief circumstances of his death are so well related by Bishop Flaget, that we will give them in his own words:*

* Letter before quoted:

"After the arrival of M. Nerinckx at the residence of the Sisters, in Missouri, he wrote to me a most affecting letter, describing the good they had accomplished in that Diocess, and the hopes which he entertained of their being one day useful to the Indians. Thence he went to visit an establishment of Flemish Jesuits, which is pretty numerous, and about ninety miles distant from the monastery. After spending some days of edifying fervour in the midst of those holy and beloved countrymen of his, he set out on his return to the monastery, and thence intended coming to Kentucky. Near St. Louis, he had an interview with an Indian chief, who promised to send him a great number of the young females of his tribe to be educated by the Sisters. He made haste to carry this news to the monastery, and his heart burned within him, whilst his imagination pictured to itself the good prospect which lay open to his hopes.

"On his road, however, was a path to a settlement of eight or ten Catholic families, who had not seen a priest during more than two years. Desirous of doing all the good in his power, he assembled them, heard their confessions, gave them instructions, and celebrated for them the Holy Sacrifice of the Mass. He was thus occupied, from a little after day-break, until towards three o'clock in the evening. Seeing the good dispositions of those Catholics, he proposed to them to build a church, in order to encourage priests to come to them: a subscription was immediately opened by those present; out of his own small means he gave ten dollars; and signatures for over nine hundred dollars were instantly affixed to the sheet.

"After all this exertion in such broiling weather, he felt feverish symptoms. These continued next day, but apparently much diminished. He wished to go to St. Genevieve, which was only fifteen or eighteen miles distant; and though the journey was short, still the exertion and the burning sun greatly increased the fever. The pastor of St. Genevieve (M. Dahman) received him with great kindness and affection. He was obliged to betake himself immediately to bed; the physicians came promptly, and paid him every attention; but to no purpose.

"M. Nerinckx was, I trust, in the eye of God, ripe for heaven; and his Lord saw that it was time to bestow upon his faithful servant the recompense of his labours. He had the use of his reason to the last, and edified all who saw him by his piety and patience. On the ninth day of his sickness, about nine in the morning, he received the Holy Viaticum and Extreme Unction, after having made his confession; and about five in the evening, he breathed out his pure soul to return to its Creator, with entire resignation, and without a struggle. The Lorettines in Missouri requested to have his body, which was accordingly conveyed to their cemetery from St. Genevieve."

The transfer of his remains to this monastery of Bethlehem, (Mo.) was made by the direction of Bishop Rosati, who had arrived at St. Genevieve on the morning after the death of the good missionary. He assisted at his funeral service, which was performed with great solemnity.*

* In a letter addressed to a friend in France, shortly after the death of M. Nerinckx, M. Odin—the present devoted Vicar Apostolic of Texas—gives some highly interesting details on the last visit of M. Nerinckx to Missouri. In the simplicity of his heart, he exclaims: "Oh! how I loved to be with him! He

M. Nerinckx had reached his 63rd year; and, during the last forty years of his life, he had laboured for the glory of God and the good of his neighbour, with a constancy, an activity, and a zeal, seldom equalled, never, perhaps, surpassed. His whole life had been one continued voluntary martyrdom and holocaust. He contemned this world, and panted only for heaven; but he ardently wished to go to paradise with a numerous escort of souls, whom he had been instrumental in rescuing from perdition, and leading to salvation. This thought seemed to engross his whole mind and soul: and his life was but a carrying of it out. That God, whom he served so long and so faithfully, has no doubt long since crowned these lofty aspirations of His humble and heroic servant.

A little before his death, M. Nerinckx had intended to found also a religious Brotherhood, bound together by the ordinary vows of poverty, chastity, and obedience; and wholly devoted, like the Lorettines, to the service of God and the good of the neighbour. He had even begun this establishment, and had already received into it some members, one of whom, James Vanrissalberghe, accompanied him on his last journey to Missouri, and assisted him in his last illness. But death cut short his design in this respect: and, deprived of its founder, the Brotherhood soon ceased to exist.

In the year 1833, his remains were translated to Kentucky, and deposited in a suitable monument

---

prescribed for me all sorts of little practices for the advancement of souls, communicated to me all that his own experience had discovered to be most advantageous for the conversion of heretics; and above all, he spoke to me frequently of the Blessed Virgin." See "Annales de la Prop. de la Foy"—vol. 2, p. 369.

erected at Loretto, the mother house of the Lorettines. This monument stands in the centre of the conventual graveyard. "The base of it is a parallelogram, about six feet long, by three wide. It is built with brick, covered with a plain oak plank, painted and sanded in imitation of stone, and surmounted by a large urn. On each side of the brick work is a projecting tablet, on which is engraved one of the inscriptions that follow:

'In memory of Rev. Charles Nerinckx, a native of Flanders, who died Aug't. 12th, 1824, in Missouri. His remains were translated to Kentucky in 1833, by brother Charles Gilbert, at the request of the Loretto Society, and interred at this place by the Rt. Rev. Bishop Flaget, and the Rev. G. I. Chabrat, Superior of the Society.'*

'M. Nerinckx came to Kentucky in 1805, and devoted himself zealously to that laborious mission, during which time he was nominated to the

* After the death of the good founder of the Lorettines, the Rev. G. I. Chabrat was appointed their superior, by the Bishop; and he continued to discharge this office until he was named Coadjutor Bishop of the Diocess. The society continued to increase and to flourish under his administration. This will appear from the following account of its present condition, for which we are indebted to notes kindly furnished us by one of the present Superiors of Loretto.

The Society now has ten different establishments, of which five are in the State of Kentucky, three in Missouri, and two in Arkansas. The total number of members, including novices, is 179; of whom 55 or 60 are attached to the establishments in Missouri and Arkansas. These last are all subject to the mother house of Loretto in Kentucky, in which latter there are at present between 30 and 40 Sisters. Since the establishment of the society, in 1812, the total number of deceased members has been 65. All the establishments have schools attached to them, in which at present more than 200 young ladies are annually educated; though, in consequence of the pecuniary difficulties of the times, this number is not so great as it was some years ago. The society continues to prepare a great many young ladies for their first communion every year; and nearly 20 orphans

Diocess of New Orleans, but he refused that dignity; and in 1812, with the approbation of the Holy See, instituted the Lorettines, or Friends of Mary, and died in performing the visitation of the Order, at St. Genevieve, Missouri, aged 63.'

"One of the end tablets has: 'Requiescat in pace:' and on the other end tablets are these words: 'Loretto's mite of esteem and veneration for its founder.' 'Do not forsake Providence, and He will never forsake you. C. N.'—this being a favourite saying of his to the nuns, at a time when Providence was almost their only dependence for the next day's dinner."*

Such was the life, such the death, and such the establishments, of the Rev. Charles Nerinckx, one of the very best priests who ever laboured on the arduous missions of America.

---

are sheltered and reared in its various establishments. A noviciate was recently established at the mother house, in which there are at present 10 novices, besides several postulants. The Jesuit Fathers of St. Mary's College are now the spiritual directors of the mother house. Such is the present condition of the Society.

* A writer in the Catholic Telegraph, giving an account of the life of M. Nerinckx, and of a visit to his tomb at Loretto. See Catholic Advocate, vol. 3. p. 10.

CHAPTER XIII.

Father David—His Early Life—The Theological Seminary.

Father David—His parentage and early youth—He studies for the Church—And is ordained—Joins the Sulpicians—Is forced to fly from France—Sails for America—Becomes a missionary in Maryland—Gives Retreats with great fruit—Resides in Georgetown College—And in Baltimore—Accompanies Bishop Flaget to Kentucky—Founds our Theological Seminary—Its early history sketched—Virtues and labours of the Seminarians—Instructions and maxims of Father David—His character—His missionary labours.

We have already had occasion to mention Father David, the intimate friend and associate, and the indefatigable co-labourer of the venerable Bishop Flaget. We must now speak more in detail of his early life, and of his invaluable services to the church of Kentucky. The history of his life and labours is, in fact, intimately connected with that of religion in our Diocess; without the former, the latter were meagre and incomplete indeed. The church of Kentucky owes him a great debt of gratitude, which will be best paid by treasuring up in the memory, and reducing to practice, his many holy instructions and exemplary virtues.[*]

[*] For many of the facts connected with the early life of Father David, we are indebted to an excellent biographical notice of him, written by an eminent ecclesiastic, and published in the Catholic Advocate, vol. vi, p. 268. seq.

John Baptist M. David was born in 1761, in a little town on the river Loire, in France, between the cities of Nantes and Angers. His parents were pious, exemplary, and ardently attached to the faith of their fathers. Though not wealthy, they were yet blessed with a competence for their own support and for the education of their offspring. Sensible of the weighty responsibility which rests on Christian parents, in regard to those tender ones whom heaven has entrusted to their charge, they determined to spare no pains nor expense that might be necessary for the Christian education of their children.

Young John Baptist gave early evidences of deep piety, of solid talents, and of an ardent thirst for learning. At the age of seven he was placed under the care of an uncle, a pious priest, who willingly took charge of his early education. By this good priest he was taught the elements of the French and Latin languages, and also those of music, for which he manifested great taste. He was enrolled in the number of *enfants de chœur*, or of the boys who served at the altar, and sung in the choir. He thus passed the first years of his life in the church, where he was reared up under the very shadow of the sanctuary.

At the age of fourteen, he was sent by his parents to a neighbouring College, conducted by the Oratorian priests. Here he distinguished himself for regularity, close application to his studies, solid talents, and, above all, for a sincere piety, which soon won him the esteem and love of both professors and fellow-students. But what all admired in him most was that sincerity and candour of soul, which formed throughout his long life the distinctive trait in his character.

THE THEOLOGICAL SEMINARY.

From his earliest childhood, the young John Baptist had manifested an ardent desire to embrace the ecclesiastical state, that he might thus devote his whole life to the service of God and of the neighbour, in the exercise of the holy ministry. His parents were delighted with these dispositions of their son; and to second his purpose, they sent him to the Diocesan Seminary of Nantes. Here he entered with ardour on his sacred studies, in which he made solid proficiency. In the year 1778, the eighteenth of his age, he received the tonsure, and, two years later, the minor orders, from the hands of the Bishop of Angers.

In the Theological Seminary he remained for about four years, during which he completed his course of studies, and took with honour the degrees of Bachelor and Master of Arts. In the twenty-second year of his age, after having duly prepared himself by a retreat of eight days, he bound himself irrevocably to the sacred ministry, by receiving the holy order of subdeaconship. He now considered himself as belonging wholly to God; and throughout the remainder of his life he never regretted nor recalled that first act of entire consecration, by which he had bound himself for ever to the service of the altar.

Shortly after he had taken this important step, with the advice of his superiors, he yielded to the earnest solicitation of one among the most wealthy and respectable citizens of Nantes, and became, for some years, private tutor in his family. Accustomed to enter heartily into every thing he undertook, he discharged this duty with such assiduity and zeal, as to win the respect of the parents and the love of the children under his charge. On the recent visit of Bishop Flaget to France, one of these came to him to enquire about his old preceptor, for whom he manifested feelings of love and gratitude which long years had not weakened nor diminished.

M. David was ordained deacon in the year 1783; and, having shortly afterwards determined to join the pious congregation of Sulpicians, he went to Paris, and remained for two years in the solitude of Issy, to complete his theological studies, and to prepare himself, by retirement and prayer, for the awful dignity of the priesthood. During this time, he edified all by his exemplary virtues, by his assiduity in study, and by the punctual regularity with which he attended to every duty of the seminarian. He was raised to the priesthood on the 24th of September, 1785.

Early in the year following, he was sent by his superiors to the Theological Seminary of Angers, then under the direction of the Sulpicians. Here he remained for about four years, discharging with industry and ability, the duties of Professor of Philosophy, Theology, and the Holy Scriptures: always enforcing his lessons by his good example. At length the storm of the French Revolution broke over Angers; and, late in the year 1790, the seminary was seized on by the revolutionary troops, and converted into an arsenal. The professors and students were compelled to fly for their lives; and M. David took shelter in a private family. In this retreat he spent his time in study, and in constant prayer to God, for light to guide him in this emergency, and for His powerful aid and protection to abridge the horrors of a revolution which was every where sacrificing the lives of the ministers of God, and threatening the very existence of the Catholic Church in France.

After nearly two years spent in this retirement, he determined, with the advice of his superiors, to sail for America, and to devote the remainder of his life to its infant and struggling missions. As we have already stated, he embarked for America in 1792, in the company of MM. Flaget and Badin. On the voyage he applied himself with such assiduity to the study of the English language, as to have already mastered its principal difficulties, ere he set foot on American soil. This is but one in a long chain of facts, which prove that he made it an invariable rule never to be idle, and never to lose a moment of his precious time.

Very soon after his arrival in the United States, Bishop Carroll ascertained that he knew enough of English to be of service on the missions, and he accordingly sent him to attend to some Catholic congregations in the lower part of Maryland. M. David had been but four months in America, when he preached his first sermon in English; and he had the consolation to find, that he was not only well understood, but that his discourse made a deep impression on his hearers. For twelve years he laboured with indefatigable zeal on this mission, in which he attended to the spiritual wants of three numerous congregations. He was cheered by the abundant fruits with which God every where blessed his labours.

Feeling that mere transient preaching is generally of but little permanent utility, he resolved to commence regular courses of instruction in the form of Retreats;* and so great was his zeal and industry, that he gave four Retreats every year to each of his congregations. The first was for the benefit of the married men; the second, for that of the married women; the third and fourth, for

* As far as our information extends, he seems to have been the first clergyman in the United States who adopted a practice, which has since proved so beneficial to religion.

that of the boys and girls. To each of these classes he gave separate sets of instructions, adapted to their respective capacities and wants.

His discourses were plain in their manner, and solid and thorough in their matter. He seldom began to treat, without exhausting a subject. At first, but few attended his Retreats: but gradually the number increased, so as to embrace almost all the members of his congregations. But he appeared to preach with as much zeal and earnestness to the few, as to the many. He was often heard to say, that the conversion or spiritual profit of even *one* soul, was sufficient to enlist all the zeal, and to call forth all the energies of the preacher.

Great were the effects, and most abundant the fruits, of M. David's labours on the missions of Maryland. On his arrival among them, he found his congregations cold and neglectful of their Christian duties; he left them fervent and exemplary. Piety every where revived; the children and servants made their first communion; the older members of the congregations became regular communicants. Few that were instructed by him could soon forget their duty: so great was the impression he left, and so thorough was the course of instruction he gave. To the portion of Maryland, in which he thus signalized his zeal, he bequeathed a rich and abundant legacy of spiritual blessings, which was destined to descend from generaiton to generation: and the good people of those parts still exhibit traces of his zeal, and still pronounce his name with reverence and gratitude.

In the year 1804, Bishop Carroll found it necessary to recall M. David from the missions, in order to send him to Georgetown College, which was then greatly in need of his services. The good missionary promptly obeyed the call, and for two years discharged, in that institution, the duties of professor, with his accustomed fidelity and ability.

In 1806, the Sulpicians of Baltimore expressed a wish to enlist his services in the Theological Seminary and the College of St. Mary's under their direction in that city. M. David belonged to this body, and he promptly repaired to the assistance of his brethren. He remained in Baltimore for nearly five years, discharging various offices in the institutions just named, and devoting all his leisure time to the duties of the sacred ministry. He laboured with so great zeal and constancy, that his constitution, naturally robust, became much impaired. Still, he was not discouraged, nor did he give himself any rest or relaxation. A pure intention of promoting the honor and glory of God, and a constant spirit of prayer, sustained him, and hallowed his every action.

When his intimate friend, the Rev. M. Flaget, was nominated first Bishop of Bardstown, M. David, as we have already seen, cheerfully offered himself to accompany the Bishop to his new Diocess in the west. Though then in his fiftieth year, and though his previous hardships had greatly weakened his health, yet his zeal had not abated; and he was fully prepared to share with his dear friend in all the hardships and privations of his rugged mission. The Bishop gratefully accepted the tender of his services; and cheerfully entered into the design of M. Emery, the venerable Superior General of the Sulpicians, who had already named him Superior of the Theological Seminary, to be organized for the new Diocess of Bardstown.

The good Bishop judged rightly, that he could not hope permanently to supply his vast Diocess with missionaries without a Theological Seminary, in which such youth of the country as manifested a vocation for the ecclesiastical state, might be diligently trained to virtue and learning. And he could not have chosen a more suitable person than the Rev. M. David, for carrying this excellent plan into execution. Reared in seminaries and colleges from his earliest youth, zealous, laborious, learned, and regular in all his habits, M. David was the very man for founding and conducting with success a theological seminary. For doing this he was, besides, blessed with a peculiar talent; and he entered on the task with all the ardour of his soul. The infant seminary became the object of all his thoughts—the idol of his heart. The founder of our Diocesan Seminary, he became the father of most of the present secular clergy of Kentucky. Long and deeply will they reverence the memory, and with tender love and gratitude will they continue to pronounce the name, of FATHER DAVID.*

We will endeavour to give a rapid sketch of the different phases in the history of the Theological Seminary founded by Father David. And we cannot do it better than in the words of the venerable founder himself,† to whose brief and summary account we will add such additional details, derived from other sources, as may be deemed interesting to the reader.

* This is the title by which he was, and is still universally known in Kentucky; and never was a title more appropriate or better deserved.

† From the letter of Father David quoted in the preceding chapter.

THE THEOLOGICAL SEMINARY. 223

"Occupied solely with the wants of his flock," says F. David, "the principal end and object of Bishop Flaget was the foundation of a seminary. Without this, it was impossible for him to have a clergy sufficient for a Diocess which extended to the sources of the Mississippi, and the Lakes of Canada. He arrived in Baltimore in July, 1810, accompanied by a subdeacon and two young laymen, the elements of his seminary, with which I had been already charged by M. Emery, the Superior General of the Sulpicians. My health was then in as bad a condition as our funds. . . . . A Canadian priest had joined us; and the boat on which we descended the Ohio became the cradle of our seminary and of the church of Kentucky."

He then gives the edifying details concerning the religious exercises performed on the boat, and states the other particulars of the journey—all of which we have spread before our readers in the preceding chapter. He then continues:

"There (at St. Stephen's,) our seminary continued its exercises for five months. The Bishop lived in a log cabin, which had but one room, and was called the 'Episcopal Palace.' The seminarians lodged in another cabin, all together, and myself in a small addition to the principal house. A good Catholic,* who had laboured for sixteen years to make an establishment for the church, then bequeathed to the Bishop a fine plantation;† and in November, (1811,) the seminary was removed thither. After five years, we finally succeeded in building a brick church,‡ sixty-five feet long, by thirty wide. The interior is not yet sufficiently ornamented, for want of means; it is,

* Mr. Howard. * The present farm of St. Thomas'.
‡ That of St. Thomas.

however, in a condition sufficiently decent for the celebration of the Divine Offices. The Bishop officiates in it on all the great feasts, and in it three ordinations have already taken place."

He next proceeds to state, that, at the date of his letter—November, 1817—there were at St. Thomas' fifteen seminarians, of whom five were studying theology, and of whom but two were able to pay annually the sum of $50 each. The number might have been doubled, if the means of the Bishop had allowed him to receive all who had applied for admission. Notwithstanding the poverty with which the infant institution had to struggle, God watched over it, and His providence did not suffer its inmates to want for any of the necessaries of life.

The young seminarians corresponded well with the parental solicitude of their good Superior. They caught his spirit, and entered heartily into all his plans for their spiritual welfare. They united manual labour with study. They cheerfully submitted to lead a painful and laborious life, in order to fit themselves for the ministry, and to prepare themselves for the privations they were destined to endure on the missions. On this subject, we will translate for our readers a portion of M. Badin's account of the early missions of Kentucky, already often quoted in these sketches.*

"The seminarians made bricks, prepared the mortar, cut wood, &c., to build the church of St. Thomas, the seminary, and the convent of Nazareth. The poverty of our infant establishments compelled them to spend their recreations in labour. Every day they devoted three hours to labour in the garden, in the fields, or in the woods.

---

* Annales," &c., vol. 1. No. 2. p. 40. *note.* See also ibid. vol. 2. p. 40, for Bishop Flaget's testimony.

Nothing could be more frugal than their table, which is also that of the two Bishops,* and in which water is their ordinary drink; nothing, at the same time, could be more simple than their dress."

Father David continues his account of the seminary, over which he presided, as follows:

"We have at length succeeded, thanks to God, in building a seminary thirty feet square. The second story, which is a garret, serves as a dormitory, and may contain twenty-five persons: it is habitable in winter. For about a year we have been able to give in it hospitabity to twelve persons belonging to the *suite* of the Bishop of Louisiana,† who is daily expected to arrive with twenty-three other companions. These will be lodged with difficulty; but our hearts will dilate with joy; and these good missionaries will perform with us an apprenticeship of the apostolic life."

As Superior of the seminary, Father David was a rigid disciplinarian. Both by word and by example he enforced exact regularity in all the exercises of the house. He was himself always amongst the first at every duty. Particularly was he indefatigable in discharging the duty of instructing the young candidates for the ministry in the sublime maxims of Christian perfection. He seemed never to grow weary of this occupation. A thorough master of the interior life himself, it was his greatest delight to conduct others into the same path of holiness. He was not satisfied with laying down general principles: he entered into the most minute details, with a zeal equalled only by his patience.

* This was written in 1822, after the consecration of Father David.
†Bishop Dubourg.

He sought to inspire the young seminarians with an ardent desire of aspiring to perfection; and of doing all their actions for the honour and glory of God. To arouse and stimulate their zeal, he often dwelt on the sublime grandeur of the ministry, which he delighted to paint as a co-operation with Christ for the salvation of souls. A favourite passage of the Holy Scriptures with him, was that containing the words of our Blessed Lord to his Apostles: "I have placed you, that you may go, and bring forth fruit, and that your fruit may remain:"* as also this other declaration of the Saviour: "I have come to cast fire upon the earth, and what will I but that it be kindled?"†

Though he sometimes rebuked faults with some severity, yet he had a tender and parental heart, which showed itself on all occasions. For all the seminarians he cherished feelings of the most paternal affection. It was his greatest happiness to see them advance in learning and improve in virtue. He rejoiced with those who rejoiced, and wept with those who wept. No one ever went to him for advice or consolation in vain. As a confessor, few could surpass him in zeal, in patience, in tenderness. But what most won him the esteem, confidence, and love of all under his charge, was his great sincerity and candour, in every thing. All who were acquainted with him, not only believed, but *felt*, that he was wholly incapable of deceiving them in the least thing.

He was always even better than his word: he was sparing of promises, and lavish in his efforts to redeem them when made. If he rebuked the faults of others, he was free to avow his own; and more than once have we heard him publicly

---

* St. John xv. 16. † St. Luke. xii. 49.

acknowledging his imperfections, and with tears imploring pardon of those under his control for whatever pain he might have unnecessarily caused them. He was in the constant habit of speaking whatever he thought, without human respect or fear of censure from others. This frankness harmonized well with the open character of the Kentuckians, and secured for him, in their bosoms, an unbounded confidence and esteem.

Those under his direction could not fail to profit by all this earnest zeal and devotedness to their welfare. They made rapid advances in the path of perfection, in which they were blessed with so able and laborious a guide. Even when he was snatched from their midst, they could not soon forget his lessons nor loose sight of his example.

We may say of him, what he so ardently wished should be verified in others: that he "has brought forth fruit," and that "his fruit has remained." He has enkindled a fire in our midst, which the coldness and neglect of generations to come will not be able to quench. He has impressed his own earnest spirit on the missions served by those whom his laborious zeal has reared. Such are some of the fruits produced by this truly good man, with whose invaluable services God was pleased to bless our infant Diocess.

But these were not all, nor even one half, of the fruits, which he brought forth, and cultivated till they were ripe for heaven. His zeal was not confined to the seminary, the labour in superintending which would appear to have sufficed for any one man. He devoted all his moments of leisure to the exercise of the holy ministry among the Catholics living in the neighbourhood of St. Thomas'. He was for several years the pastor of this congregation; and, besides the church, he attended to several neighbouring stations, on Thursdays, when his duties did not require his présence at the seminary. He also visited the congregation at Bardstown once a month. Constant labour was the atmosphere he breathed, and the very element in which he lived. He was most happy, when most occupied. During his long life, he, perhaps, spent as few idle hours as any other man that ever lived.

CHAPTER XIV.

The Sisters of Charity in Kentucky.

Father David, their Founder—The objects of the Sisterhood—Its humble beginning—And early history—Its rapid growth—And extended usefulness—Branch establishments—Removal to the present situation—Present condition of the Society—A precious legacy.

BESIDES attending to the seminary and to the missions, Father David set about laying the foundations of another institution, which was afterwards destined to become the ornament and pride of the Diocess, and which was admirable even in its rude beginnings. We allude to the establishment of the Sisters of Charity in Kentucky, who justly look up to him as their father and founder.

We will devote the present chapter to a rapid sketch of the origin, design, and early progress, of this Society. Without doing this, in fact, our sketches, both of the life of Father David and of the religious history of Kentucky, would be very incomplete.*

The foundation of the Sisters of Charity in Kentucky dates back to the year 1812; one year and a half after the arrival of Bishop Flaget in his new Diocess, and about twelve months after the Theological Seminary, under charge of Father Da-

* For the principal facts and dates of the following statement we are indebted to notes kindly furnished by the present Superiors of the Nazareth Institution.

vid, had been removed from St. Stephen's to the farm of St. Thomas. At this time, the excellent Superior of the seminary, with the advice and consent of Bishop Flaget, conceived the idea of founding a community of religious females, who, secluded from the world, might devote themselves wholly to the service of God and the good of the neighbour.

The new society was to be wholly under the control of the Bishop, and of the ecclesiastical superior whom he might appoint. Besides aspiring to the practice of religious perfection, by fulfilling the three ordinary vows of poverty, chastity, and obedience, the members of the Sisterhood were to devote their lives to such works of mercy, both corporal and spiritual, in behalf of the neighbour, as might come within their reach; and also to apply themselves to the education of young persons of their own sex, in all the branches of female instruction. To these occupations they were to add the instruction of poor children and servants in the catechism, and the visiting of the sick, without distinction of creed, as far as might be compatible with the other duties of their institute.

Such was the original plan of the society. So soon as the intentions of the Bishop were known in the several congregations of his Diocess, there were found several pious ladies who professed a willingness to enter the establishment, and to devote their lives to the objects which its projectors proposed. In November, 1812, two pious ladies of mature age, Sister Teresa Carico and Miss Elizabeth Wells, took possession of a small log house contiguous to the church of St Thomas. Their house consisted of but one room below and one above, and a cabin adjoining, which served as a kitchen. They commenced their work of charity by manufacturing clothing for those belonging to the seminary of St. Thomas, then in its infancy.

On the 21st of January following, 1813, another member was added to the community, in the person of Sister Catharine Spalding. On the same day, the Superior, Father David, presented to them the provisional rules which he had already drawn up, unfolding the nature, objects, and duties of the new society. On the same occasion, he also read, and fully explained to those present, an order of the day, which he had written out, for the regulation of the exercises of the community; and this was still farther organized by the temporary appointment of the oldest member as Superior, until the society should be sufficiently numerous to proceed to a regular election, according to the provisions of the rule.

At this time, the house in which the Sisters lived was so poor as to be unprovided with even the most necessary articles of furniture. They bore this and other privations with great cheerfulness; and, from the date last mentioned, they began gradually to form themselves into a religious community, by observing the rules which they had just received. As yet, however, they had no religious uniform, but continued to wear the dress in which they had entered the community.

Such was the humble commencement of the Society of Sisters of Charity in Kentucky. Nevertheless, with the Divine blessing, it was soon destined to increase in number, and to prosper, even beyond the most sanguine expectations of its saintly founder. On Easter Monday, April, 1813, the community was farther increased, by the entrance of two additional members, Sisters Mary Beaven and Harriet Gardiner.

In June of the same year, the Sisters, being now six in number, made a spiritual retreat of seven days, under the direction of Father David; and, at the close of it, proceeded to the election of a Superior, and of officers, from their own body. Sister Catharine Spalding was chosen the first Mother Superior, Sister Harriet Gardiner, Mother's Assistant, and Sister Betsey Wells, Procuratrix. At this first election ever held in the society, there were present, Bishop Flaget, Father David, and the Rev. G. I. Chabrat. On the occasion the Bishop made the Sisters a very moving exhortation, on the nature of the duties they were undertaking to perform, and on the obligations they contracted in embracing the religious life. The ceremony was closed with the episcopal benediction.

The society continued to increase every successive year. The Sisters edified all by their piety and laborious life. They devoted their time chiefly to supplying the wants of the theological seminary. For two years they continued to observe their provisional rule, patiently awaiting the decision of their Bishop, and of their Rev. founder, as to what Order or Society they would associate themselves.

At length it was determined that they should embrace the rules of the Sisters of Charity, founded in France, nearly two centuries before, by St. Vincent of Paul. A copy of these rules had been brought over to the United States from France, by Bishop Flaget, at the request of Archbishop Carroll; and they had been already adopted, with some modifications to suit the country, by the religious society of Sisters of Charity, lately established at Emmettsburg, Maryland. Upon mature reflection, it was decided that the regulations of this excellent institute were more conformable than any other to the views and intentions of the Bishop and of Father David, as well as to the wishes of, and the objects contemplated by, the members of the new society.

At the same time, the Sisters adopted a religious uniform of their own manufacture, consisting of a habit and cape of black, similar to the dress which they now wear; and of a cap, which was at first black, but which, after two or three years, was, with the approbation of their Superior, exchanged for one that was white. This last colour was thought more convenient and economical, as well as more comfortable than that worn by the Sisters of Charity in France.

For greater convenience and retirement, the Sisters had already removed their residence to the distance of about half a mile from the church and seminary of St. Thomas. In 1814, an additional log house was put up, with the aid of the seminarians, adjoining the one in which they resided. It was intended for a female school, which was shortly afterwards opened. Hitherto, the sisters had walked daily to the church of St. Thomas, to hear Mass: but now, having more room, they fitted up a small chapel in an upper apartment, where the Blessed Sacrament was kept, and the Holy Sacrifice offered up as often as was convenient: they, however, still continued to attend church at St. Thomas' on Sundays and festivals.

From the year 1815, the Sisters commenced and kept up a boarding-school which was as much patronized as could have been anticipated, considering the location and the novelty of such an establishment in Kentucky. The number of pupils continued to be small, never exceeding thirty, until the year 1822, when the institution was transferred to its present location, two and a half miles north of Bardstown.

In the summer of 1816, the Sisters had, by their industry and economy, accumulated means sufficient for the building of a small frame chapel, which the increased size of the family rendered necessary. On its completion, the Blessed Sacrament was transferred to it with great solemnity, the Sisters and their pupils following in the procession.

During the time they spent at their establishment on the farm of St. Thomas', they lost no opportunity to qualify themselves as teachers. Their indefatigable founder devoted all his leisure hours to their instruction in the various branches which they were afterwards to teach. Thus they were enabled gradually to carry out their plan of educating young persons of their own sex. They succeeded so well, that, in 1818, they found themselves in a situation to erect a large brick school-house, in which fifty boarders might be easily accommodated; and also to put up two other out buildings, one of brick, and the other of stone. Their school also continued to increase each successive year.

The number of members in the community had increased so fast, that the Sisters were soon enabled to form branch establishments in different places. On the feast of the Nativity of the Blessed Virgin, 8th of September, 1819, three Sisters—Harriet Gardiner, Polly Beaven, and Nancy Lynch—left the mother house, to establish a day-school in Bardstown. The new establishment was called Bethlehem, and was opened in a house which had been previously contracted for by Father David. This school continued to flourish for many years, and was the means of doing great good to the children of the town.

In the following year, another colony of three Sisters was sent to found a school in Breckenridge county, Kentucky. But, after they had endured much sickness, and struggled with many difficulties, their Superiors deemed it advisable to recall them, and to abandon the enterprise for the present.

The attempt made during the same year, 1820, to establish a school of the society in Union county, met with better success. To this distant place, Sister Angela Spink, Sister Frances Gardiner, and another, were sent by their Superiors, to open a school on the plantation destined for the church, which the society afterwards purchased. This portion of Kentucky being then but newly settled, and totally unprovided with the most common conveniences of life, the good Sisters who laboured there had to endure many privations and hardships for several years. But, by dint of patient industry and perseverance, they finally succeeded, with the divine assistance, in establishing there a very respectable boarding school, which still continues to flourish.

The society had now existed for more than eight years. During all this time, the Sisters had been employed in carrying on their school, and in improving themselves, in order that they might be fully adequate to teach all the branches of education. They had also aided the seminary, by manufacturing all the clothing worn by the seminarians, as likewise that of the servants. They moreover had done whatever sewing was needed for the altar and church of St. Thomas. In a word, they had rendered to the seminary and to the church generally, all the services in their power.

P

During all this time, and for many years afterwards, they had a very hard and laborious life, having very little assistance from servants, being obliged frequently to provide and cut their own wood, and always to do their own cooking and washing, and to manufacture their own clothing, to cultivate their own garden, and even sometimes to labour in the fields. To all these hardships and privations they submitted without a murmur, consoled and strengthened by the grace of God, to whose service they had dedicated themselves, and cheered by the voice of their good founder, who comforted them amidst all their sufferings.

In 1821, after the establishment of St. Joseph's College, and the removal of the seminary to Bardstown, two Sisters were sent to reside near the college, in order to do the sewing of both institutions, and to perform other useful services. Shortly afterwards their number was increased, and then they took charge of the wardrobe and infirmary of the college; and also superintended the kitchen and refectory. They continued to perform these services till the year 1834, when they were recalled to the mother house by their Superiors, who had need of their services for duties more immediately connected with their vocation.

The year 1822 formed an epoch in the history of the society. It marks the date of the removal of the mother establishment from the farm of St. Thomas', to its present situation. During the twelve years which elapsed since the birth of the Sisterhood, it had rapidly increased, and had become strong enough, not only to conduct a boarding-school at the principal establishment, but also to establish several branches in different parts of Kentucky. The land on which the mother house stood did not belong to the Sisters; and the will of Mr. Howard, bestowing it for the benefit of the Catholic church in Kentucky, was of such a nature as to render it impossible for them to obtain any portion of it by purchase. Under these circumstances, it was deemed advisable and expedient, for the utility and permanency of the society, that some other situation should be selected.

They accordingly purchased the present site of the parent institution, which they were enabled to do, chiefly through the means generously left at their disposal by Mrs. O'Connor of Baltimore, who had just joined the Sisterhood. Their own slender means had been already exhausted in the improvements made on their first establishment near St. Thomas'. In removing, they were necessarily compelled to sacrifice all these improvements, as well as the resources they had accumulated during ten years of patient toil. They had to recommence every thing at the new motherhouse, which was called *Nazareth*, like that which they left on the farm of St. Thomas.

The removal was effected on the 11th of June, 1822. In the month of March, preceding, three Sisters, with two orphan girls, and the only two servants then belonging to the institution, had been sent to make the necessary preparations for the removal of the entire community. A small wooden building, the study of preacher Lapsley,* the former proprietor of the place, had been fitted up as a temporary chapel; and there Father David had celebrated the Holy Sacrifice, invoking, at the same time, a blessing on the house which was destined for the community.

* A Presbyterian minister, whose name has been already mentioned in these Sketches, in connection with the Very Rev. M. Badin.

At the time of their removal, the community numbered about thirty-eight members. The school was small, but, from this date, it began rapidly to increase. To afford room to the numerous pupils, it soon became necessary to erect temporary cabins for the accommodation of the community. The same motive, and other reasons, caused the discontinuance of a day-school which had been previously opened.

The society not only prospered at home, but continued to send out colonies for the formation of branch establishments. In April, 1823, Mother Catharine Spalding,* with three other Sisters, set out for Scott county, Kentucky, to found the school of St. Catharine, which, some years later, was removed to Lexington, where it has continued to flourish ever since.

In March, 1824, another colony of four Sisters, under the superintendence of Sister Harriet Gardiner, was sent to form a school at Vincennes, at that time under the jurisdiction of Bishop Flaget. The school succeeded for several years, though the Sisters had to encounter many difficulties, and to endure many privations, the greatest of which was, that, owing to the scarcity of clergymen in Indiana at that time, they were often left for weeks, and even months, without the means of hearing Mass or of approaching the Holy Sacraments. Finally, for sufficient reasons, the establishment was abandoned, in 1838, and the Sisters attached to it were recalled by their Superiors to Nazareth.

---

* As we have seen, she was the first Mother Superior of the society; and she was subsequently selected at five different times. The term of service for the Mother is three years; so that she has been Superior altogether, eighteen years. The other Superiors elected by the society, were: Mother Frances Gardiner, Mother Angela Spink, and Mother Agnes Higdon.

Having succeeded in their school even beyond their own anticipations, the Sisters now determined to improve their place by additional buildings. The first thing they thought of was a church, which they erected in the summer of 1824. It was a neat brick edifice, amply sufficient, not only for the community, but likewise for the numerous pupils attached to the boarding-school.

Notwithstanding their very limited means, they next undertook the building of the present large and commodious edifice for a boarding-school; and though many timid persons sought to dissuade them from an undertaking apparently so far beyond their resources, yet they persevered, and succeeded in completing it without much difficulty. In its accomplishment they were greatly aided by the kind indulgence of the merchants of Bardstown, who, by generously offering to furnish them with whatever they needed, and to await their own convenience for the payment, enabled them to employ all their means on the building. Thus, within six years after their removal to the present institution, they had expended about $20,000 on the improvement of the place.

The Institution of Nazareth continued to increase yearly in usefulness and popularity. The Sisterhood also increased in number every year. And in proportion as God blessed their labours, they extended the sphere of their usefulness. In 1831 Mother Catharine Spalding, with three other Sisters, went to Louisville to open a day-school, which was commenced in the basement story of the St. Louis Church. It soon became numerous, and has continued to flourish to this day. To this was lately added a free-school for girls, which is also numerously attended.

Two years later, preparations were made for building a house on the lot adjoining the church, for a female Orphan Asylum. This charitable institution soon became prosperous; and two years after its foundation, it was removed to the beautiful situation, on Jefferson Street, which had been purchased for the purpose by the Nazareth Institution. This latter had already been incorporated, with a very favourable charter, by the Legislature of Kentucky.

Finally, in August, 1842, a new school, conducted by Sisters of the society, was opened in Nashville, Tennessee, under the auspices of the Rt. Rev. Dr. Miles. Though yet in its infancy, it has flourished even beyond the most sanguine expectations of its friends.

The following table will exhibit the present condition of the society, and of the establishments under its direction.

Number of Professed Sisters, - 67
    Do. of Novices, - - - - 9
    Do. Boarders at the Nazareth Academy, 120
    Do. at St. Vincent's, in Union county, 35
Number of boarders at St. Catharine's,
    Lexington, - - - - 22
    Do. Day-scholars, do. do. - 40
Number of Boarders at St. Mary's Academy, Nashville, - - - - 18
    Do. Day-scholars, do. do. - 47
    Do. Day-scholars at Presentation Academy, Louisville, - - - 50
    Do. do. do. Free-school, do., 75
    Do. Orphans at St. Vincent's Asylum, do. 40
Total of Sisters, - - - 76
Total of scholars, including orphans, 447

The society thus educates yearly between four and five hundred girls, including forty orphans which it has been the means of rescuing from misery and degradation. And the number is not now so great, as it has been in previous years, owing chiefly to the difficulties of the times.

Father David continued to be the Superior of the society for twenty years, when age and infirmity compelled him to retire from its management. He had watched over the infancy, and he lived to be cheered by the rapid growth and extended usefulness of the Sisterhood. While preparing to descend to the tomb, he was consoled by the virtues of those whom he had trained in the path of perfection, and by the immense good they were doing to religion. And, after some more years of weary pilgrimage, he was destined to breathe his last at the institution he had founded, and to bequeathe his remains to those whom he had spent so many years in forming to Christian perfection. But he bequeathed to them and to all, a more precious legacy still—the memory of his virtues and of his instructions!

CHAPTER XV.

The New Cathedral of St. Joseph's—Consecration of Father David—His Writings, Death, and Character.

Removal of the Seminary to Bardstown—Erection of the Cathedral—Liberal subscriptions—Obstacles—Dedication of the Cathedral—The edifice described—Its paintings and ornaments—Father David named Bishop—Accepts with reluctance—His poverty—His Consecration—His zeal redoubles—His zeal for the rubrics—And taste for Music—His qualities as pastor of the Cathedral—As a preacher—And as a confessor—The splendid services of the Cathedral—A refreshing reminiscence—Testimony of eye-witnesses—The remainder of Father David's life—His zeal for the faith—His oral discussion with Hall—His controversial sermons and writings—His other writings—His happy death—And character.

In the year 1818, Father David removed to Bardstown, with a portion of the seminarians of whom he was Superior.* Many reasons induced this change of location. Bishop Flaget wished to reside in the place which was his episcopal See, and he was desirous of being surrounded by his young seminarians, as a father by his children. The new Cathedral of St. Joseph's was then in progress of erection, and the establishment of a

---

* Only those who were more advanced in their studies removed to Bardstown. The others remained at St. Thomas', which, for some years, continued to be a preparatory theological seminary, to which was annexed an elementary school.

THE NEW CATHEDRAL. 243

College was contemplated. The services of the seminarians would be needed in the college during the week, and in the cathedral on Sundays and Festivals. Such were some of the principal motives for the removal of the seminary from St. Thomas to Bardstown.

During the first eight years of his residence in Kentucky, Bishop Flaget had no Cathedral, other than the poor chapel at St. Stephen's, and the small church of St. Thomas'. His poverty, as well as his continual occupations, rendered it impossible for him to undertake the erection of a suitable church for this purpose. His people, too, were as poor as their Bishop; and hence the latter, however much and ardently he desired it, was compelled to defer the undertaking for so many years. We will here quote the language of Father David, on this subject* already often referred to.

"That which has occupied us most is the building of a Cathedral at Bardstown. Though the Bishop had conceived this design immediately on his arrival, he had not, however, yet ventured on its execution: but Providence has at length removed all obstacles in a wonderful manner. A good Catholic carpenter† from Baltimore has offered his services for this purpose; and the amount of the first subscription was found to be from twelve to fourteen thousand dollars. Bardstown alone, which scarcely equals in size one of our large villages in France, subscribed five thousand dollars."

Many citizens of Bardstown, who were not Catholics, subscribed liberally for this purpose. The Cathedral was commenced, and the work was prosecuted with ardour and spirit. The Catholics

* Dated November 20th, 1817, nearly two years before the completion of the Cathedral.
† John Rogers, the architect of the Cathedral.

vied with each other in zeal and liberality, for the completion of an edifice, which was to be the pride and glory of themselves and of their children. But many unforeseen obstacles arose. The subscription was found to be insufficient; and, from one of those sudden pecuniary revulsions common to all commercial countries, and no where more frequent than in the United States, many who had subscribed had become totally unable to pay the amount of their subscription. All our elder citizens remember the heavy pecuniary pressure and distress of the years 1819 and following.

In this emergency, the good Bishop came generously to the assistance of his people, to the full amount of his means, which were, however, as yet very slender. The work continued to progress; and the new Cathedral was nearly completed by the summer of 1819. On the 8th day of August, of this year, it was solemnly dedicated to Almighty God, under the invocation of St. Joseph. With a heart overflowing with joy and gratitude to God, the Bishop performed the magnificent ceremony of the dedication, according to all the rites prescribed in the Roman Pontifical. He was on this day surrounded by almost all his clergy, and by the seminarians; and the seremony was performed in the presence of an immense concourse of people from all parts of the surrounding country. Long and gratefully will that day be remembered by the Catholics of Kentucky. It marks an æra in the history of our infant church.

The Cathedral is a neat and beautiful specimen of architecture, of the Corinthian order;* and its

* It is not entirely according to all the rules of the pure Grecian Corinthian style: the capitals have the Corinthian floral leaves, without the involutes. The portico is supported dy six beautiful columns of the Ionic order. This was completed only some years later.

THE NEW CATHEDRAL.

dimensions are one hundred and twenty feet in length—including the beautiful semicircular sanctuary—by seventy-four feet in breadth. The ceiling of the centre aisle is arched, and flanked on each side with a row of four beautiful columns, besides the pilasters of the sanctuary. The ceiling of the side aisles is groined; and it was intended by the architect to have the side walls decorated with pilasters in the same style of architecture, but the limited funds of the church did not permit him to carry out this plan. The steeple is a well proportioned and beautifully tapering spire, nearly one hundred and fifty feet in height, to the summit of the cross with which it is surmounted. It is provided with a large bell, procured from France by the present Coadjutor Bishop of the Diocess.

An organ, and two superb paintings, the one representing the Crucifixion, and the other, the Conversion of William, Duke of Brienne, by St. Bernard, were placed in the church. They had been procured from Belgium by the venerable M. Nerinckx; and were by him presented to the Bishop for the new Cathedral. To these paintings were subsequently added several others which had been presented to the Bishop by the King of Naples, and the Sovereign Pontiff, Leo XII.*

The Cathedral was also provided with rich suits of vestments, golden candlesticks, a golden tabernacle, and other splendid ornaments, presented to the Bishop by the present King and Queen

---

* These fine paintings, with that of St. Bernard and of St. Charles Borromeo, were lately removed to Louisville by the Bishop, on the transfer of the episcopal See to that city.

of the French.* In a word, the Cathedral is a beautiful and well decorated edifice; and it will long remain an evidence of the zeal and liberality of our Bishop and of the Catholics of the congregation attached to it, as well as a monument of the ability and exquisite taste of its architect.

Father David had been long the bosom friend and intimate associate of Bishop Flaget. Weighed down with the labours and solicitude of his vast Diocess, in the visitation of which he was compelled to be often absent from home for months at a time, the Bishop determined to petition the Sovereign Pontiff to have his old friend nominated his Coadjutor. The latter would then be able better to supply his absence, and would also be invested with more power and authority for doing good, and for rearing up, and forming the character of the young clergy placed under his care. Though a few years† older than the Bishop, yet the health of Father David was still robust, and so regular had he ever been in all his habits, that he bid fair yet to live to be able to labour in the vineyard for many years to come.

Father David accepted with great reluctance the proffered appointment. He could be induced to yield to the urgent wishes of his friend and Superior, and to the voice of Rome, only by the conviction which was forced on his mind, that such was the will of God; and that, as Bishop, he could best promote the glory of God and the salvation of souls. He had ever taught the duty of

---

* These, too, were removed to Louisville, on the translation of the Episcopal See to that city. The old Cathedral is, however, still amply provided with every thing that is necessary for its decoration, and for Divine Service.

† About three years.

implicit* obedience to the voice of superiors; and, in regard to himself, he was always consistent with his own principles. No matter how great or how painful the sacrifice, he was prepared cheerfully to make it, whenever the command of his superior made it a duty.

He received his appointment as Bishop in the fall of 1817; but nearly two years elapsed before his consecration. Besides his reluctance to accept the dignity, other reasons caused this delay. He was himself blessed with so much of that holy poverty, which he was in the habit of extolling to others, that he had not wherewith to make the necessary preparations for his consecration.† He had no means of procuring the episcopal habiliments, or other necessary articles for furnishing his episcopal chapel. His Bishop was scarcely able to succour him in this emergency; and he was compelled patiently to await the arrival of the necessary assistance from France. In the letter to a friend in his native country, already often quoted in these pages, he mentions his poverty, and begs him to procure and send from France the necessary articles for his consecration.

The ceremony of his consecration took place in the new Cathedral, in the presence of a vast concourse of people, on the Feast of the Assumption of the Blessed Virgin, the 15th of August, 1819; the Octave of the consecration of the Cathedral. Bishop Flaget was the consecrator; and, having been unable to procure the attendance of any other Prelate, he was assisted on the occasion by two among the oldest clergymen of the Diocess.

* *Blind obedience* was a favorite term with him.
† He loved this poverty even unto death: he left no property behind him, and could bequeathe nothing to his friends but his virtues.

After his consecration, Father David changed in nothing his former manner of life. He was still the plain, humble, and mortified man of prayer; the same regular, zealous, and indefatigable minister of God. From this time his zeal seemed to have received a new impulse: he now belonged more entirely to God, and his whole energies were to be consecrated still more fully, if possible, to the good of religion and to the salvation of souls. Living in the midst of his seminarians and clergy, eating at the same table, and joining with them in every exercise, he was at once the father and the model of both clergy and people. Into the former he laboured unceasingly to infuse the true spirit of the ecclesiastical state; in the latter he spared no pains to build up the sublime edifice of the Christian life.

One thing that he inculcated with particular force on the minds of his young clergy, was a zeal for the decency of divine worship. He was very fond of the *rubrics,* in which he was thoroughly versed. He trained the seminarians to an exact observance of all the ceremonies prescribed in the Roman Missal, Ceremonial, and Ritual, as fully explained in the copious and admirable decisions of the Roman Congregation of Rites. He employed every effort to promote this exact observance; and his zeal was aroused at the omission or improper performance of the least ceremony. In his instructions to the seminarians, he often dwelt in great detail on this branch of ecclesiastical education.

From his earliest youth, he had cherished and cultivated the natural taste for music with which he had been blessed. He loved the grave severity of the venerable Gregorian chant, and could not brook the slightest departure from it in the church of God. He spared no labour to form the choir of the Cathedral; and for many years, he himself acted as organist and leader of the choir. His greatest delight seemed to be to unite with others in singing the praises of God, in that simple and soul-stirring melody, handed down to us by our fathers in the faith.

After he had been consecrated Bishop, he discharged for many years the office of chief pastor of the Cathedral. The ceaseless labours required by his triple charge of Superior of the Seminary, Superior of the Sisters of Charity, and Coadjutor Bishop of the Diocess, did not prevent him from devoting much of his time to the exercise of the holy ministry in the congregation of St. Joseph's. He visited the sick and the poor, he preached, he heard confessions, he gave spiritual instructions, he administered the Sacraments, with indefatigable zeal. He lost not a moment of his precious time. Impressed with the lofty dignity of the ministry, and with the importance of aiding in the salvation of souls ransomed with the blood of Christ, he willingly devoted his whole energies to this sublime work.

As a preacher, though not naturally very eloquent, he was eminently successful in imparting his own ideas and spirit to his hearers. His sermons were plain, solid, well connected, closely reasoned, and full of wholesome instruction. Every one saw, in the plain earnestness of his manner, that he was himself fully convinced of, and deeply imbued with, the holy truths and maxims which he unfolded.

But it was in the confessional that his zeal abounded most; and it was there that his success was most signalized. He there made an impression which time and the oblivious tendency of poor human nature could not soon obliterate. His numerous penitents yet remember and profit by the instructions which they there received. And long and gratefully will the congregation of St. Joseph's treasure up the lessons, enforced by the example, of their oldest and most warmly cherished pastor.

During all the time of which we are treating, the Bishops lived in common with their seminarians, and, on every Sunday and Festival, appeared at the head of their clergy in all the services of the Cathedral. We cannot recall those happy days without a feeling of pride and of happiness. No one, who has seen the venerable Patriarch of the west officiating in his Cathedral, can ever forget the impression then made on his mind. Even Protestants, who at that time often attended the Cathedral, were deeply impressed with the touching and soul-stirring spectacle they there witnessed. Never, perhaps, in the United States, were the ceremonies of our sublime service performed with more solemnity and impressiveness.

We will be pardoned for dwelling somewhat on this interesting subject, and for furnishing some extracts from letters written at the time by those who were engaged in, or witnessed this beautiful exhibition of our ceremonial, in the centre of a country, through which, but a few years before, the wild beast and the savage alone had wandered. There is something striking and moving in this melody of the divine praises, breaking forth from the walls of a beautiful Cathedral, but newly erected in the centre of what had so lately been an unreclaimed wilderness! It is pleasing and instructive to revive reminiscences so refreshing to the soul.

The first extract we will give is from a letter of

Bishop Flaget himself to the directors of the French Association for the Propagation of the Faith.* It will appear from it, that the venerable Patriarch was himself touched by the spectacle which he witnessed, and of which he made so prominent a part, in his new Cathedral.

"Nothing could be more astonishing and edifying at the same time, than to see the Bishop officiate pontifically in his Cathedral, with deacon and subdeacon, both students of the seminary, and surrounded by more than fifteen young seminarians, tonsured or in minor orders, clad in cassock and surplice, and singing as well as if they had been trained in Paris itself. Many priests have been already reared in the seminary: their piety and their talents would render them distinguished even in Europe; and some of them are excellent preachers and very good controvertists."

To this we will add the testimony† of a young Propagandist, who about that time visited Kentucky, and thus related his impressions of what he saw and felt:

"l have just arrived from Kentucky, whither I went to fulfill certain commissions towards the holy Bishop Flaget and some members of his clergy. This Prelate showed me his famous establishments and his Cathedral. Accompanying me himself on horseback, he made me visit his convents, his seminaries and his colleges: for we must already speak in the plural number of all these establishments, scattered in the midst of the forest. I avow to you, sir, that if ever I was penetrated with deep feeling, it was while assisting at the Holy Sacrifice in the Cathedral on a Sunday.

* Published in the "Annales," &c., vol. 2. p. 40. seq. No. for May, 1826.
† Published ibid, p. 42.

Torrents of tears flowed from my eyes. The ceremonies, all performed with the greatest propriety, according to the Roman rite; the chant at once grave and touching; the attendant clergy pious and modest;—every thing impressed me so strongly, that I almost believed myself in the midst of one of the finest churches of Rome, which I had before thought could not be equalled any where else in the world. From the bottom of my heart, I poured forth prayers to God for this worthy Bishop, for France, and for those who, by their generosity, had contributed to have the good God so well worshipped in the midst of the waving forests."

Many other testimonies of a similar character might be alleged, pourtraying the spirit and the worship of these golden days of the church of Kentucky. But these must suffice: the reminiscences of the older portion of our readers may easily supply the rest. We must now return to Father David, and endeavour feebly to sketch the remaining portion of his history, which, like that of his venerable associate, is identified with that of the church of Kentucky.

For more than sixteen years he continued to be the Superior of the theological seminary which he had founded, and over the welfare of which he had watched with sleepless vigilance. His declining years and increasing duties now compelled him to resign this charge, and to commit the destinies of the institution to younger hands. Still, he continued to manifest an interest in its welfare, and to devote to the spiritual benefit of the seminarians all the time he could spare from his other duties. He delighted to give Retreats; and he had written out an admirable course of meditations for this purpose.

He manifested as much zeal for the maintainance of the faith, as for the preservation of morals. As a controvertist, he was clear, solid, logical, learned, thorough, and convincing. These characters appeared both in his sermons, and in his controversial writings.

Shortly after he had been consecrated Bishop, a Presbyterian preacher by the name of Hall, who then resided in Springfield, was in the habit of visiting Bardstown for the purpose of attacking the Catholics, whose numbers were then greatly increasing, while their institutions were springing up about this town. He was a man of strong frame and of stentorian lungs, and as bitter and violent is his denunciations, as he was confident and reckless in his assertions. He was gifted with a certain stormy eloquence, which made an impression on those, with whom declamation passes for argument, and assertion for proof. That by this description we do him no injustice, we appeal to the testimony of all the impartial.

Father David had been explaining, in the Cathedral, in a series of discourses, various points of Catholic doctrine, and, among others, that which regards the use and relative respect paid to relics and images. The bitter attacks of the preacher on Catholic doctrines had induced him to undertake this course of explanatory and *defensive* lectures on the various points impugned or misrepresented. Preacher Hall gave out that, on a certain day, he would preach in the Court-house of Bardstown, on this same subject of images, and would prove the Catholic church guilty of gross idolatry.

Though much averse to oral discussion, which seldom ends in any thing except a widening of the breach and the greater embittering of prejudice, yet Father David felt compelled, under all the circumstances, to meet the Reverend preacher, and to answer his objections. A large concourse of people were in attendance, on the appointed day; and Mr. Hall opened the discussion, with a discourse of two hours in length, in which he gave full play to his lungs, and a wide range to the subjects he brought up as matter of accusation against Roman Catholics.

When he had concluded, Father David arose, and in a calm, solid, temperate and argumentative discourse of about the same length, answered the minister's objections, and laid down the grounds of the Catholic faith and practice on the subject of images. His discourse made a deep impression on his hearers, which was not destroyed by the declamatory rejoinder of the preacher. Father David wished to bring him to close quarters, and to reduce the discussion to a simple and logical form; but the preacher refused this, and also another request—to reduce his objections to writing, that the Bishop might be able to answer them in the same way. After having tired out the audience in his long rejoinder, Mr. Hall abruptly dismissed the meeting.

There was, of course, a diversity of opinion as to the merits of the discussion, according to the respective religious tenets or prejudices of the hearers. But many intelligent Protestants were heard to praise the calm manner and solid reasoning of Father David: and a very talented Protestant lawyer, on being asked his opinion of the debate, remarked, quaintly and pointedly: "that while Bishop David was preaching, the admirers of Mr. Hall looked like—owls when the sun was shining."*

* This caustic remark is ascribed to the famous and lamented John Hayes, by nature one of the greatest orators whom Kentucky ever produced.

Circumstances not having allowed him fully to answer the objections made in the second discourse of Mr. Hall, Father David resolved to give, in writing, a plain statement and a temperate defence of the Catholic doctrine on the subject of images and relics. Another motive for this publication was the wish to spread before the whole reading community, most of whom had not been able to attend the discussion, the whole matter in controversy. This he did in a pamphlet of 64 pages, entitled: "Vindication of the Catholic Doctrine concerning the Use and Veneration of Images, the Honor and Invocation of Saints, and the Keeping and Honoring of their Relics."*

This pamphlet exhausted the subject, and presented an unanswerable array of evidence on the articles in controversy. Mr. Hall published a "Reply," which drew forth from Father David another pamphlet of 106 pages, entitled: "Defence of the Vindication of the Catholic Doctrine concerning the Use and Veneration of Images, &c., in answer to the 'Reply' of Rev. Nathan Hall."† The minister did not attempt a reply to this publication, which accordingly closed the controversy, leaving Father David master of the field.

About the same time, Father David published his celebrated "Address to his brethren of other professions; On the Rule of Faith"‡ a pamphlet of 56 pages, remarkable for its clear and logical method, its temperate spirit, and its unanswerable reasoning. Preacher Hall had delivered a discourse on the same subject in the Court-house at Bardstown: and Father David had sent him, by a

* Published in Louisville, by S. Penn, 1821.
† Published in Lexington, Ky., by James W. Palmer, 1823.
‡ Published by S. Penn, Louisville, 1822.

young divine, a series of questions* on the subject, which he had declined answering. In the "Address," these questions are taken up and discussed with the thoroughness which marks every thing from the pen of Father David. It is, in a brief compass, one of the best arguments we have ever seen on the subject: and we may here express a hope that this and his other controversial writings will be shortly republished.

Controversy was not the only subject on which Father David wrote. He had already composed and published in Baltimore the "True Piety,†" one of the best of our books of devotion. At a later period in life, he wrote several very solid articles for the Metropolitan Magazine, published in Baltimore; and when old age and infirmity compelled him to retire from the active duties of the ministry, he employed his time in translating various spiritual works of Saint Liguori, and of Bellarmine. The last translation he made was that of Bellarmine's beautiful little work "On the Felicity of the Saints." This was a foreshadowing, in his own mind and heart, of those blessed realities of heavenly bliss, which he was soon to taste.

He continued faithful to all his spiritual exercises, as well as laborious and indefatigable in his duties, to his last breath. The evening of his life was spent in constant preparation for death. As when in the evening the sun, after sinking below the horizon, tinges with beautiful and varied colours the clouds which hang over the western sky;

---

* We intend giving these questions, together with some other papers, in an Appendix to these Sketches. See Appendix No. III. p. —

† This Prayer Book, like many other works, has since been *improved* for the worse: and Father David was wont to call the new editions, with a smile, the *false* "True Pieties."

so also, in the evening of his life, the gathering clouds of sickness and of death, were lighted up by the sun of another world, which faith opened to his view!

He died as he had lived. On the 12th of July, 1841, he quietly breathed his last, at Nazareth, the Sisters of which Institution had watched over him with tender solicitude during his last illness. He was interred in their cemetery. He had reached the eighty-first year of his life, the fifty-sixth of his priesthood, and the twenty-second of his episcopacy.

It is not necessary for us to pronounce his eulogy. To those who knew him, this were unnecessary: and to those who were not personally acquainted with him, the facts contained in this and the previous chapter will suffice to give some insight into his character.

Sincerity and candour in all things were, perhaps, the most distinctive traits in his character. He was what he appeared to be. He had less of human respect than is usually found among men. He always told you plainly what he thought; and you might rely upon the sincerity of his opinion, as much as on the soundness of his judgment. He was also, as we have already remarked, entirely consistent with his own principles. If he taught prompt obedience to others, he always practiced it himself, no matter how much pain it cost him; and this even after he had been consecrated Bishop. If he was somewhat rigid towards others, he was much more stern to himself. He never sought to impose upon others a burden which he did not cheerfully bear himself.

He was laborious, and always occupied in doing something useful. He never lost a moment in idleness. He was as regular in all his habits, and as punctual to all his exercises and appointments, as he was industrious and indefatigable. Regularity became a second nature with him. And this accounts for the great labours he was able to undergo, and the immense good he was the instrument of effecting. We can in no other way explain how he was able to fulfil so many seemingly incompatible duties, and how he could find time for all his employments.

Gifted in an eminent degree with the spirit of prayer, he was always united with God, in all his actions. He laboured, not for men, but for God; not for earth, but for heaven. His ambition aspired to a heavenly crown of unfading glory; he spurned all else.

In one word, he was the faithful fellow-labourer of our Bishop, the founder of our Seminary and of the Sisterhood of Charity in Kentucky, and the FATHER and Model of our clergy and people. In their memory and in their hearts is his monument reared, and his epitaph written, in indelible characters :—he needs none other!

CHAPTER XVI.

Rev. Messrs. O'Flynn and Derigaud.

Rev. F. O'Flynn—His early life—Emigration to America—And arrival in Kentucky—His appearance and piety—Incident showing his eloquence—His infirm health—And return to France—Rev. M. Derigaud—His early life—Ordination—Virtues—Zeal and labours—A religious brotherhood—His edifying death.

WE will endeavour, in the present chapter, to furnish brief notices of two among the oldest and most zealous of our missionaries: the Rev. Messrs. O'Flynn and Derigaud. We regret our inability to do full justice to the memory of either. Unable to find any written or printed account of their lives, we are compelled to confine ourselves to such facts as we have been able to glean from some of the older Catholics of Kentucky.*

Rev. Mr. O'Flynn was a native of Ireland. At an early age, he was sent to France, where he went through a regular course of studies, and was promoted to the priesthood. Previous to his ordination, he entered the religious order of Franciscans, to the austere obligations of which he appears to have continued faithful until death. After his religious profession and ordination he remained in France for many years; and he was

---

* What we will say of Rev. Mr. O'Flynn rests chiefly upon the authority of the Very Rev. S. T. Badin: the facts concerning Rev. M. Derigaud have been derived from various respectable sources.

as thoroughly conversant with the French, as he was with the English, language.

In consequence of the troubled condition of Europe, during the years which followed the French Revolution, F. O'Flynn, with the approbation of his Superiors, sought shelter in the United States, to the struggling missions of which he determined to devote the remainder of his life. He landed on our shores about the year 1807; and shortly afterwards made a tender of his services to Bishop Carroll, who sent him to Kentucky. He was then, probably, more than fifty years of age; his frame was very slight, and his constitution and health very delicate. Yet he did not shrink from the laborious duties connected with the missions of Kentucky.

He reached our State in the year 1808; and immediately afterwards engaged with zeal in the active duties of the missionary life, which he continued to discharge for nearly eight years, residing chiefly with the Very Rev. M. Badin, at St. Stephen's. He was a man of prayer and of very retiring habits. He was very short-sighted, and rather eccentric in his manners. He cared little for dress, and was very lowly in his appearance. He was likewise very diffident; and it was with difficulty that he could be induced to preach. Yet he is described as having been remarkably eloquent in the pulpit, in which he manifested all the warmth and energy of his countrymen. As an evidence of his eloquence, we will relate an incident connected wtth the building of the first brick Catholic church in Lexington.

In the year 1801, the Rev. Mr. Thayer had purchased a log house in the lower part of the city, which was subsequently used as a Catholic chapel for many years. The number of Catholics in that vicinity having greatly increased, M. Badin determined to erect a more spacious and suitable church. As the Catholics were chiefly Irish, or of Irish descent, he resolved to open the subscription for this purpose on St. Patrick's day, in the year 1810. He accordingly announced, some weeks previously, that the panegyric of Ireland's patron Saint would be preached that year by the Rev. F. O'Flynn, in the Court-house of Lexington.

F. O'Flynn was then in Scott county: but when M. Badin communicated to him the intelligence of the appointment, the old gentleman hung down his head, and said, with a rich brogue, that he "could not preach on the occasion; that he had no sermon prepared; and that he could not do justice to the subject." M. Badin insisted; but F. O'Flynn persisted in his refusal. It was with the greatest difficulty, that M. Badin could induce him to make his appearance at all in Lexington on the appointed day.

The announcement had created a great sensation, and the Court-house was filled to overflowing. M. Badin was sadly puzzled to know how to proceed; for he did not wish himself to preach the panegyric, and F. O'Flynn, though on the platform, still declined. At length he announced to the audience, that he would make some preliminary remarks, after which he had no doubt that his Reverend friend could be induced to address them.

F. O'Flynn at length arose. His dress and whole appearance were very lowly; and he commenced in an embarrassed and trembling voice;—every one expected an entire failure. Soon, however, his embarrassment ceased; he kindled with his subject; and, for more than an hour, he kept that large assemblage enchained. All were lost in astonishment at the success of the unpromising orator. Seldom had such a burst of genuine eloquence been heard in Lexington. More than three hundred dollars were subscribed on the spot, for the erection of the new church; and shortly afterwards, the amount had increased to three thousand dollars. Protestants contributed as liberally as Catholics. Among the former, we may mention with praise, Captain Nathaniel Hart and Col. Joe Daviess.*

F. O'Flynn became more and more infirm; and at length he was compelled to retire from a mission beset with so many hardships. The last nine months that he spent in Kentucky, were passed by him at the residence of a countryman, Captain Peter Wickham, who lived at the distance of four miles from Bardstown. In the fall of 1816, he left Kentucky for France, having been recalled by his Superiors. Of his subsequent life we know nothing, except that he acted for some years as chaplain to a pious and wealthy French family.

M. Derigaud was a native of France. He came to the United States with Bishop Flaget, in 1810. As yet, though perhaps more than thirty years of age, he had not commenced his theological studies. On the arrival of the Bishop in Kentucky, in 1811, he entered the theological seminary founded by Father David. After having completed the regular course of studies, he was ordained priest by Bishop Flaget, in the church of St. Thomas, on the first day of January, 1817.

*The liberality of the Protestants was likewise greatly stimulated by the bigotry of many who made every effort to prevent the erection of the church, or even the purchase of a lot on which it might be built. About the same time, three thousand dollars were also subscribed, in a great measure by Protestants, for building a church in Louisville.

He was not a man of great talents or learning; but he was as eminent for piety and zeal, as he was remarkable for skill in the management of temporal affairs. He devoted himself to the holy ministry with all the energy of his soul; and he was a living model of the virtues he taught to others. His health, naturally feeble, had been greatly impaired by the severe course of studies through which he had passed, after he had reached the years of manhood. He bore his sufferings with exemplary patience; and, notwithstanding his bad health, continued to labour with unremitting zeal, until the close of his life. During the ten years of his ministry in Kentucky, he was instrumental in effecting great good.

On the removal of the strictly theological department of the seminary to Bardstown, in 1818, M. Derigaud was left in charge of St. Thomas', where such of the seminarians remained, as had not yet entered upon the study of Divinity. Annexed to the preparatory department of the seminary, was also an elementary school, which continued to flourish for many years. Many of the present clergy of Kentucky still remember, with great reverence and affection, the virtues of M. Derigaud, who trained them up in the path of virtue and learning, in the seminary of St. Thomas.

Bishop Flaget had long wished to establish a brotherhood of religious men, who, besides aspiring to christian perfection, by the observance of the three simple vows of poverty, chastity, and obediance, might also aid the missionaries as catechists and teachers of elementary schools, and in the management of temporal affairs. He wished to found a society similar to that of the "Brothers of the Christian Doctrine," who have done so much good for religion in various parts of christendom. Several pious young men offered themselves for this purpose; and the foundation of the new brotherhood was laid at St. Thomas' seminary, about the year 1826. M. Derigaud directed the exercises of the infant society, the members of which at first bound themselves by vows for only three years.*

In the spring of 1827, the Brothers removed to a farm in Casey county, Ky., which had been obtained for their establishment. M. Derigaud accompanied them as Superior. But his health, which had been declining for some years, now entirely failed; and he lingered but a few months. He died in that county, in the summer of the same year, with the most edifying sentiments of faith and piety. The good Bishop Flaget visited and comforted him in his last sickness. His remains were brought back to St. Thomas' seminary, where they were solemnly interred. Not long after the death of their saintly Superior, the Brotherhood was dissolved.

The piety, the laborious zeal, the fortitude, and the many virtues of M. Derigaud, will be long remembered in Kentucky, where his memory is deservedly cherished.

---

* They were, soon after their establishment, ten in number; and almost all of them exercised some mechanical trade. See the "Annales," &c., vol. 3. p. 200.

CHAPTER XVII.

The Rev. William Byrne and Rev. George A. M. Elder.

Two Christian friends—Two founders of Colleges—Rev. Wm. Byrne—His early life—His ordination—His zeal and missionary labours—Founds St. Mary's College—His unshaken constancy in adversity—His qualities as a preacher—His virtues and instructions—Falls a martyr of charity—Rev. G. A. M. Elder—His early life—And missionary labours—His amiability of character—Founds St. Joseph's College—A touching incident—His indefatigable zeal—His pious and edifying death.

On the 18th of September, in the year 1819, the new Cathedral of St. Joseph's at Bardstown, was thronged at an early hour, by a multitude, who had come to witness an important and moving ceremony. But a month had elapsed since the solemn episcopal consecration of Father David had taken place in this same church; and but a few days more than a month, since the church itself had been dedicated to God.

Though less solemn than the two ceremonies just mentioned, that of which we are speaking was almost equally impressive. It was the raising of two young men to the sublime dignity of the priesthood. It was the first time, that an ordination of the kind had taken place in the Cathedral; and the first time, too, that Bishop David performed this ceremony. Those two young priests were the first who solemnly prostrated themselves before that altar, to utter their vows of eternal consecration to God, in the holy ministry: they were, also, the first fruits of the episcopacy of Father David.

There were other circumstances which tended to impart additional interest to the scene to which we allude. The two persons, who reverently knelt before that altar to receive the sacerdotal ordination, were from different countries and continents: the one was a native of Ireland, the other of Kentucky; one was from the old, the other, from the new world. They were united by the bonds of a common faith, drawn yet more closely by a common love and charity. Their hearts had been long blended together by the mutual sympathies of a tender Christian friendship, which hallowed and ennobled the feelings of natural affection. Both were destined to do much good for religion in Kentucky; both too were to be the founders of colleges for the Christian education of youth; and both, after having given bright examples of priestly virtues, to breathe their last in the midst of their labours and usefulness.

Few of our missionaries, in recent times, have laboured with more indefatigable zeal, or have succeeded in effecting more good, than the two of whom we are speaking. The Rev. Wm. Byrne was the founder of St. Mary's; and the Rev. George A. M. Elder, of St. Joseph's College. Both institutions were established about the same time; both have met with many reverses, have had to struggle with many difficulties, and have passed through a fiery ordeal; both have been very useful, and have reflected great honor on Catholicity in Kentucky. And though the lives of the two good priests who founded them are still fresh in the minds of almost all our readers, and appear to be too recent to constitute the matter of history; yet we will be pardoned for devoting one chapter of these Sketches to a brief biographical notice of them.

* The Rev. Wm. Byrne was born of poor, but respectable and pious parents, in the county of Wicklow, Ireland, about the year 1780. He was one of a large family of children, and his father dying when he was yet quite young, the care of his widowed mother and of the family, devolved, in a great measure, on him. He fulfilled the trust thus committed to him by heaven, with all the earnest disinterestedness for which he was ever after so conspicuous. He had neither opportunity nor means to acquire a classical education: he could only learn the common elementary branches, and for a knowledge of these, he seems to have been indebted to a pious uncle. This was the more painful to him, as from his earliest boyhood, he had an ardent desire to become a priest, and to labour for the salvation of souls. While yet a boy, he heard read from the altar, the passage from the Apocalypse which represents the virgins as following the Lamb, whithersoever He goeth—and from that moment he resolved to consecrate his virginity to God. But he could bide his time, and trust in Providence. The bloody scenes of the "Rebellion" in 1798, made a lasting impression on his youthful mind. He sympathized deeply with the Irish patriots, and he had many near relations who fought under their banner at Vinegar Hill. Often has he described to us in glowing language

---

* In our notice of Rev. W. Byrne, we abridge a biographical sketch of his life and labours, published in the Catholic Advocate for June 1843; and republished in the Catholic Cabinet of St. Louis, No. for February, 1844.

the closing horrors of that bloody struggle, when the beautiful scenery of Wicklow was marred and desolated; and even his own mother's cottage was threatened with the flames. By night, you might then behold one half of that beautiful county lighted up, from hill-top and valley, by the burning houses and cottages of the more odious "rebels."

After remaining with his mother until he had passed his twenty-fifth year, he found that he could make the necessary arrangements for coming to the United States; and one leading motive for this step, was a hope that he might thus be enabled the more speedily to carry into effect his darling project, of devoting himself to God in the holy ministry. Not long after his arrival in America, he entered Georgetown College, and applied for admission into the Society of Jesuits. He was received on probation, and made his thirty days' retreat. After remaining, however, for some months at Georgetown, he ascertained that, in consequence of his advanced age, and his neglected studies, he could not hope, at least for many years, to be ordained in the Society of Jesus; and not wishing to confine himself to the humble office of a simple lay-brother in the Society, when he thought he had a vocation for the priesthood, he resolved to leave Georgetown, and to seek counsel, as to his future life, of the venerable founder of the American Hierarchy—Archbishop Carroll.

The Archbishop received him kindly, heard him patiently, entered into all his views, and advised him to apply for admission into Mt. St. Mary's College, Emmittsburg. The late excellent Bishop Dubois, then President of this Institution, received him with open arms, pointed out his future course of study, and, with the tender charity of a father, encouraged him to proceed in his undertaking. Finding in him a great talent for managing youth, he assigned to him the office of Prefect in the institution, and from the vigilance, activity and tact of Mr. Byrne, in the discharge of his important office, he derived great satisfaction and relief in the most responsible station of President.

Like St. Ignatius, Mr. Byrne began to study Latin, when near the age of thirty; and he often cheered himself on by so bright an example. Less energetic minds would have given up the undertaking as impracticable; but his, like a vessel riding the waves, always rose with the difficulties it encountered. His labours were hallowed by religion, and sweetened by the tender offices of friendship. At Mt. St. Mary's he become acquainted with the late Rev. G. A. M. Elder, and, though different in disposition, and seemingly uncongenial in temperament, yet these two contracted an intimate and tender christian friendship, which lasted through life, and contributed much to the happiness as well as to the usefulness of both.

To prosecute more rapidly his sacred studies, Mr. Byrne repaired to the Theological Seminary of St. Mary's, Baltimore, which was then in a flourishing condition, under the newly constituted "Marian Faculty," composed of Doctors Tessier, Deluol, and Damphoux. Here, however, Providence permitted that he should encounter new difficulties. He had not been long in Baltimore, when, owing to circumstances which it is not necessary here to detail, he left the seminary. It is proper, however, here to record the fact, that he ever entertained and expressed for the distinguished gentlemen of that institution, sentiments of the greatest respect: and though he often spoke on the subject of his leaving Baltimore, he is not known to have uttered one unkind word of any of them. Of the late venerable Dr. Tessier, in particular, he was wont to speak in terms of the highest eulogy, and his pupils were as much conversant with the character and virtues of this truly good man, as if they had been acquainted with him all their lives.

He had been ordained subdeacon, and had therefore made an irrevocable vow to attach himself to the holy ministry: nor had he, when leaving Baltimore, the most distant idea of abandoning his vocation. He threw himself into the arms of Providence, and Providence directed his course westward. At Pittsburgh, he met with the venerable Bishop Flaget, who willingly accepted the tender of his services for the Diocess of Bardstown. The fact, that he was to labour in the same field with his dear friend Mr. Elder, and that, toiling side by side, they would sweeten the labours of the ministry by the soothing words of friendship, was an additional reason for attaching him to the choice he thus made. After some preparation at the seminary of St. Thomas, he and his friend Mr. Elder were both raised to the holy order of priesthood, in the new Cathedral of St. Joseph, at Bardstown, by the late Rt. Rev. Dr. David. They were the first priests ordained in this Cathedral, and the first ordained by Bishop David.

Shortly after his ordination, Mr. Byrne was appointed pastor of the congregation of St. Charles and of Holy Mary's, and of the adjoining stations. Though his health had been much impaired by a long and rigid course of study, yet he laboured in his new charge with the most indefatigable industry. He was always at his post, and never was known to miss an appointment. Whether sick or well, he might be seen, by day and by night, on horseback, visiting the sick, or attending his congregations or stations. His zeal was fed by labours and difficulties, as fire is fed by fuel. Besides his ordinary duties, he visited monthly the congregation of Louisville, more than sixty miles distant. As a preacher, he was not eloquent nor pathetic—but his discourses were plain, solid and instructive. His style was different from any which we find laid down in books on rhetoric—it might be called the *pointed.* He had a quick eye to observe the faults and deficiencies of his flock; and many who would not be led to the practice of virtue by the honeyed tones of persuasion, were at least often deterred from open vice by his pointed invectives from the pulpit. He eradicated many evil customs, and did much, both by word and example, to stimulate that spirit of sincere piety, for which those congregations are now so conspicuous.

He had lived so long in colleges, and had so long fulfilled the disagreeable office of Prefect, that he had become disgusted with that kind of life, and had firmly resolved never more to engage in it; and he was not much in the habit of changing his resolutions. Yet, the ignorance of the children in his various congregations, and the consequent difficulty of teaching them their religious duties, whilst most of them could not read, made him think seriously about establishing some institution for elementary instruction, by which this inconvenience might be remedied. The difficulties were great and appalling. But what were difficulties to him? They only quickened his zeal and nerved his resolution. He had neither money to build, nor men to conduct such an institution. But his energy supplied every difficulty. Once he had overcome his great repugnance to the undertaking, by persuading himself that it would promote the glory of God, and the good of his neighbour, all other obstacles vanished. He laid his plans before the Bishop, who had already entertained similar views, and who warmly approved them, encouraging his zeal with a solicitude truly paternal.

He immediately set about his task. The first thing to be done was to procure a site for the seminary. He purchased a farm, and paid for it by subscriptions raised among those favourable to his undertaking. As there was however but little money in the country at the time, he had great difficulty in raising the necessary amount, and especially in converting into cash the articles of produce subscribed by many. The farm paid for, the next thing was to erect suitable buildings. An old stone distillery on the premises, was soon fitted up for the purpose of an academy of learning. Mr. Byrne was himself almost constantly with the workmen, and labouring with them bareheaded, under a scorching sun. He had made an arrangement with the parents of children, that every thing contributed by them to the institution, either in money or work, should be refunded in tuition, which was to be at the very lowest rates. The parents were to pay nothing for board, only furnishing a certain quota of provisions per session. A plan so reasonable, and so fully adapted to the wants of the community could not fail to be successful. At length the long and anxiously expected day for the opening of the new school arrived, and it was on that day filled to overflowing. It was early in the spring of the year, 1821: and the new institution was called St. Mary's Seminary.

Thus were laid the foundations of a school, which, with more trials and difficulties than have perhaps fallen to the lot of any other institution, has subsisted with ever increasing popularity, for twenty-two years, and has at length taken its stand among the first chartered Colleges of the country. It was founded by *one man*, amidst difficulties which would have appalled almost any other—it was sustained for more than twelve years by the indomitable energy of *one man*. It boasted no money endowment, but it could boast an endowment far more noble—unquenchable zeal, hallowed by religion! The Rev. Mr. Byrne was President, sole disciplinarian, sole prefect, sole treasurer, and at first almost sole professor—he filled every office. And at the same time, he was often compelled to attend missionary calls. Yet he found time for every thing. Often have we known him after all had retired to rest, to go several miles on horseback, to attend a sick call, which he could not find time to attend during the day, and after returning and taking a brief repose, to be the first one up in the morning. His quick eye immediately discovered those who possessed the greatest talent, and amidst all his other occupations, he found time to train up several of those for teachers. Thus in less than a year he had raised up a body of tutors and officers, who subsequently relieved him of much labour, and continued their studies, whilst engaged in teaching those branches which they had already learned.

The seminary had become very popular throughout Kentucky: its strict discipline, and the moral and literary advancement of its pupils, were justly admired. Its founder had liquidated almost all its debts, and had nearly completed an additional building for the accommodation of more students,

when God permitted the whole to be consumed by
fire! He was absent in Louisville at the time,
and we remember well the sadness which sat on
his brow when on the next day he rode into the
enclosure, and beheld the smouldering ruins of
what had cost him years of anxious toil! Yet
the suddenness of the shock did not unnerve
him—it gave him new energy. In a few short
months St. Mary's Seminary arose from its ashes
fresher and more beautiful than ever!

During the months in which the new college
was being erected, Mr. Byrne toiled day and night;
he was not a mere looker-on, but he took part in
the work. While not thus employed, he was engaged in giving instructions to several of his
more advanced students, whom he retained with
him. In a few years he had recovered from the
pecuniary embarrassment consequent upon the
late accident by fire—he had also paid the debts
of the new building, and had an additional edifice
almost completed, when in one night, by another
severe visitation of Providence, this last was consumed by fire, involving him in a debt of more
than four thousand dollars! He was not discouraged by this second misfortune, and offered up
the Holy Sacrifice the next morning in thanksgiving to God for having preserved the main building. While those who came to condole with him
seemed sad and dejected, he treated the matter
lightly, and observed, smiling, that his only cause
of grief was the loss of his hat, which he had forgotten in the new building on the evening previous!

Nothing daunted, he rebuilt the burnt edifice
on a more enlarged plan, and in a few years was
enabled, by patient industry, and rigid economy,
to pay all his debts, and to place the Institution on

a firm and enduring foundation. It may here be proper to glance at the advantages which St. Mary's Seminary has bestowed upon the country, especially during the twelve years, from 1821 to 1833, that it was under the immediate superintendence of its founder. During all that time, the number of students ranged from eighty to one hundred and twenty: and taking one hundred as the average number, we ascertain that the Institution gave instruction, partial or complete, to at least 1200 youths. These were from all parts of the State, and many of them, on their return to their respective neighbourhoods, established private schools, which they endeavoured to assimilate to their *alma mater*. Thus the benefits of education were not confined to those who had been students of St. Mary's Seminary; this institution gave an impulse to knowledge, which affected the whole State, and extended even to the adjoining States. And all this good must be attributed to the energy of one man! Those who know how difficult it is to found, and how much more difficult it is to keep up a literary institution, must be impelled by these facts to give him more credit, than is usually awarded in such cases.

We now come to an act in his life which displays his character more perhaps than any other, and which must forever endear his name to St. Mary's College, and immortalize it with posterity. He had founded St. Mary's—had clung to it amidst all its misfortunes and vicissitudes, for twelve years—he had twice raised it up from its ruins—he had spent thousands on thousands of dollars upon it; the property was his own, the fruit of his own industry; and he made a free donation of it, while living, to the society of Jesuits, believing them much better qualified to conduct it than himself, and thinking that he could be more usefully employed elsewhere. Though advanced in age, and worn out in constitution, yet he thought of renewing in his declining years, the scenes of his more vigorous manhood.

He had been on a visit to Nashville, and having seen the necessity of an institution such as St. Mary's at that place, where the Catholic religion had to contend with neglect and scandals, he had resolved to make it the theatre of his future labours. In a letter to Bishop Flaget, he observed, that all he needed in leaving St. Mary's to found a new institution, was his horse, and ten dollars, to bear his travelling expenses! Some time before this, he had conceived a similar idea in regard to an establishment near Paducah, in Jackson's Purchase. This last enterprise he had however abandoned, probably because he had reason to believe, that his absence at that time might have been detrimental to the interests of St. Mary's: at least it was not because he deemed such an undertaking impracticable; for whoever knew him, must have learned that to *him* few things appeared or were impracticable. He had made up his mind in regard to his undertaking at Nashville, and he delayed it for a short time, only to aid for a season his friend, Rev. Mr. Elder, in the administration of St. Joseph's, which was then labouring under pecuniary difficulties.

But God was satisfied with his previous labours, privations, and sacrifices, and called him to Himself. He allowed him to breathe his last in the arms of the Fathers of the Society of Jesus, whom he had always respected, and with whom, at Georgetown, he had first learned to breathe the pure atmosphere of a religious life. But in the closing scene of his life God wished to give us a bright example of virtue the most heroic. He had sacrificed bodily comfort, by a long course of privations and of toils—he had sacrificed the fruit of all his labours, by one generous donation, made for the love of God—he was now to sacrifice his life, and fall a victim of divine and fraternal charity! The *cholera* came with all its fearful horrors: consternation seized upon the spirits of all. It was an awful storm, which bowed down even the oaks of the forest. But there was one spirit which quailed not—the Rev. William Byrne was ready to live or to die, as might be the will of God! In common with all his brethren of the ministry, he exposed himself to danger, wherever duty called; but he had greater reasons than any of them to fear the fatal disease.

He had been for many years subject to a chronical complaint, very analogous to the *cholera* in its symptoms, and whenever he exposed himself to rain or to cold, as he did whenever duty required, he might be seen for hours writhing in the very agonies of death—with cramps of the stomach, and spasms just like those of a cholera patient. He was well aware of all this, and he had reason to predict that if ever he should take the cholera, he would fall a victim to it, being a subject already predisposed to its attacks, without having longer strength of constitution to struggle successfully against them. Under these circumstances, he cheerfully answered a call to visit a poor negro woman, dying with that disease. He was not bound to answer the call by any pastoral charge, but he felt himself bound, by the more general consideration of Catholic charity and zeal. Before going, he was heard to say, that it would probably cause his death. He went; prepared her for death, and came home himself to die!

With the disease upon him, he yet said Mass the next morning—from the altar he went to his bed of death, and five hours after he had terminated that hallowed sacrifice, he offered cheerfully the sacrifice of his life. It was the 5th of June, 1833.

One would think that he was reading of the saints or martyrs of old—but he is only reading of the closing act in the life of one who lived and moved in the midst of us, and whose life, while he was living, was not sufficiently appreciated. The minister of God may well exclaim: may the Lord, in his mercy, grant me the happiness to die a death so worthy of a priest! "May my soul die the death of the just, and may my last end be like unto their's!"

The Rev. George A. M. Elder was born in Washington—now Marion—county, Kentucky, in the year 1793. His parents enjoyed a moderate competence, and were full of zeal for the Catholic faith. His mother was a convert. They spared no pains to make a good impression on the tender minds of their children, and to rear them in the knowledge and practice of Christian virtue. The young George gave early evidences of piety, and of that amiable disposition which characterized him throughout life. He manifested, from his most tender childhood, an ardent thirst for learning, and gave indications of a wish to study for the church. His parents did every thing in their power to foster these good dispositions, by giving him every opportunity to cultivate his mind, in the few schools with which Kentucky was blessed at that early day.

At the age of about eighteen, he was sent to the flourishing College of Emmittsburg, Maryland. Here he remained for several years, prosecuting his classical studies, in order to qualify himself for entering on the study of Theology. Here, too, he became acquainted with Mr. Byrne, with whom he formed that intimate Christian friendship which continued throughout life, and which even death could not sever.

With a view to prosecute the study of divinity with greater advantage, he accompanied his friend to the Theological Seminary of St. Mary's, Baltimore, conducted by the Sulpicians. In this institution, he completed with credit his theological course; and then returned to Kentucky, where he was soon after rejoined by his friend. As we have already seen, both were raised to the priesthood by Bishop David, in the new Cathedral of St. Joseph's, on the same day, the 18th of September, 1819.

Soon after his ordination, the subject of our notice entered upon the active duties of the holy ministry, in the congregation attached to the Cathedral. Here he laboured with great zeal and efficiency for several years. The Diocesan seminary had already been removed to Bardstown; and, like the other clergymen living in this town, the Rev. Mr. Elder resided at the seminary recently erected, and ate at the same table with the seminarians and the two Rt. Rev. Bishops.

The people of Bardstown had long expressed a wish to have a school there established for the education of their children. The good Bishop Flaget now resolved to comply with this wish; and he selected Mr. Elder to be the founder and first President of the infant establishment. As no buildings had been as yet erected for the purpose, the school, composed at first entirely of day-scholars, was opened in the basement story of the theological seminary. The seminarians assisted he Rev. President in the duties of the school, which was numerously attended. Thus, about the year 1820, were laid the humble foundations of St. Joseph's College. Its cradle was the cellar of the seminary.

The number of scholars daily increasing, the President determined, with the approbation of the Bishop, to undertake the erection of a separate building for the college. The south wing of St. Joseph's College was soon put up, and paid for chiefly from the proceeds of the day-school. Boarders were now received, and the institution was soon filled to overflowing. The success of the establishment surpassed the most sanguine expectations of its projectors. The number of boarders was soon afterwards (in May, 1825) greatly increased, by fifty-four young men brought up to it from the south by the Rev. M. Martial, a special friend of Bishop Flaget.* This was the commencement of that southern patronage, which was destined to render the institution so flourishing in after days; and also, on the subsequent heavy pecuniary derangement of the south, to bring upon it so great an amount of pecuniary embarrassment and responsibility!

The increasing patronage of the College soon rendered necessary the erection of new buildings for the accommodation of the students. The north wing, and, subsequently, the front, or main college edifice, were rapidly put up. The President spared no labour to promote the welfare and prosperity of the institution, which was soon incorporated by the Legislature of Kentucky, and

* They had belonged to a southern college, in the management of which M. Martial was concerned. When circumstances caused the dissolution of this institution, the students were transferred to St. Joseph's College. See the Annales, &c. vol. 3. p. 184.

became one of the most flourishing colleges of the west. It has educated many youths of the most distinguished families in the western and southern States.

The accomplished manners and amiable character of the Rev. Mr. Elder, gave him a peculiar facility for the management of youth. He secured the esteem and won the hearts of all under his charge. He was like a kind parent in the midst of his affectionate children. The esteem, love, and confidence of both parents and children, did much to enlarge the patronage, and to secure the permanent prosperity of the institution. The chief, and, perhaps, the only fault he had, as President, was on the amiable side—a too great mildness and indulgence in enforcing discipline.

But it is not, perhaps, as founder or president of a college, that the character of the Rev. Mr. Elder exhibits itself in the best light. It is not the mere activity of mind and body, the mere zeal for promoting education, or the unalterable meekness and amiability of his disposition, that is most estimable in his character. As a Christian priest, possessing in a high degree the virtues of his exalted station, he has still greater claims on our love and admiration. He was pious and exemplary in his conduct, regular in all the devotions of the priesthood, and zealous and laborious for the salvation of souls.

The following touching incident, selected almost at random, from a hundred of a similar nature, will illustrate his tender charity towards the poor. We relate it in the words of the one who pronounced his funeral oration; and can vouch for the entire accuracy of the account.

"About 11 o'clock, on a very cold, bleak night, in the winter of 1836–7, a Reverend gentleman discovered a man whose health was particularly delicate, who was hungry and almost naked, stand- at the college door. It seemed that he had sought shelter in other places, and had been refused. He had begged for assistance, but it had been denied him by those who knew not what it was to *be* benevolent, and who could look with a proud, unpitying eye upon suffering humanity. The gentleman who discovered him, immediately conducted him to Mr. Elder, by whom he was received with the kindest welcome, and who immediately placed before him such food as could be obtained at that hour, to satisfy his craving appetite.

"The next thought was about preparing some place for the poor man to lodge. All had retired to rest; and there was but one bed in the apartment—the one on which Mr. Elder himself was accustomed to repose. But his generous heart could not brook the thought of occupying that, while a poor, miserable, unhealthy stranger, was couchless under his roof. He immediately spread the bed before the fire, resigned it entirely to his guest, whom he invited to repose; and very soon the poor man was unconscious of his wretchedness in sleep. Shortly afterwards—perhaps, while watching on that very night—Mr. Elder composed some verses in reference to the circumstance, every line of which speaks volumes for the benevolence and charity of his heart. Some of them I will repeat.

"THE POOR MAN."

"The Stranger asks to be received,
 He stands imploring at my door;
Of health, of roof, of couch bereaved,
 Can *he* the wintry blast endure?

Thou shalt not, Stranger, farther stray!
 Thy sickly frame too feeble seems,

"To bear the cold and hunger. Stay,
   And lose thy cares in pleasant dreams.

Thou may'st not wander hence to-night,
   The winds so fiercely howling round;
A stouter heart might yield to fright;—
   The ruthless blasts so fiercely sound!

Come, seat thee there, and cheerful be!
   My hearth, and board, and bed be thine!
For glad I am a guest to see,
   To break my bread and taste my wine.

For why have I these gifts in store,
   If not to share with those who need?
Then freely eat!—But first adore
   The Father at whose hands we feed.

God bless the man who loves the poor!
   God spare the poor from want and cold!
And grant me this, (I ask no more;)
   To give, and not to hoard my gold!"*

The Rev. Mr. Elder continued his labours in connection with St. Joseph's College for nearly the whole of the twenty last years of his life. For only two or three years was this occupation changed for the active duties of the missionary life, in Scott county and throughout the central portion of Kentucky. On his retirement from the College, the office of President was discharged with great vigour and success, by the Rev. I. A. Reynolds—the present distinguished Bishop of Charleston. Upon the resignation of the presidency by the Rev. Mr. Reynolds, Mr. Elder was induced again to accept the office, which he continued to hold till his death.

His health was, however, already beginning to decline, under the weight of his heavy and long continued labours. It received an additional

---

* An "Eulogy on the life and character of the late Rev. G. A. M. Elder—delivered before the Eurodelphian Society of St. Joseph's College, on Thursday, 25th of October, 1838. By J. D. Grant."—Catholic Advocate, vol. 3. p. 316. seqq.

shock from the exposure and fatigue which accompanied and followed the disastrous burning of the main college building, on the 25th of January, 1837. He never recovered from this blow, which not only went to his heart, but also greatly impaired his already feeble constitution.

For many years he had been subject to a violent palpitation of the heart. This disease had been probably caused by over-exertion, while a student at Emmittsburg. Each year it exhibited symptoms more and more alarming; and at length, in combination with fever, it caused his death, on the 28th day of September, 1838—the forty-fifth year of his age, and the twentieth of his priesthood.

Few men were more universally beloved and regretted. He had not, he could not have had, *one* personal enemy. His unalterable sweetness would have subdued all enmity, even if any had existed. The reverence felt for his memory was attested by the vast concourse of persons who attended his funeral. The funeral procession was more than half a mile long. Never, perhaps, was such a funeral witnessed in this portion of the country. Persons attended without distinction of creed or sect. They all looked on him as an ornament and benefactor of society.

His death was, in every respect, worthy of his exemplary and blameless life. Those who saw him during his last painful illness of two weeks' duration, cannot easily forget the impression the spectacle must have made on their minds. We will give, in the language of an eye-witness, some edifying details connected with his last sickness, and his death.*

"In the midst of the most painful agonies of his

* From the obituary notice published in the Catholic Advo-

sickness, he lost nothing of his usual calmness of mind. To his last breath, he was patient, without murmuring; he was even cheerful, though enduring the most excruciating sufferings. He received the last Sacraments of the church with a fervour the most edifying, answering the usual prayers with hands clasped and eyes uplifted to heaven. After he had received the Holy Eucharist, he burst forth into a canticle of praise and thanksgiving to God, interspersed with appropriate passages from the Psalms, which he repeated with so much feeling and unction, as to draw tears from those present. When it was suggested by the clergyman who attended him, that he would exhaust his strength, he immediately acquiesced, and became silent, seemingly absorbed in prayer.

"He frequently asked those in attendance to read to him some of the Psalms; and he himself pointed out such as were his special favourites: as the fiftieth, beginning, 'Have mercy on me, O Lord, according to Thy great mercy;' and the eighty-eighth, 'The mercies of the Lord I will sing for ever.'

"He retained his faculties to the last, with the exception of an occasional incoherency when he awoke from slumber, or when his pains were most acute. But even in these wanderings of mind, he often spoke of pious subjects. During his last agony, almost every word he uttered showed that his mind and heart were directed towards heaven. Such were the following aspirations which he repeated many times, especially the first one: "My God and my Saviour! I love Thee with my whole heart, and with my whole mind, and with my whole strength, for ever and ever! Amen.' 'Come

cate, (vol. 3. p. 276-7) with some slight changes in the phraseology.

nearer to me, O my Savour! Come nearer!' 'I am crucified with Christ, *crucified, crucified,* to the world!'

"While the departing prayer was recited, he remained silent and collected, with his hands joined before his breast. Almost his last words were passages from the fiftieth Psalm, and the aspirations given above. He often looked at, and reverently kissed, the crucifix, which had been placed on his breast, to remind him, in that last and dreadful hour, of the death of Jesus Christ. During the last half hour of his life, he did not speak, but still held his hands clasped before his breast, and expired in that attitude of prayer.

"Such scenes as this must make even the sternest infidel acknowledge the power of religion! They console the Christian, and strengthen his faith. In witnessing them all will exclaim: 'May my soul die the death of the just, and may my last end be like to theirs.' "*

We must present an extract from the testimony of another individual—a Protestant—who witnessed that moving death-bed scene.

"On the night on which he died, I visited him. When I reached the door, a solemnly interesting, but melancholy scene presented itself to my view. In one corner of the room stood the couch upon which rested my dying friend. By his side kneeled the clergyman in attendance, breathing softly, but audibly, a prayer in his behalf. The room was filled with kneeling, weeping friends. In one part of it you might have observed a disconsolate, almost broken-hearted sister, with her streaming eyes turned towards heaven, and her lips moving as if in prayer. There was the aged father, the

* Numbers, xxxiii. 10.

very picture of the deep, but calm grief of his venerable age. I involuntarily paused; for it seemed as though some unearthly voice whispered me thus:

> 'Tread lightly o'er the threshold, and leave there
> The vanities of earth, and every pulse
> Of worldliness, as unfit garments. For the place
> Thou enterest is filled with heaven,
> And angels hover there, to bear away in peace
> The waiting spirit of the friend thou lovest.'

" . . . . . His voice was nearly spent; yet each low, soft whisper, sounded as the vibration of some harp whose strings were swept by airs of heaven. Each word he uttered was rich with love of God and his fellow-men. And although his manly form lay prostrate, yet his soul seemed lifted above, and to be only waiting for the call of his Maker, to accompany a bright band of ministering spirits which seemed hovering around him, to join the company of ceaseless worshippers around the throne of God. In a few brief moments, with the cross upon his breast, his hands clasped before him, and his eyes turned towards heaven, the angel of death removed the curtain which conceals, and his soul took its flight into, the world of spirits."*

* "Eulogy," &c., before quoted.

CHAPTER XVIII.

The Jubilee of 1826-7—*Statistics of the Diocess at its close—Conclusion.*

The nature of a Jubilee—And of an Indulgence in general—The utility of Indulgences shown—The Jubilee of 1826-7 in Kentucky—Its commencement—Progress—And astonishing results—Edifying examples—Conversions of Protestants—Statistics of the Diocess—The Rev. Mr. Kenrick—Reflections—The Patriarch of the West.

On his accession to the Pontificate, Pope Leo XII. proclaimed a Jubilee throughout Christendom. The voice of the Chief Pastor was heard even in the midst of the waving forests of our State; and it here made so deep an impression, and awakened so many to faith and repentance, that the date of the Jubilee which it proclaimed marks an epoch in the church history of Kentucky. We intend to devote the present chapter —the last of these Sketches—to a summary account of this Jubilee, which is yet vividly remembered by all the older Catholics of our Diocess.

A Jubilee is an ample form of Plenary Indulgence published at the beginning, and at intervals of every quarter, of a century; as well as on great occasions of rejoicing or of calamity: such as the accession of a Sovereign Pontiff, or a season of imminent peril to the church. This form of Indulgence has been in use in the church for nearly five centuries and a half;* and it has been found invariably useful in reviving piety among the people, and in awakening sinners to conversion. Like the Jewish Jubilee of old, it was always viewed as a special season of mercy and grace, in which the bonds of iniquity were to be broken, the long standing debts of sin to be cancelled; the sinner to rest from his evil ways, and the worldling to repose from the feverish excitements of earthly affairs, and to turn his attention to the things of eternity.† So beneficial were found to be the results of the first Jubilees proclaimed by the Sovereign Pontiffs, that it was soon determined to publish them more frequently than had been at first intended. The interval between successive Jubilees, originally a century, was afterwards reduced to a half, and finally to a quarter of a century—which last is the present discipline.

The immense spiritual benefits which have, at all times and in all places, resulted from the Jubilee, are of themselves sufficient to establish the fallacy of the Protestant assertion: that the doctrine of Indulgences operates as an encouragement to the commission of sin. According to its very nature, an Indulgence, instead of fostering, necessarily excludes sin, by awakening repentance and stimulating the sinner to approach the Sacraments of Penance and the Holy Eucharist. An Indulgence is not a remission of sin, nor of the eternal punishment due to it, but only of the *temporal* penalty, which often remains due after the

---

* The first Jubilee was celebrated in the year 1300; and it was proclaimed by Pope Boniface VIII., who, among other things, alleged the example of the Jubilee ordained by God for the Jews.

† For an account of the Jewish Jubilee, see Leviticus, ch. xxv., and Numbers, ch. xxxvi.

sin itself has been forgiven. It is a mere sequel to the Sacrament of Penance. No one can receive the benefit of an Indulgence, unless his sins have been already forgiven by God, and he himself be in the state of grace. So that, a necessary condition for obtaining the Indulgence, is a sincere repentance of heart, with a confession and a firm purpose of amendment.

Besides the great benefit of an Indulgence in thus powerfully stimulating the sinner to repentance, a Jubilee offers another signal advantage to the Christian world. It brings about a union of prayer among Christians scattered over the surface of the earth. It displays, in a most striking manner, the Unity and Catholicity of the Church. It causes all differences of language, of cast, of political sentiment, to disappear; and prompts all Christians to prostrate themselves in humble prayer before the common altars of a common religion. It causes the voice of a heart-felt repentance to ascend simultaneously from every portion of the earth, and to offer a holy violence to heaven in the eloquent pleading for mercy. If, where two or three disciples are assembled together in prayer, the Lord is in the midst of them; if, when even one sinner does penance, angels carry up the falling penitential tear to the heavenly court, where the intelligence causes a jubilee of joy and exultation; what will be the approval of God, and what the joy of the heavenly host, when the whole world unites in prayer and in doing penance? Only the Catholic Church, with its indissoluble unity and its wide-spread extension, can present spectacles at once so thrilling and so sublime, as that of the whole world thus uniting in prayer!

These reflections naturally grow out of the Jubilee of 1825–6,* of the promulgation of which in our Diocess we will now proceed to treat in some detail. The blessings arising from this great season of mercy and benediction are still fresh in the memory of most of our readers. For stating those benefits, and describing the exercises which accompanied them, we possess an advantage which we have seldom enjoyed while writing out these Sketches, that of ample printed documents. A full account of this Jubilee was written in French by those who participated in its exercises, and was transmitted to the Association for the Propagation of the Faith in France. Hence we have little more to do than to condense this statement, and to translate into English its more interesting portions.†

The exercises of the Jubilee began among the clergy, assembled in a Spiritual Retreat at Bardstown: and they were immediately afterwards followed up in the various congregations of the Diocess, beginning with that attached to the Cathedral. In a letter addressed by the venerable Bishop Flaget to M. Badin,‡ dated Louisville, September 29, 1826, we find the following interesting account of the exercises of the Jubilee, and of the fruits attending them among the clergy and faithful of the Diocess.

"You will learn with pleasure, how we have proceeded to gain the Indulgence of the Jubilee. On the first day of September, all my missionaries

---

* This Jubilee was the more solemn from the circumstance, that, besides occurring at the regular interval—the commencement of the second quarter in the present century—it was intended also to commemorate the elevation of Leo XII. to the Chair of St. Peter.

† The documents alluded to are found in the "Annales de la Propagation de la Foy," vol. 3. p. 183, seqq.

‡ Then in Paris, France.

assembled at the theological Seminary in Bardstown. All of us made together a Retreat of eight days, during which we endeavoured to comply with all the conditions prescribed in the Pontifical Bull. On the 10th of September, being vested in Pontificals, I opened the Jubilee for the congregation of the Cathedral. It lasted for eight days, during which a sermon was preached at 10 o'clock A. M., a conference was given at 3, P. M., and another sermon, on the great truths of our holy religion, was delivered by candle-light. During the week following, the same plan was followed at St. Thomas', with the exception that but one sermon was given in the day. At present we are engaged in giving the same exercises at Louisville, where a sermon is daily preached at the church, and a conference given every evening in the Court-house. I have with me four young missionaries who are doing great good.

"The young Mr. Kenrick,* a student of Propaganda, presides over the conferences, and answers the objections against the Catholic doctrine. It is impossible for me to tell you of all the good which results from these conferences: Protestants relish them even more than Catholics. We have had the consolation to see a great number of old sinners make strong efforts to gain the Indulgence of the Jubilee. Many Protestants are deeply impressed. . . . . . But, my God! how many difficulties have they to overcome on the part of their preachers and their relations! Six months are allotted to each congregation to gain the Indulgence. I give Confirmation wherever the Jubilee is proclaimed. Nearly a year will be necessary for the visitation of the whole Diocess, in making which

* The present learned and excellent Bishop of Philadelphia.

I shall be accompanied by Rev. Mr. Kenrick and two or three other missionaries. With what pleasure have I entered on this Apostolic career! And if the consolations which I at present feel should go on increasing, they will afford me happiness enough for this world: I will say, with the greatest pleasure, the *nunc dimittis* at the end of the Jubilee, provided my debts will have been liquidated by that time. For the love of God, aid in drawing me out of this abyss!"*

In the same collection, from which we have translated the portion of Bishop Flaget's letter just given, we find a much fuller account of the Jubilee. As this document is well written and very edifying, and as besides, it contains a valuable statistical account of the condition of Catholicity in Kentucky at that time, we will be pardoned for translating it entire.†

"The promulgation of the Jubilee has been for the Diocess of Bardstown an epoch of the most abundant benedictions. The zeal with which the faithful every where performed the exercises; the modesty and recollection they exhibited; and, above all, the eagerness they manifested to approach the Tribunal of Penance and the Holy Table; all prove, that, while the Vicar of Jesus Christ opened on earth the treasures of the church, God was pleased, from high heaven, to cast an eye of mercy on this portion of the New World, and to prepare, beforehand, so to speak, the graces which he was to scatter over it with a sort of profusion.

"Under circumstances so favourable to the spiritual good of the flock confided to his care, Bish-

---

* "Annales," &c., vol. 3. p. 183-4.
† Ibid. p. 206. seqq.

op Flaget did not think that he ought to spare himself. He hesitated not to put himself at the head of his missionaries; and, despite the fatigue inseparable from long journeys, he wished to share with them in all the labours, as well as in all the consolations, of a ministry as august as it is painful.

"Two years had been allowed him by the Pontiff for the promulgation of the Jubilee in all the parts of his vast Diocess. He himself granted six months to each congregation, for the same purpose, in order that all might be the more easily enabled to gather its fruits. The conditions prescribed for gaining the Indulgence were: to visit, at four, or at least at three, different times the church of the congregation; to assist at all the public exercises as far as practicable; to recite the Litany of the Saints, with some other stated prayers; and finally, to say five *Our Fathers* and five *Hail Marys*, according to the intentions of the Sovereign Pontiff.

"As to the order and nature of the exercises, they were not every where the same: it was necessary to adapt them to places and circumstances. At the Cathedral, they commenced with the celebration of the Holy Sacrifice of the Mass. This was immediately followed by the sermon, after which the prayers above indicated were recited. At three o'clock, P. M., a conference took place between two priests, on some dogmatical point. At half past six o'clock in the evening, another sermon was delivered for the convenience of the citizens of Bardstown, both Catholic and Protestant, who might not have been able during the day to attend the meetings. These exercises continued for eight days; and this was likewise observed in all the other congregations, except in

STATISTICS OF THE DIOCESS. 295

those where the number of Catholics was very inconsiderable. In the latter, however, but two instructions were given on each day.

"Although the churches were crowded, yet the slightest disorder never occurred. The attention to the word of God was constantly kept up, and what was yet more consoling, the effects of the sermons were admirable. It would have been difficult to behold a greater concourse of persons at the tribunal of penance. At four o'clock in the morning, and even at two o'clock, in the congregation of St. Charles,* although it was the month of December, in the middle of winter, a large crowd of persons, of whom many had travelled several miles, pressed for admission at the door of the church. Scarcely had it been opened, when the places destined for hearing confessions were thronged, and they did not cease to be so until late in the evening. Among the faithful, many remained the whole day without taking nourishment, and even without changing their places, for fear of being deprived of the consolations after which they so ardently sighed: yet, notwithstanding all the care they thus took, many were compelled to wait till after the conclusion of the exercises, before they could share in the graces flowing from the Sacrament of Penance.

"All hearts appeared to be truly moved. This was seen in the vividness of the sorrow and in the abundance of tears, which accompanied the confession of their sins. Sinners of the most inveterate habits were seen weeping over their past wanderings, and prepared to make the greatest sacrifices to amend their lives. Many, too, profitted

---

* This was one of the principal congregations of the good M. Nerinckx; and the zeal there manifested during the Jubilee, proves that his lessons had not been forgotten.

by this happy season to renew marriages contracted before Protestant ministers, and rendered null by the impediment of infidelity. Others, surmounting all false shame, repaired previous sacrilegious confessions. All, in fine, gave extraordinary evidence of repentance, and showed a firm resolution to lead for the future, lives more Christian, or more perfect.

"During the week of the Jubilee, all temporal affairs seemed forgotten; only those of the soul were attended to : and as the greater part of the Catholics came from a distance of eight, ten, or twelve miles, they remained during the whole day in the church. They did not leave it, for a moment, except to take a frugal repast on the grass, or in the adjoining wood. Not only did the labourers and farmers, who constituted the majority of the Catholics, give these beautiful examples of fervour and zeal, but persons of every condition— merchants, physicians, magistrates, legislators— showed themselves equally eager to profit by the graces of heaven. Human respect, so powerful under other circumstances, had given way to more noble sentiments : and all thought of nothing else but of giving open and public evidences of their strong attachment to a religion, which was the only source of their consolation and happiness.

"Such was the edifying spectacle which Kentucky presented during those days of benediction. Perhaps the fruits of the Jubilee were more abundant here than in any other part of the Christian world, if we take into the account the small number of Catholics. Scarcely was there to be found one in twenty, who proved recreant to the voice of God, and to the call of the church. We may be persuaded of this by the number of those who received the Holy Communion and Confirmation,

STATISTICS OF THE DIOCESS.

as shown by the account kept by the missionaries in each congregation."

This number is exhibited by the same writer in the following statistical table.

Congregations.	Counties.	Number of Communions.	Number of Confirmations.
Cathedral,	Nelson,	450	30
St. Thomas,	Do.	150	30
Louisville,	Jefferson,	50	20
St. John Baptist,	Bullitt,	70	24
St. Michael,	Nelson,	250	60
St. Benedict,	Spencer,	50	20
St. Charles,	Washington,	450	160
St. Mary's,	Do.	300	60
Loretto,	Do.	110	40
St. Pius,	Scott,	250	60
St. Peter,	Fayette,	30	00
St. Rose,	Washington,	800	260
St. Hubert,	Do.	290	110
Holy Cross,	Do.	495	160
Do. do.	Nelson,	120	55
St. Vincent,	Do.	100	00
Sacred Heart,	Union,	150	60
Do. do.	Daviess,	40	7
St. Anthony,	Breckenridge,	70	26
St. Romuald,	Do.	50	14
St. Theresa,	Meade,	70	20
Total number,		4,345.	1,216.

"Thus the whole number of communicants during the time of the Jubilee, amounted to four thousand three hundred and forty-five. If we add to this number those who afterwards went to communion, after having commenced their preparation during the time of the Jubilee, the number will exceed six thousand.* The whole number of Confirmations was twelve hundred and sixteen.

"Three congregations in the eastern, and three in the western, portion of the Diocess, remain as yet unvisited; which, together with those already named, makes the total number of congregations in the Diocess exceed thirty.

"The Protestants also participated, at least to some extent, in this general movement. About fifty of them re-entered the bosom of the Catholic church. Many of these received Baptism. Many others expressed a desire to hear the principles of the Catholic faith again explained. They acknowledged that the prejudices, which they had hitherto entertained, rested upon no solid foundation.

"In the conferences, objections the most specious and the most difficult, were set forth and answered with a clearness and a force which left nothing to be desired, and precluded any reply. These conferences were conducted by the Rev. Mr. Kenrick, a young Irish priest, as remarkable for his piety as for the extent of his knowledge, the vivacity of his mind, and the natural eloquence with which he expresses himself. The sectarian preachers were often reduced to silence. A Methodist preacher, called, very inappropriately, Light, wished to profit by the absence of Mr. Kenrick, to sustain the honour of his sect. He succeeded only in drawing down upon himself the humiliation of a public refutation, to which he did not think proper to make any reply. Another preacher of the Anglican Church met with a similar fate. Finally, a Presbyterian preacher, more ardent, having ventured to attack Mr. Kenrick

*The present number of communicants in the Diocess probably exceeds ten thousand.

publicly, was answered so triumphantly, that, when he wished to speak in rejoinder, he was abandoned by Protestants as well as Catholics."*

Such were the fruits of the famous Jubilee of 1826-7 in our Diocess, as unfolded by two eyewitnesses. Great must have been the delight and consolation experienced by the venerable Bishop Flaget, in thus seeing all his previous apostolic labours crowned with such wonderful success. He had been but fifteen years in Kentucky, and already his infant Diocess had produced fruits as abundant and mature, as many other Diocesses of much greater antiquity. Institutions of learning and of charity had sprung up in great numbers around him, which by their prosperity and usefulness had far surpassed his most sanguine expectations. A new clergy, formed by Father David, in his own newly established Diocesan Seminary, now issued forth, full of vigour and zeal, to aid their Bishop in the laborious duties of the missionary life. All, both clergy and laity, looked on him as a father; and he viewed them as his children. He lived in their midst, eating and drinking with them, sharing in all their privations, rejoicing with them in their joy, and mingling his tears with theirs in their sorrows. Those were truly the golden days of the church of Kentucky.

What had been, but a few short years before, a vast and unreclaimed wilderness, inhabited only by the wild beast and the yet fiercer savage, had now become a blooming garden of Christianity, in which the flowers of piety sent forth their sweet fragrance, and in which the fruits of virtue were gathered in abundance. Churches, many of

---

* This preacher was the Rev. Mr. Sneed; and the occurrence alluded to, still fresh in the memory of many among our readers, took place in Springfield, Washington county.

them neat, and some of them, as the Cathedral of Bardstown, very beautiful, had sprung up in the midst of the waving forests: and, on Sundays and Festivals, they were crowded with worshippers, reverently kneeling, and piously assisting at the tremendous Sacrifice of the New Law. The public worship was performed according to all the prescriptions of the ceremonial; and the prayers of the faithful were wafted to heaven with the sounds of heavenly music, and clouds of ascending incense. The finger of God had wrought this wonderful change!

In the other portions of the great West, originally under the episcopal jurisdiction of the Bishop of Kentucky, the improvement, in a religious point of view, has been no less remarkable. Truly does the venerable Bishop Flaget deserve the appellation, which he has often received—of **PATRIARCH OF THE WEST.**

APPENDIX.

APPENDIX.

We will throw into an Appendix a few documents which we had at first thought of giving in the text. They may prove interesting to at least a portion of our readers; and may be deemed worth preserving.

(No. I.)

The Latin Poem, or "Carmen Sacrum" of the Rev. M. Badin, composed on occasion of the arrival of Bishop Flaget in Kentucky, in June, 1811.

This poem was translated into English by that ripe scholar, and particular friend of M. Badin, Mr. Kean O'Hara, of Frankfort. We will give our readers his translation of only the concluding portion, as the whole poem would be too long for insertion. M. Badin thus addresses the new Bishop:

> "Bishop of Barda! May high heaven shed
> Its choicest blessings on thy reverend head:
> And may thy flock and clergy ever share
> In all thy joys, as objects of thy care.
> Thou shalt be blessed; and may thy Diocess
> In equal blessings hold an equal place.
> Be this thy crown of glory and reward,
> That he who in the name of our dread Lord
> Doth come, shall blessed be. 'Tis rightly meet,
> That I, precursor of my Pontiff's feet,
> The humblest servant of the Prince of Peace,
> Should be diminished; and that he increase,

Whose high succession from St. Peter flows,
And who, as Christ's *vicarius* clearly shows
An unimpeached authority to guide
The flock o'er which he's destined to preside.

And now, O God! since that my eyes behold
This great salvation granted to Thy fold,
Prepared to spread Thy truth from shore to shore,
And teach mankind Religion's sacred lore;
O! let Thy servant now depart in peace!
Since false delusions shall henceforward cease,
And the bright sun of Christian truth shall rise,
To guide a pious race to reach the skies!
O Christian souls! with loud accord rejoice!
And praise your gracious God with one harmonious voice."

(No. II.)

THE "EPICEDIUM," OR LATIN POEM, WRITTEN BY THE REV. M. BADIN, ON OCCASION OF THE DEATH OF COL. JOE DAVIESS, AT THE BATTLE OF TIPPECANOE, NOV. 7TH, 1811.

This is, perhaps, the sweetest Latin poem ever written by M. Badin. It strongly reminds us of some of Virgil's Eclogues. As we have already seen, Col. Joe Daviess was a warm friend of M. Badin, who, in this Epicedium, pours out his soul in mingled strains of patriotism and friendship.

We will give the Poem entire, in the elegant English translation of it made by Dr. Mitchell of New York.

"A happy autumn, with accustomed cheer,
Had in profusion decked the fruitful year;

And elms, presaging winter's dreary reign,
Had spread their drooping foliage round the plain:
When fame's loud trump the vault of ether rends,
As thus the true, but mournful, news she sends:

Pretending peace, the faithless savage bands
By night in blood imbued their murd'rous hands,
With lead and steel and unexpected force,
Assailed and slew the Leader of the horse ;
Pierced by three wounds, the brave Commander fell.
The routed foes sent forth a hideous yell,
Till death o'ertook them with relentless frown,
And flames vindictive triumphed through their town.

A Comet's glare foretold this sad event,
The quaking Earth confirmed the dire portent ;
E'en Wabash slow his shores and islands laves,
As thick with gore he rolls his viscid waves.

The Dryads deeply sigh, sweet Hymen faints,
Refusing comforts 'midst embittered plaints :
The Muses silent sit, while Friendship weeps,
On hand and arm the crape of mourning keeps,
And in incessant tears her eye-lids steeps.

Yet what avails a never-ending woe?
The fates obdurate disegard its flow ;
But Themis eyes the scene with kinder view,
Decides the meed of praise to merit due,
And thus, with mind from doubt and error free,
In solemn words declares her just decree :

'Brave Daviess' bust shall decorate the wall
Where courts and juries meet within my hall ;
The civic oak shall round his temples twine,
And victor laurel rival twigs combine ;
The Legislature pay the debt of grief,
And Clio's pen inscribe the historic leaf:
Cypress the field shall shelter with its shade,
And for his noble heart an urn be made ;

A marble tomb shall faithful friendship rear,
To guard his ashes with peculiar care :
Heroic Daviess this our age shall sing,
Heroic Daviess future ages ring ;
In eloquence among the foremost found,
In peace and war with deathless glory crowned.'

Life occupies a small and bounded place,
But glory's as unlimited as space.
They who to country give their dying breath,
Shall live immortal, and shall conquer death ;
Their great examples times to come inflame,
To shed their patriot blood for everlasting fame."

(No. III.)

A List of Questions, sent by Father David to the Rev. Nathan H. Hall, on the Rule of Faith.

These questions were intended to show the uncertainty and difficulties of the Protestant Rule of Faith, which admits nothing that is not contained in the Bible, as explained by the private judgment of each individual. Mr. Hall, perhaps for a very obvious reason, never answered these questions. In fact, they exhibit a close train of reasoning, wholly unanswerable by the Protestant. They cover the whole ground of the controversy on the Rule of Faith ; and show us how logical was the mind of Father David, and how directly it went to the point at issue. His "Address," &c. to Protestants, on the Rule of Faith, is but an answer to these questions, and an unfolding of the principles they envelope.

The questions are as follows:—and we entreat every sincere Protestant to read and ponder them well:

"Is not the first act of faith to be made on the Scripture itself, to wit: I believe that this book contains the true word of God; that is, all the books written by inspired writers, and none but such as were written by them? How can any one ascertain this from the Scripture itself? Does any book in the Bible determine the number of canonical books? And if it did, how shall I know that this book itself is canonical?

"Through what channel have these books been handed down to posterity? How shall I know that they have been preserved in their integrity, and free from interpolation? Is this to be known from the Scripture itself?

"Should these points be settled, how shall every individual be assured that he has a good translation? That the translators neither mistook nor wilfully altered the original text?

"Supposing this also to be settled, how will those do, who cannot read? Or who have not time to read? Have, really, all the believers among Presbyterians, Baptists, &c.; in a word, among those who make the Scripture the sole Rule of Faith, formed their faith from it? Or, did they not believe, and were they not Presbyterians, Baptists, &c., before they began to read? Must a man who begins to read the Bible be absolutely without faith? If he has faith, by what rule has he formed it? If he has none, how can he be saved, in case he die before he has read the whole Bible? And must a man, who reads the Bible, be without faith until he has read the whole? If not, when may he begin to have faith?

"How did the primitive Christians do, before the sacred books of the New Testament were written? Had they no faith? How did Christians form their faith before the fifteenth century, when the art of printing was unknown and few could procure a Bible?

"Suppose all the preceding questions were solved to every one's satisfaction, more difficulties still offer themselves. How can any one ascertain that he has attained the true sense of every text in which he thinks he discovers an article of faith? How is he to reconcile the apparent contradictions between text and text? To solve the objections of those, who understand them in an opposite sense?

"When he hears that the Scripture is an infallible Rule of Faith, an infallible judge of controversy; how is he to understand this? Of the Scripture uninterpreted or interpreted? If uninterpreted, how can he hear a judge that is dumb? If interpreted, he must ask, is the interpreter fallible or infallible? If fallible, he cannot rely on his interpretations. If infallible, who is he? His preacher? But the preacher himself disclaims infallibility. His own private judgment? But this also he cannot deem infallible. The Holy Ghost? But first, how does he know that there is a Holy Ghost? This is a point of faith to be known by the Rule of Faith, to wit: the Scripture. But this he cannot know till he has already ascertained the sense of it. Secondly, how can he be assured that he is inspired by the Holy Ghost, when he sees the very fathers of the Reformation, Luther, Zwinglius, and Calvin, wrangling so much about the plainest texts of Scripture? When he sees the numberless sects, who take the Scripture for their sole Rule of Faith, so widely differ from one another?"

FINIS.

Religion in America
Series II

An Arno Press Collection

Adler, Felix. **Creed and Deed:** A Series of Discourses. New York, 1877.

Alexander, Archibald. **Evidences of the Authenticity, Inspiration, and Canonical Authority of the Holy Scriptures.** Philadelphia, 1836.

Allen, Joseph Henry. **Our Liberal Movement in Theology:** Chiefly as Shown in Recollections of the History of Unitarianism in New England. 3rd edition. Boston, 1892.

American Temperance Society. **Permanent Temperance Documents of the American Temperance Society.** Boston, 1835.

American Tract Society. **The American Tract Society Documents,** 1824-1925. New York, 1972.

Bacon, Leonard. **The Genesis of the New England Churches.** New York, 1874.

Bartlett, S[amuel] C. **Historical Sketches of the Missions of the American Board.** New York, 1972.

Beecher, Lyman. **Lyman Beecher and the Reform of Society:** Four Sermons, 1804-1828. New York, 1972.

[Bishop, Isabella Lucy Bird.] **The Aspects of Religion in the United States of America.** London, 1859.

Bowden, James. **The History of the Society of Friends in America.** London, 1850, 1854. Two volumes in one.

Briggs, Charles Augustus. **Inaugural Address and Defense,** 1891-1893. New York, 1972.

Colwell, Stephen. **The Position of Christianity in the United States,** in Its Relations with Our Political Institutions, and Specially with Reference to Religious Instruction in the Public Schools. Philadelphia, 1854.

Dalcho, Frederick. **An Historical Account of the Protestant Episcopal Church, in South-Carolina,** from the First Settlement of the Province, to the War of the Revolution. Charleston, 1820.

Elliott, Walter. **The Life of Father Hecker.** New York, 1891.

Gibbons, James Cardinal. **A Retrospect of Fifty Years.** Baltimore, 1916. Two volumes in one.

Hammond, L[ily] H[ardy]. **Race and the South:** Two Studies, 1914-1922. New York, 1972.

Hayden, A[mos] S. **Early History of the Disciples in the Western Reserve, Ohio;** With Biographical Sketches of the Principal Agents in their Religious Movement. Cincinnati, 1875.

Hinke, William J., editor. **Life and Letters of the Rev. John Philip Boehm:** Founder of the Reformed Church in Pennsylvania, 1683-1749. Philadelphia, 1916.

Hopkins, Samuel. **A Treatise on the Millennium.** Boston, 1793.

Kallen, Horace M. **Judaism at Bay:** Essays Toward the Adjustment of Judaism to Modernity. New York, 1932.

Kreider, Harry Julius. **Lutheranism in Colonial New York.** New York, 1942.

Loughborough, J. N. **The Great Second Advent Movement:** Its Rise and Progress. Washington, 1905.

M'Clure, David and Elijah Parish. **Memoirs of the Rev. Eleazar Wheelock, D.D.** Newburyport, 1811.

McKinney, Richard I. **Religion in Higher Education Among Negroes.** New Haven, 1945.

Mayhew, Jonathan. **Observations on the Charter and Conduct of the Society for the Propagation of the Gospel in Foreign Parts;** Designed to Shew Their Non-conformity to Each Other. Boston, 1763.

Mott, John R. **The Evangelization of the World in this Generation.** New York, 1900.

Payne, Bishop Daniel A. **Sermons and Addresses,** 1853-1891. New York, 1972.

Phillips, C[harles] H. **The History of the Colored Methodist Episcopal Church in America:** Comprising Its Organization, Subsequent Development, and Present Status. Jackson, Tenn., 1898.

Reverend Elhanan Winchester: Biography and Letters. New York, 1972.

Riggs, Stephen R. **Tah-Koo Wah-Kan; Or, the Gospel Among the Dakotas.** Boston, 1869.

Rogers, Elder John. **The Biography of Eld. Barton Warren Stone, Written by Himself:** With Additions and Reflections. Cincinnati, 1847.

Booth-Tucker, Frederick. **The Salvation Army in America:** Selected Reports, 1899-1903. New York, 1972.

Satolli, Francis Archbishop. **Loyalty to Church and State.** Baltimore, 1895.

Schaff, Philip. **Church and State in the United States** or the American Idea of Religious Liberty and its Practical Effects with Official Documents. New York and London, 1888. (Reprinted from *Papers of the American Historical Association,* Vol. II, No. 4.)

Smith, Horace Wemyss. **Life and Correspondence of the Rev. William Smith, D.D.** Philadelphia, 1879, 1880. Two volumes in one.

Spalding, M[artin] J. **Sketches of the Early Catholic Missions of Kentucky;** From Their Commencement in 1787 to the Jubilee of 1826-7. Louisville, 1844.

Steiner, Bernard C., editor. **Rev. Thomas Bray:** His Life and Selected Works Relating to Maryland. Baltimore, 1901. (Reprinted from *Maryland Historical Society Fund Publication,* No. 37.)

To Win the West: Missionary Viewpoints, 1814-1815. New York, 1972.

Wayland, Francis and H. L. Wayland. **A Memoir of the Life and Labors of Francis Wayland, D.D., LL.D.** New York, 1867. Two volumes in one.

Willard, Frances E. **Woman and Temperance:** Or, the Work and Workers of the Woman's Christian Temperance Union. Hartford, 1883.